# Inside Digital Advertising

For Caroline and Zeynep

# Inside Digital Advertising

Platforms, Power, and Material Politics

Donald MacKenzie and
Koray Caliskan

polity

Copyright © Donald MacKenzie and Koray Caliskan 2025

The right of Donald MacKenzie and Koray Caliskan to be identified as Authors of this Work has been asserted in accordance with the UK Copyright, Designs and Patents Act 1988.

First published in 2025 by Polity Press Ltd.

Polity Press Ltd.
65 Bridge Street
Cambridge CB2 1UR, UK

Polity Press Ltd.
111 River Street
Hoboken, NJ 07030, USA

All rights reserved. Except for the quotation of short passages for the purpose of criticism and review, no part of this publication may be reproduced, stored in a retrieval system or transmitted, in any form or by any means, electronic, mechanical, photocopying, recording or otherwise, without the prior permission of the publisher.

ISBN-13: 978-1-5095-6863-5
ISBN-13: 978-1-5095-6864-2(pb)

A catalogue record for this book is available from the British Library.

[LoC number here]

Typeset in 11 on 14pt Warnock Pro
by Cheshire Typesetting Ltd, Cuddington, Cheshire
Printed and bound in Great Britain by 4edge Limited

The publisher has used its best endeavours to ensure that the URLs for external websites referred to in this book are correct and active at the time of going to press. However, the publisher has no responsibility for the websites and can make no guarantee that a site will remain live or that the content is or will remain appropriate.

Every effort has been made to trace all copyright holders, but if any have been overlooked the publisher will be pleased to include any necessary credits in any subsequent reprint or edition.

For further information on Polity, visit our website:
politybooks.com

# Contents

*Acknowledgments* vi

1 Introduction 1
2 Display Ads, Cookies, and the Open Marketplace 29
3 Money Machines and the Characteristics of Digital Advertising 47
4 Hacking the System 80
5 Enfolding Your Phone 109
6 Digital Advertising's Tensions 135
7 Conclusion 162

*Notes* 194
*References* 210
*Index* 238

# Acknowledgments

We are enormously grateful to Frances Burgess, Addie McGowan, and Charlotte Rommerskirchen, the other members of our Edinburgh University/The New School team researching digital advertising. Frances managed the entire project, including its finances, organized research trips, maintained a project bibliography, and word-processed successive drafts of both this book and the papers we are drawing on. Addie, a digital-advertising practitioner as well as impressive academic, gave us vital insights and has influenced this book in multiple ways. Charlotte has led our work on the regulation of advertising, and her influence is also strong on what we say about that here. Although not a formal team member, Neil Marchant has made an invaluable contribution, transcribing our many interviews (some conducted in noisy cafes and restaurants) with remarkable accuracy and in a very timely way.

We are also very grateful to John Thompson at Polity Press for welcoming this book so warmly, and to two anonymous referees for helpful suggestions for revisions. The Columbia University Sociology Department's workshop, Science, Knowledge, and Technology, generously hosted three seminars on our research in 2023–5. Feedback from those seminars and the other audiences to whom we have presented this work has made a major contribution to our evolving thinking. Donald particularly thanks Jean Czerlinski Whitmore Ortega, who has been an invaluable guide, both to technologies central to digital advertising and intellectual issues that the field raises.

We owe a huge debt of gratitude to our interviewees from within digital advertising without whom we couldn't have written this book. They took time out from their busy lives to introduce us to the field's practicalities, systems, and conflicts. We also thank the organizers of sector meetings who allowed us to attend, often free of charge or at a reduced rate. The funding for our research came primarily from a research grant from the UK Economic and Social Research Council (ES/V015362/1), with initial exploratory interviews funded by an earlier ESRC project (ES/R003173/1). The book draws on three existing articles: MacKenzie, Caliskan, and Rommerskirchen (2023), McGowan, MacKenzie, and Caliskan (2024), and MacKenzie (2024). We are grateful to our co-authors and the copyright holders for allowing us to reuse this material here. And we would also like to thank the many existing researchers on advertising (whose work we discuss in chapter 1) for welcoming us into their community.

Needless to say, any errors are our responsibility. We have learned an enormous amount from those to whom we have spoken, but we apologize if we have got anything wrong. We hope, though, that our informants in digital advertising, generous as they were with their time and input, will judge this book to be an insightful, sometimes critical, but, above all, fair account of the world in which they spend their working lives.

# 1

# Introduction

Enter a query into a search engine. Visit a news organization's website, or another site that has to make money from its visitors. Or go to your favorite social media platform. In the fraction of a second before what you're looking for appears, a great deal happens behind the scenes. Your single action can trigger at least one, and sometimes more than a hundred, near-instantaneous automated auctions of the opportunity to show an advert on your screen. Globally, the process is repeated almost unimaginably often: over 100 billion digital ads are shown daily, and as many as two trillion ad auctions take place.[1]

This book is about what goes on behind the scenes, on this gigantic scale, in those crucial fractions of a second. In the words of three campaigners against political manipulation, the digital world is often "like a one-way mirror." Those behind the mirror "can see the public, but the public cannot see them," and so "don't know who is trying to influence them" (Ravel, Woolley, and Sridharan 2019: 6).[2] Digital advertising's systems use a variety of tools to help them "see the public." Cookies, which we will discuss in chapter 2, are the best-known example – you have probably "consented" to them several times already today – but we still encounter digitally savvy people who don't know that their mobile phone has a unique identifier number. If advertising technology systems can access it, they can build a picture of your activity across apps, helping them, for example, to decide how much to bid for the opportunity to show you an ad. Android phones' identifier numbers can generally be accessed, but Apple has blocked default access to iPhones' identifiers, sparking controversy and disruption within digital advertising that we focus on in chapter 5.

The risk to privacy in using cookies, identifier numbers, or other technologies to "see" users is only one of the crucial issues involved in digital advertising. The winning bid in any one ad auction – and thus the revenue from showing a single ad – is normally tiny, often just a fraction of a cent, but multiplied by the trillions of ads shown annually it accumulates.[3] Aggregate revenue from digital advertising globally totaled around US$612 billion in 2023, and it is rising (Lebow 2024). That income stream funds the everyday digital world, sometimes in part, sometimes completely. Without it, Google Search, which you probably use many times daily, would not exist, nor would Google Maps or your favorite social media platform – or, at least, you would have to pay for those services. Many of the news and other websites you visit, games you play, or apps you use could not survive without advertising income.

Another issue is that the trillions of daily automated ad auctions aren't abstract economic operations: they are material computations. Some happen on your own phone or laptop, almost always without you knowing. Others happen in datacenters: huge, normally windowless, warehouses, each housing tens of thousands or more computers. Wherever it happens, an ad auction consumes electricity, as does the transmission of an ad to your device and the rendering of it on your screen. Some of that electricity may be from renewable sources, but much of it involves carbon emissions.

On average, showing just one digital ad to one user involves emitting a little puff of carbon dioxide sufficiently big that if it were cigarette smoke you would be able to see it: it's somewhere between a tenth and a whole pint of carbon dioxide (MacKenzie 2023).[4] And there are over 100 billion – perhaps as many as 400 billion (Kotila 2021) – such puffs every day. Digital advertising is responsible for, very roughly, around a tenth of information and communication technology's global emissions (Pärssinen et al. 2018).

So what goes on behind the one-way mirror matters. We'll begin our account of it in chapter 2 with digital advertising's original, still very important, main form: "display ads," in other words ads shown to you simply because you are visiting a webpage or using an app, without you necessarily having demonstrated any interest in a purchase. Display ads now account for around 30% of revenues from digital advertising (IAB 2022), and originally were the preserve of what participants often call digital advertising's "open marketplace," inhabited by a multiplicity of generally small or medium-sized firms.

Then, in chapter 3, we'll move to the two global leviathans of digital advertising: Google and Facebook, now renamed Meta Platforms Inc. Meta's platforms show display ads, but the mechanism by which they are sold is utterly different from the traditional open marketplace. Google was the crucial exponent of another of the most important forms of digital advertising: search advertising, the ads that appear when you search for something of commercial interest. This quickly became a bigger money earner than display ads, and now accounts for a little over 40% of digital-advertising revenues (IAB 2022). The field's remaining sectors, which we will not discuss in any detail, include advertising on connected television/video-streaming services (just over 20% of total revenues), and a number of smaller sectors such as digital audio and the digital equivalent of classified ads (in aggregate around 8% of revenues).

Digital advertising is economically extremely concentrated. Alphabet, which is Google's parent company, received around 39% of all digital advertising revenues globally in 2023, and

Meta about 22%.[5] Between them, therefore, the two leviathans of digital advertising have a market share of around 60%, but their position is not always as impregnable as that figure might suggest. In chapter 4, we will examine a major challenge to Google and, in chapter 5, a very different challenge to Facebook/Meta. Chapter 6 discusses how advertising's human practitioners navigate the complexities and perils of their world, and chapter 7 draws out the book's lessons.

## Our approach

When you first take a glimpse behind the one-way mirror, one aspect of what you see doesn't surprise you too much. Digital advertising is a market or, rather, a set of markets. There are providers of a "supply" of advertising opportunities: the big platforms such as Google, YouTube, Facebook, Instagram, TikTok, and Amazon; and smaller publishers such as news organizations, owners of other websites that make money from advertising, games developers, and connected television/streaming services such as Netflix. And there is "demand" for those advertising opportunities from advertisers, both big and small, and from the advertising agencies that work on their behalf. The distinction between supply and demand is built into the field's terminology. Publishers often sell advertising opportunities via what are called "supply-side platforms," or SSPs, and advertisers almost always delegate to "demand-side platforms," or DSPs, the technologically very demanding task of bidding in the trillions of auctions that SSPs run.

When, however, you start to look closely, more surprising things come into view. For example, what's bought and sold are quite often only apparent advertising opportunities: for instance, ads that can't be seen by human eyes, perhaps because they are "shown" in a browser tab other than the one that's open on the user's screen, or where the "viewer" is a computerized "bot" simulating a human audience. And demand and supply are often far less distinct than you might imagine. For instance, the advertisers or advertising agencies that constitute the "demand" for advertising often don't themselves decide whether to bid in Google's or Meta's auctions, and if so how much to bid: they leave these decisions to those platforms, in other words to "supply."

To understand digital advertising, we therefore need an approach that goes beyond simple, standard economics. Our work is a contribution to the burgeoning interdisciplinary field of "market studies," succinctly described in a recent introduction to it as "an effort to understand and unscramble the entangled knot of practices, agents, devices and infrastructures that constitute markets" (Geiger at al. 2024: 1). More specifically, we work at the intersection of economic sociology and science and technology studies (STS), two academic fields that have interacted productively since the late 1990s. Crucial in bringing them together was the French STS scholar and economic sociologist Michel Callon, especially in his pioneering edited collection, *The Laws of the Markets* (Callon 1998).

What Callon and STS scholars more generally bring to market studies is close attention to the role in economic life of measurement (from centuries-old weights and measures to today's digital metrics), systematic practices such as those of accounting, the cognitive tools employed in those practices, and physical things and material devices, whether as old as clay tablets or as sophisticated as the ultrafast algorithmic trading systems that now play a dominant role in many financial markets (MacKenzie 2021). Those are not matters of mere detail, STS-influenced scholars argue, but can shape economic life profoundly. A strong, specific form of that argument is the thesis of the "performativity of economics": the idea that economics – which needs to be conceived of here quite broadly, not just as the academic discipline – is not simply the analysis of economic phenomena "from the outside," but at least sometimes is enacted – i.e., "performed" – within economic life (Callon 1998, 2007).[6] Mathematical models of financial markets, for example, sometimes influence patterns of prices in those markets (MacKenzie 2006; MacKenzie and Millo 2003).

Callon is a central member of a group of scholars within STS – including his colleague, the late, much-missed Bruno Latour, and also, among many others, Madeleine Akrich, John Law, and Annemarie Mol – who developed what is sometimes called "actor-network theory." To present this in full is beyond the scope of this book (see, e.g, Latour 2005), but one productive way of thinking about it is as a shift from a sociology of nouns – "the economy," "society," "culture" – to a sociology of verbs. The economy, for example, should not be thought of as an already existing "thing," but as something that constantly has to be brought into being, that constantly needs to be enacted. The researcher's focus thus needs to shift from "the economy" to "economization" (Caliskan and Callon 2009, 2010), in other words, to the rendering of relations and entities as "economic." Digital advertising, for instance, involves the attempt – sometimes successful, sometimes not, as we shall see in this book – to turn your attention to your phone or laptop's screen (itself not an intrinsically economic phenomenon) into something economically valuable. In other words, digital advertising seeks to "economize" your attention, indeed to "marketize" it, to turn it into something that can be bought and sold as an advertising opportunity.

Another crucial aspect of the work of Callon and those influenced by him is consistent attention to materiality. That is at the heart of the threefold overall argument of *Inside Digital Advertising*. First, we are going to revive an old term, *megamachine*, to capture the materiality, the scale, and the environmental impact of digital advertising's technologies. Second, we will emphasize what we'll call the *material political economy* of those technologies. Like any machine, advertising's megamachines can be designed and configured in materially different ways, and the differences are often economically consequential and in a broad sense political. Third, those issues are at the heart of *platform power*. That power is multifaceted and sociotechnical – i.e., inextricably both social and technological – and in chapter 7 we will lay out what this book reveals about its components.

## Megamachines and material political economy

When computers first became everyday devices, it was easy to think of the digital world as somehow non-material: as "virtual," as constituting a realm of "cyberspace" that was inherently different from the mundane materiality of daily life.[7] No longer. It has become inescapably clear that the digital world is underpinned by a vast, energy-consuming, ever-growing infrastructure. Anyone who still needed convincing of this would surely have changed their mind in September 2024, when it was announced that a mothballed nuclear reactor at the most famous civil nuclear site in the United States, Three Mile Island in the Susquehanna River, was being brought back on stream in a 20-year deal to supply power to Microsoft's computer datacenters (McCormick and Smyth 2024: and see Figure 1.1 below). The following month, Google and Amazon both signed deals with start-up companies developing "small modular" nuclear reactors. Google, for example, has ordered at least six from Kairos Power, which is designing reactors that will be cooled with molten lithium and beryllium fluoride salts, not the traditional water (Moore 2024; Smyth 2024).

The term *megamachine*, which we are using to capture the sheer scale of the materiality of today's digital world, was coined by the social critic and polymath Lewis Mumford to refer to "a radically new type of social organization": the armies of disciplined people who, though equipped with only basic tools, built giant monuments such as the Pyramids and the flood control and irrigation systems of ancient empires. They formed

**Figure 1.1 Powering the digital economy**
The nuclear energy site at Three Mile Island in the Susquehanna River in 2014, photographed from Middletown, Pennsylvania. On the right, with steam rising from them, are the cooling towers of reactor Unit 1, now being recommissioned to power Microsoft's datacenters. On the left are the cooling towers of Unit 2, no longer operational. Unit 2's near-meltdown in 1979 remains the most serious civil nuclear power incident in the US

"an archetypal machine," but one "composed of human parts," writes Mumford (1967: 11). In more recent times, Mumford went on to argue, "the ancient megamachine" has been "resurrected" with alarming consequences, and given "a more perfect technological structure, capable of planetary and even interplanetary extension. . . . With nuclear energy, electrical communication, and the computer, all the necessary components of a modernized megamachine at last became available" (Mumford 1971: 166, 274).

We are in no sense followers of Mumford, and examining his – in our view, overly broadbrush – criticism of centralized technologies and "the technocratic prison" (Mumford 1971: 435) would lead us far beyond the confines of our topic.[8] His tendency to think and write about "the megamachine" in the singular is not helpful: for us, megamachines are inherently plural. It is nevertheless useful to have a word, "megamachine," to capture large-scale assemblages of people and machines that often have characteristics quite different from those of their component parts. The presence of people, it is worth emphasizing, remains important. Even Google, developer and operator of the archetypal digital megamachine, still employs large numbers of people: its parent corporation, Alphabet, had 182,500 employees in December 2023.[9] Although digital advertising's core processes are automated, human beings, personal relationships among them, and their interests and beliefs are all still crucial to the design, construction, and use of its systems.

The relationship of today's digital megamachines to their non-human components is that they *inhabit* giant assemblages of physical machines. "Inhabit" is the correct word because the particular physical machines that make up a megamachine can change from minute to minute. A digital megamachine is in that sense a *meta*machine: a material computational process, or set of processes, running on a huge, possibly ever-changing, set of physical machines.

The megamachines discussed in this book are of two main types. The first inhabit a giant, tightly integrated assemblage of physical machines, with a single corporate owner, such as Google/Alphabet or Meta. Those assemblages, discussed in chapter 3, are not simply accidental aggregates but, to a substantial extent, consciously designed, and their component parts work together, not always seamlessly, but with relatively limited friction.

Google Search, which we will discuss in more detail in chapter 3, has a strong claim to be the original digital megamachine of this first kind. The title of an early article by three Google engineers, "Web Search for a Planet" (Barroso, Dean, and Hölzle 2003), gives a sense of the magnitude of Google's ambition: to have its systems ingest and index nearly the entirety of the already extremely large World Wide Web. That goal was already hugely demanding even at Google's launch in 1998, and its difficulty grew roughly a million-fold over the following decade,

**Figure 1.2 Housing a megamachine**
This photograph by Robert Webster of the Google datacenter, Mayes County, Oklahoma gives a sense of the physical size of Google's "warehouse-scale" computers.

as the number of Google searches and the number of webpages to be searched each increased by a factor of around a thousand (Dean 2010).

To achieve *scale* (a crucial characteristic of the powerful platforms discussed in this book), Google's engineers had to rethink what a computer was. It shouldn't be thought of as a single machine, they realized, but as an ensemble of thousands, tens of thousands, or even more computers packed into a datacenter, such as that shown in Figure 1.2. "[W]e must treat the datacenter itself as one massive warehouse-scale computer," wrote Google engineers Luiz André Barroso and Urs Hölzle (2009: vi). As we will discuss in chapter 3, the individual computers on which Search and other Google services ran were cheap, individually unreliable machines, but by fusing them together into a few dozen giant "warehouse-scale" computers, each housed in a strategically located datacenter to ensure worldwide coverage, key processes could run uninterrupted, globally, even in the face of multiple failures of these individual machines.

A megamachine of this first type, involving giant streams of data ("big data," as it was starting to be called) being processed by warehouse-scale computers with a single corporate owner, can still be programmed by the owner's engineers. The task, however, needs to be tackled differently from the traditional programming of an individual computer. Crucial to this was what was to become a hugely influential approach to programming, MapReduce, first developed at Google in 2003 (and described publicly in 2004) by two engineers central to the programming of Google Search, Sanjay Ghemawat and Jeff Dean.[10]

MapReduce enabled Google's programmers to divide up a giant computational task among huge numbers of machines without having themselves to tackle the complexities of fusing individually unreliable machines into a smoothly functioning megamachine. With MapReduce, the "run-time system," not the human programmer, "takes care of the details of partitioning the input data, scheduling the program's execution across a set of machines, handling machine failures, and managing the required inter-machine communication" (Dean and Ghemawat 2004: 1).

The second type of megamachine that we will discuss has no single owner and is an emergent assemblage rather than consciously designed. While parts of it can be programmed, it cannot be programmed as a whole. Its component parts operate more or less in concert, but typically with greater friction than megamachines of the first type. Digital advertising's longest-established form, Web-display advertising (discussed in chapters 2 and 4) is, for example, a megamachine of this second type. It consists in good part of a plethora of interacting systems deployed by large numbers of different firms, mostly of modest size. Google's systems also play central roles in that megamachine, but their centrality is fiercely contested, as we shall see in chapter 4.

Megamachines and giant warehouses stuffed with tens of thousands of computer servers may seem very alien from everyday life, but these megamachines also inhabit your laptop and your smartphone. You can hold your phone in the palm of your hand, and if its battery still has charge it can run without interaction with the external world, but it is often part of at least one megamachine, some parts of which can be so big that they can almost be seen from space.[11] If, for example, your phone is an iPhone, much of the time it forms part of a megamachine owned and controlled by Apple. Use your phone, however, for a Google Search, and that megamachine clicks into action. Use it to visit a social media platform, and your phone then forms part of that platform's megamachine. The other apps you use, the ads you are shown within them, the elaborate apparatus that seeks, often with some difficulty, to measure and optimize the efficacy of those ads – those are often contested material terrain, with different megamachines contending for control.

Our reason for conceptualizing digital advertising, and digital economies more generally, as consisting in good part of megamachines is not simply to underline their scale but to emphasize *design*. Machines can be designed differently, and material practices can be conducted differently, and which ways prevail is often not simply an issue of technical efficiency but also of power relations, sometimes including those of class, race, and gender.[12] Megamachines, too, can be designed and configured differently, and we would argue that it is important consciously and explicitly to consider how to redesign megamachines even of the second, emergent rather than planned, type.

That is in part an issue of environmental politics, given megamachines' huge consumption of energy and water, the latter used in datacenters' cooling systems to dissipate the heat generated by enormous arrays of computer servers. But there are other crucial design issues too, including one that we explore in chapters 4 and 5. Should your phone or your laptop simply be a relatively passive appendage to the relevant megamachine, sending information on your digital activities to the megamachine's more central systems, and receiving from them ads decided on by those systems? Or should your device play a more active role, itself running auctions for your attention, and storing important data, such as the record of your taps on ads, in its own memory, rather than immediately sending that data to other parts of the megamachine?

Issues such as those make clear that digital economies are not simply *material* economies (as their huge electricity consumption makes evident) but spheres of material *political* economy. The challenges to Google and Facebook/Meta, which we will discuss in chapters 4 and 5, were attempts to reconfigure megamachines, attempts that were economically consequential and, in a broad sense, political. The initiative we describe in chapter 4, for example – to move a crucial part of the market for Web-display ads away from Google's datacenters and into your laptop or phone – involved an effort to change the balance of power between Google and publishers (especially news publishers) and to boost publishers' advertising revenues. It was thus a prime example of material political economy.

Our notion of material political economy has its roots in science and technology studies, in particular the idea of "material politics" put forward by John Law and Annemarie Mol (2008) and Andrew Barry (2013). Again, we think about materiality in terms of verbs, not nouns. In particular, don't take "material political economy" to mean an emphasis on the hardware of computer systems rather than software. Instead, think about material political economy in terms of the difference between the verbs *should*, *must*, and *can*.

For example, Apple's challenge (described in chapter 5) to Facebook/Meta, other mobile-phone apps, and in-app advertisers involved Apple materially restricting their access to the identifier number of each iPhone, known as its IDFA (Identifier for Advertisers). Apple could have said that app developers *should not* use IDFAs to track users without their permission, or even that they *must not* do this. Instead, as we will see in chapter 5, Apple's engineers altered iPhones' operating system so that app developers *cannot* do this, unless that system contains the electronic record of a tap by the user materially consenting to tracking. That, for us, makes Apple's move an instance of material political economy, a change in *what can and cannot happen*, which is economically consequential and in a broad sense political. And the fact that the change was implemented in code – it took the form of an operating system update, rather than an alteration to the physical hardware of iPhones – doesn't stop it being material political economy.

The change that Apple's engineers made also teaches us something important about megamachines. They can be socially powerful and physically big – "macro" – but they can pivot on things that seem merely "technical" and are sometimes physically tiny: "micro." The crucial identifier, your iPhone's IDFA, is an example. It is a 32-digit number electronically encoded in a tiny portion of the silicon-chip memory of a small device that you carry around with you almost all the time. If you have an Android phone, its memory contains an equivalent 32-digit number, Google's version of Apple's IDFA. Physically minuscule, these numbers make a big difference. As we will describe in chapter 5, their reliable functioning helped platforms that took the form of mobile-phone apps gain size, global scope, and power.

A megamachine, at least of the first of the two types discussed above, is a "solid durable macro-actor," to borrow a phrase from Michel Callon and Bruno Latour's first exposition in English of their actor-network theory (1981: 283). As they emphasize, however, we should not take the existence of such macro-actors for granted, but always investigate how they come into being. An actor – in Callon and Latour's view, "[a]ny element which bends space around itself," not just a human being – "grows with the number of relations he or she can put, as we say, in black boxes," which function reliably, and the contents of which "no longer need . . . to be reconsidered" (1981: 284–6). That process, according to Callon and Latour, is what creates macro-actors such as megamachines and, at least in part, is what gives them their power. MapReduce, for example, was centrally involved in that process as it played out in Google: it put the megamachine's complexities into what could be treated as a reliably operating opaque box, so enabling Google's programmers to write code that would run on a giant scale, but without their having themselves continually to wrestle with those complexities.

The crucial role of Apple's IDFAs in megamachines that take the form of mobile-phone apps meant that when Apple in 2021 made default access to IDFAs by apps and advertising systems impossible, it was seriously disruptive. That case is a little unusual, though, in that making something impossible to do is an extreme form of material political economy, one that is difficult to achieve given the unpredictability of technical systems and the ingenuity of human beings seeking to subvert them. Making something hard or awkward to do is more common. Latour gives a simple everyday example: the keys to many European hotel rooms, prior to today's swipe cards. To avoid the nuisance and expense of having a new key cut, or perhaps for security reasons, hotel owners wanted to stop guests leaving the hotel with their keys in their pockets or bags. As Latour points out, one way of doing that – the *should* way – was to have a sign saying: "Please leave your room key at the front desk before you go out." A "should," however, can always be ignored, and even changing the sign to "you *must* leave your key at the desk" might have been insufficient. So hotel owners acted materially, and had a heavy weight added to each key, so that it was awkward for the guest to carry the key around (Latour 1991: 104).

Issues of what it is possible, quick, even easy, to do – and what is awkward, slow, or impossible to do – are pervasive in digital life and appear many times in the chapters that follow. Sometimes, there is a clear intention: Apple's senior managers and engineers plainly knew what they were doing when they were restricted access to iPhones' IDFAs. Material systems, though, are not simply the result of human intentionality. They often have features or exhibit behavior that nobody intended, and it would be mistaken to restrict our discussion to features of such systems only where there is evidence of human intent. Sometimes, indeed, we simply lack the data to infer intent, an issue that we will discuss in the section below on our data sources.

## Platforms and platform power

At the core of digital advertising are a small number of platform-owning corporations, notably Alphabet (Google's parent), Meta, and Amazon. How should their platforms be conceived of and analyzed?

One approach we take is to think of a platform as a "stack" of economization processes, in the sense (already explained) of processes that render things economic. A "stack" is a layered, interacting set of computational processes, and our interviewees often refer to the various systems employed in the advertising market, such as the demand-side and supply-side systems referred to above and the ad servers that we will discuss in chapters 2 and 4, as the advertising technology or "AdTech stack."

What we see as stacked in a platform, however, are not just computational processes but processes of economization. Again, digital advertising offers a simple example. As noted above, users' attention is marketized. But marketization is not the only mode of economization. Gifts are a form of economization, at least when they are viewed, as they are by anthropologists, as carrying with them obligations, as creating a non-monetary form of debt. So is barter, again if conceived of anthropologically as something more complicated than just exchange without the medium of money: as "dynamic, self-contradictory, and open-ended ... deriv[ing] from, and creat[ing] relationships" (Humphrey and Hugh-Jones 1992: 11, 17).

Google, for example, marketizes users' search queries, although, as already suggested, it is often Google's own systems, not advertisers themselves, that bid in the billions of auctions that determine which ads are shown in response to a commercially relevant search term. Google, however, also "gifts" or barters ordinary, "organic" search results (i.e., the results that aren't ads) to users, who in return provide the platform with potentially valuable data: see, e.g., Elder-Vass (2016) and Fourcade and Kluttz (2020).[13] How best materially to configure this stacking is a crucial problem for the developers of platforms, as we shall see when we discuss in chapter 3 the early years of both Google and Facebook, the founders of which were acutely aware of the possibility of getting this wrong.

We lay out the view of platforms as stacked economization processes elsewhere (Caliskan, MacKenzie, and Callon 2024; Caliskan, Callon, and MacKenzie forthcoming). Here, however, we think it is also important to tackle the issue of *platform power*, which is an essential counterpart of our notions of megamachine and material political economy. There's a widespread, correct intuition that platforms of the kind discussed in this book are powerful. The best-known expression of that intuition is Shoshana Zuboff's *The Age of Surveillance Capitalism* (2019), which famously portrays nearly all-powerful surveillance capitalists, of which the big digital platforms (especially, in her view, Google's platforms) are the prototype. Surveillance capitalists' systems "know everything *about us*" and "not only *know* our behavior but also *shape* our behavior at scale" (Zuboff 2019: 8, 11; emphases in original). That argument, in our view, is overstated: digital advertisers' data is often "broken data" in the sense of Pink et al. (2018), and while advertisers might *wish* to shape behavior, their capacity actually to do that is frequently quite limited.

That platform power can be overstated does not, however, imply that it does not exist. It is, as we've said, intrinsically multidimensional. Zuboff is right that one aspect of it is "data power." Big Tech platforms "own vast quantities of user information" (Iliadis and Russo 2016: 1), even if they usually do not in any simple sense "marketize" or sell that data: they hoard it, making it an asset, and can thus "control and manage the very information markets depend upon" (Birch 2023: 14). Platforms also have "algorithmic power," in Taina Bucher's sense: "[i]n ranking, classifying, sorting, predicting, and processing data, algorithms are political in the sense that they help to make the world appear in certain ways rather than others" (2018: 3). And the big-platform corporations enjoy a degree of market dominance within digital advertising that troubles regulators such as the United Kingdom's Competition and Markets Authority (CMA 2020).

In this book, however, we also follow platform researchers Thomas Poell, David Nieborg, and colleagues, and seek to go beyond "monolithic perspectives on platform dominance," such as Zuboff's, and to broaden the "conceptualisation of platform power" (Poell, Nieborg, and Duffy 2023: 1391; van Dijck, Nieborg, and Poell 2019: 1). In particular, we will emphasize platform power's megamachine materiality. For example, Google's capacity to build reliable "warehouse-scale" computers out of large numbers of cheap, individually fallible machines, and its ability to use MapReduce to simplify the programming of those computers were vital components of its platform power.

We will also highlight the importance to platform power of *systematicity*, which again we've already touched on implicitly. An instructive contrast here is between Google's integrated AdTech stack and the rest of the "open marketplace" in Web-display ads, with its large number of smaller firms and only partial centralization via Google's systems. The open marketplace operates at megamachine scale, but frictions and "broken data" abound, for example in the process of "cookie matching" that we will touch upon in chapter 3. In contrast, Google operates an integrated system (as Rieder 2022 emphasizes), and that was and is important to its platform power, forming for example a major obstacle to the material challenge to Google that is the focus of chapter 4.

## Data sources

Our investigation of digital advertising draws upon three sources of data. First is the trade press, in particular the daily *Ad Exchanger*, which covers digital advertising in particular depth.[14] Second, we have participated in six face-to-face advertising-sector conferences (three in the United States, three in the United Kingdom), twelve online conferences, 39 other online events such as webinars, and two online training courses. Formal presentations to these conferences and webinars frequently resemble sales pitches, but conference panels and smaller events are less scripted, as, e.g., were a short-lived flurry of AdTech discussions on Clubhouse. Even the sales pitches indirectly helped us identify tensions within digital advertising because they often implicitly position the product/service in question as a response to them.

Third, we have conducted 119 interviews with 96 practitioners of digital advertising, publishers, and related technical specialists. Interviews are semi-structured, typically 45–60 minutes long, and all but six were audio-recorded and transcribed. Apart from two particularly well-known (and therefore hard to anonymize) interviewees who have given us their permission to name them, we refer to interviewees using two-letter codes, assigned chronologically by the date of our (first) interview with them: see Table 1.1. Our canvas was initially deliberately broad: we sought interviewees from across digital advertising and at first simply pursued any opportunity to speak to people with firsthand experience of its practices and systems. It is only a slight exaggeration to say that initially we spoke to anyone who would speak to us.

Gradually, our data collection became more analytically led. We immersed ourselves thoroughly in the field, reading the trade press, taking part in as many sector meetings as possible, following the sector's debates, and gradually learning about the field's systems, practices, organizations, and specialized terminology. Immersion enabled us to identify specific systems, practices, and episodes (such as Apple's 2021 restrictions on apps' access to iPhones' IDFAs) that are of particular analytical interest, and where possible to focus interviews on those, also seeking out further interviewees with involvement in them. Convenience, snowballing, and the analytically led selection of interviewees and evolving, interviewee-specific questions ruled out even rudimentary quantitative analysis ("N percent said X; M percent said Y") of interviews but brought benefits in the concrete depth of what we learned. Proceeding iteratively in this way is inherently slow (our research began in 2019 and continues) but that has its virtues in providing insights into change through time.

We make no claim that our interviewees are in any sense "representative." There is almost certainly overrepresentation of people in more senior positions because they are easier for us to identify and often more confident in speaking to researchers. Women are underrepresented: only a quarter (29 out of 119) of our interviews are with women. Our research is almost entirely restricted to digital advertising in the United States and Europe (see Table 1.1). We haven't, for example, tried to investigate China, which is very different culturally and politically, with a large but differently structured advertising sector.

A shortcoming of a different kind is that we have found that Big Tech platforms often sharply constrain what employees can say about internal matters, making them wary of being interviewed and/or sometimes very guarded in what they say. In particular, we were not able to interview employees of either Meta or Apple for this book, so lack firsthand fieldwork data on internal processes in those corporations.

That creates a methodological danger that we have been careful to avoid: the risk involved, in the case of large corporations that are complex organizations, of inferring a unified corporate

## Table 1.1  Interviewees

| | US | UK | Continental Europe | India | Total |
|---|---|---|---|---|---|
| Advertiser | AE, AG, AH, CV, DE, DF, DG, DQ | AF | AQ, CC, CD, CE | CF | 14 |
| Advertising agency | AB, AK, AL, AM, CJ, CK, DO | AI, AP, AX, AZ, BB, BL, CG, CL | AJ, AV, DL, DM, DN | | 20 |
| "Demand-side-oriented" AdTech, eg Demand-Side Platform (DSP) | AN, BI, CM, CO, CP, CR, DH, DI, DR | AC, AO, AU, AY, DD | CH | | 15 |
| "Supply-side-oriented" AdTech, e.g. Supply-Side Platform (SSP) | AS, BJ, BK, BQ, BR, BS, BT, BW, BX, BZ, CB, CN, CS, DK | BE, BF, BP | AT | | 18 |
| Major platform | AA, CQ, DC, DP | | | AR | 5 |
| Other publisher | BN, BU, BV, BY, CA, CT, CU, CW, CY, CZ, DB | AW, BA, BC, BD, BG, BH, BO, DJ | | | 19 |
| Technical specialist, auditor, etc. | BD, CW, DA | BM, CI | | | 5 |
| Total | 56 | 27 | 12 | 1 | 96 |

*Note*: Two-letter labels are chronological by the date of our first interview with the person in question. AA and AB were first interviewed in 2019; AC-AH in 2020; AI-BN in 2021; BO-CO in 2022; CP-DD in 2023; DE-DR in 2024.

intent. "Politics," including material politics, is to be found not only in the interactions among big corporations and between them and the wider world, including government, but also *within* them. Sometimes at least, what looks like a corporation's in which the advertiser often pays simply to have their ad shown; the second by systems such as Google Search ads, in which advertisers pay only if users click on their ads (see chapter 3).

More is at stake in the divide between the two forms than simply pricing mechanisms in the narrow sense, as Beuscart and Mellet (2013) argue, and we view understanding the divide as vital when researching digital advertising: see, for example, the final section of our chapter 3. The first form, "pay per ad," was and is often associated with a world of digital advertising that involves advertisers seeking to boost their brands, advertising agencies that often have their roots in pre-digital practices, and, at least sometimes, digital versions of traditional media. The second world of digital advertising, characterized by "pay per click," is the domain of platforms that are quite different from traditional media, of advertisers that seek a "direct response," such as an immediate purchase, and (as we have found in our interviews) of advertising practitioners who often view themselves quite differently from their pre-digital counterparts.[16]

This group of researchers, especially Beauvisage (Beauvisage 2023; Mellet and Beauvisage 2020), have also worked on the most studied aspect of digital advertising, cookies, which we discuss below in chapter 2. Others who have made important contributions on that topic include Jones (2020, 2024: see p. ••) and Crain (2021). We have also been influenced strongly by Beauvisage and colleagues (2023), an insightful study, which we draw on in chapter 6, of the collision between traditional human-guided targeting of advertising to particular sociodemographic groups and targeting by machine-learning-based optimization systems, targeting that is "post-demographic" in the sense of Rogers (2009).

The collision between human guidance and automated optimization raises the issue of whether the latter involves a partial loss of human agency by advertising's practitioners, an issue central to chapter 6. Another influence on our discussion of that issue is work by Annmarie Ryan and colleagues, who distinguish between AdTech practices that enhance practitioners' agency, and those that "equip but limit the agency of the marketer" (Ryan et al. 2023: 480). As discussed in chapter 6, however, a formulation stronger than theirs seems to us to be justified. Human practitioners, especially in direct-response advertising, the second of the two worlds of digital advertising identified by Beuscart and Mellet (2013), are being in some respects "de-agenced," stripped of capacities that were often crucial to the self-conception of their pre-digital counterparts.

Another long-term contributor to the literature on advertising is Robert Cluley. Drawing on the work of Gilles Deleuze (1992) on "societies of control," Cluley and Stephen Brown elegantly formulate a crucial aspect of digital advertising, closely related to the issues that we have just discussed, which is that it treats "consumers not as *fixed individuals* but as *dividualized consumers* – that is to say, collections of data that can be exposed, dissected and segmented into new marketable groups" (Cluley and Brown 2015: 107; the term "dividual" is Deleuze's).

Cluley (2018) focuses on a seemingly more mundane but actually crucial issue that we have also already touched on in this chapter – that many ads are not actually viewable in any meaningful sense by human beings – and describes an industry initiative to create a standard measure of viewability. Cluley (2020) characterizes data as "political," a characterization with which we heartily agree (on data politics, see Ruppert, Isin, and Bigo 2017), and documents another important conflict around a failed initiative to restrict tracking. Cluley (2025) reports the results of an in-depth ethnographic study of a company providing rapid evaluation (by paid cohorts of subjects) of the relative effectiveness of different advertisements.

Consumers' reactions to advertising are, of course, a topic worth study in its own right. Heath, Cluley, and O'Malley (2017) focus on users' resistance to advertising and marketing. Minna Ruckenstein and Julia Granroth (2020) analyze a related issue, the pervasive tension between users' dislike/fear of "creepy" tracking and the "pleasurable moments of being 'seen' by the market" (Ruckenstein and Granroth 2020: 12). That tension is no longer simply "external" (i.e., felt by advertising's audiences) but has now transposed itself into digital advertising itself in the form of the increasing restrictions that we will discuss in chapter 5 and 6. These restrictions partially *de-individualize* advertising's audiences in a way that has yet to be fully taken into account in the literature, which has tended to focus on how platforms and algorithms construct and act upon individuals.[17]

Despite the relative youth of digital advertising (as we will discuss in chapter 2, it began to gather momentum only in the mid-1990s), historical studies of it are accumulating. Smith (2015) contains a useful account of digital advertising's early years, based in good part on firsthand contact with those involved. McGuigan (2023) is an excellent, primary-source-based examination of the computerization and optimization efforts that form digital advertising's prehistory. He investigates, in particular, what he refers to as the "archaeology" of four crucial aspects (four "affordances") of digital advertising: "programmability," "addressability" (i.e., targeting), "shoppability" (direct response), and "accountability," the measurement of advertising's effectiveness (McGuigan 2023: 132).[18] We build upon that in our discussion of the characteristics of digital advertising at the end of chapter 3, and like McGuigan we too see optimization as crucial, both to the field's practices and to its claims to legitimacy.

Matthew Crain's similarly impressive *Profit Over Privacy* (2021), which we draw on especially in our chapter 2, picks up the story, especially of Web-display advertising, from its beginnings in the mid-1990s to around 2008. Meg Leta Jones is another insightful, broadly historical, scholar. Her first book (Jones 2016) does not deal directly with advertising, but her recent *The Character of Consent* (2024) builds on her journal articles (notably Jones 2019, 2020) and develops a fine interwoven history of relevant technologies, especially cookies, of constructions of the person – as "data subject," "user," "consumer," etc. – and of the relevant law.

The automated auctions at the heart of digital advertising have not so far been a major focus of the literature on it, but three important contributions do throw light upon them. Alaimo and Kallinikos (2018) helpfully examine the standard that defines the digital objects that are traded in open-display ad markets. Viljoen, Goldenfein, and McGuigan (2021) discuss auctions in the context of a broader study of the role – especially the legitimatory role – of the academic economics of mechanism design, while the legal scholar Dana Srinivasan (2020) discusses the auctions on which we will focus in chapter 4 in the context of a broader account of Google's dominant role in digital advertising.

Despite the multiple strengths of the literature we have just reviewed, it also needs to be said that its coverage of digital advertising is patchy. Most notably, despite the importance of the mobile-app economy and the central role of advertising in that economy, advertising in and of apps has seldom been examined in any depth. The central existing contribution is David Nieborg's (2017) examination of the "player commodity": in effect, the buying and selling of players of mobile-phone games. This builds on his pioneering investigation (Nieborg 2015) of the paradigmatic free-to-play game Candy Crush Saga, a game that is our central example in chapter 5. Nieborg's work links back to an important contribution to the Marxist-inspired political economy of media, Dallas Smythe's (1977) account of the "audience commodity" in pre-digital advertising, for example on broadcast television.[19]

What Smythe highlighted nearly 50 years ago was the buying and selling of, for instance, access to the screens of those watching specific TV programs, who had aggregate sociodemographic characteristics that could often be inferred by studying the viewing habits of nationally representative panels of viewers. Broadcast TV audiences, however, were not knowable at the level of individuals. In the 1990s, though, the newly invented

World Wide Web did more than offer a new medium via which to advertise. It soon also offered — especially via cookies, introduced in 1994 — ways of recording not just aggregate audience characteristics but individual actions, so making possible new ways of targeting advertising and measuring its effectiveness. Display ads on the Web are therefore an appropriate starting point, in the next chapter, for our account of digital advertising.

# 2

# Display Ads, Cookies, and the Open Marketplace

Digital advertising began, in the mid-1990s, with display ads shown – at first with only minimal targeting – to visitors to websites. Nowadays, display ads can be videos or sometimes even games, but originally they were simple, static combinations of an image or images and text. They were, however, clickable, with the click usually taking you to the advertiser's website, where you could learn more about the product or service being advertised, and perhaps buy it there and then.

This chapter discusses the emergence of display ads on the Web and their relations to the evolution of the Web itself, to the browsers that enable websites to be rendered on users' screens, and to a crucial innovation that gave the Web a "memory" and left a long-standing mark on digital advertising: the cookie. We will see how the material form of the market for Web-display ads has changed. Originally, buying and selling involved face-to-face contact between human beings, perhaps over Madison Avenue's traditionally lavish expense-account lunches or dinners, but from 2006 onward it increasingly moved inside machines.

That shift gave birth to what practitioners at the time called "programmatic advertising." That name has stuck, but we won't use it because it is confusing: the big systems that we will describe in chapter 3 – which practitioners often call "walled gardens," in contrast to the world whose origins are described in this chapter – are in a literal sense equally programmatic. Instead, we will highlight that contrast (which, curiously, the literature on digital advertising discussed in the previous chapter has given little explicit attention to) by adopting a different practitioners' term: the "open marketplace."

As its name suggests, barriers to entry to the open marketplace are low. Most of the firms that populate it are small, and competition among them is often fierce. The open marketplace is decentralized and sometimes a little chaotic, and there is frequently only limited policing. It is less distant from today's pervasive imaginaries of a "market" than the walled gardens are, as we will discuss in chapter 6. But the form the open marketplace in Web-display ads takes is not an economic inevitability, nor the result of some imagined greater efficiency of a market. It has its roots in the materiality of the Web, as the final part of the chapter will show by contrasting it with the later, materially quite different, world of display ads within apps.

## The Web, display ads, and the dot-com bubble

When display ads first appeared in 1994, the Web (then often called the "World Wide Web") was only four years old. Its origins were far from commercial. Famously, it began as a 1989–90 proposal by physicist and computer scientist Tim Berners-Lee for how his employer, Geneva's multinational CERN laboratory for particle physics, should organize and make accessible its growing, ever-changing body of documentation.[1] In December 1990, the Web was just a single prototype website and a rudimentary browser with which to access it, both physically existing on Berners-Lee's desktop computer (Berners-Lee 2010: 80).

By June 1993, there were still no more than about 130 websites worldwide, and the United States had only around a couple of dozen ISPs (Internet Service Providers) via which those sites could be accessed from people's homes.[2] But the Web was growing fast, doubling in size every three months or less, helped by the development of browsers that integrated the display of text and images on the user's screen: first Mosaic in 1993, and then, crucially, Netscape Communications Corporation's Navigator in 1994. (Earlier browsers rendered images separately, in much the same way as they appear, sometimes even today, in preprints of scientific papers.) By January 1996, there were around 100,000 websites, and by August that year nearly 3,000 ISPs provided US businesses and households with access to them, although still nearly always slow, "dial-up" access via conventional telephone lines.

Many of the new websites created in the mid-1990s had a commercial orientation. Amazon, for example, was founded in 1994, and eBay in 1995. Among them was HotWired (hotwired.com), set up in 1994 by the new, widely read technology magazine *Wired* as a complement to its print version. HotWired was an experiment to see what could be done with the new medium of the Web, but one that was expected from the start to earn its keep: Andrew Anker, the venture capitalist who had become *Wired*'s Chief Technology Officer, saw HotWired as "building a business." That could not be done by charging visitors to the site: even if they were willing to pay, at the start of 1994 there was not yet any widely available secure way of using a credit card online. So, says Anker, "there was . . . no other way to make money but getting advertisers to pay."[3]

Corporations already advertised in *Wired*'s print magazine, so – via the magazine's print-ad sales team – Anker was able to persuade a number of them also to advertise on its new website. The specific ad that has become famous – it's usually regarded as the start of Web-display advertising – was created in 1994 by Joe McCambley and his colleagues at a new digitally oriented marketing agency, Modern Media, for their client, the US telecoms giant, AT&T (McCambley 2013). It was a simple horizontal digital banner, complementing a traditional AT&T advertising campaign pivoting around the slogan "you will." AT&T's name did not appear in the banner. It simply asked: "Have you ever clicked your mouse right HERE?" An arrow pointed to the answer: "YOU WILL." Users who actually clicked there were taken to another page on HotWired's website, which showed a map of the world, AT&T's name and logo, and links to a dozen or so cultural websites, mainly those of art galleries.[4]

Users *did* click, at a rate measured by code on HotWired's site of 44% (McCambley 2013). *Wired*'s sales team went on to strike further direct deals with other advertisers' marketing departments to have their ad or ads embedded in HotWired's website for a fixed period of time. "$10,000 was a round number that made the numbers [HotWired's finances] work," says Anker, "and we tried it and everybody sort of seemed to buy it." The website was divided into sections, and "we matched up an advertiser to a section." The same banner ad for Volvo, for example, always appeared above HotWired's "On the Road" section, even if the user "hit reload . . . There was no idea of targeting."[5]

HotWired demonstrated that it was possible to fund a website by showing ads. That fact quickly became interwoven with huge enthusiasm in the late 1990 for the stock of the new Web-based commercial enterprises: the "dot-com bubble." On August 5, 1995, the pioneering Web-browser developer, Netscape, yet to make a profit, launched on the stock market, with its shares priced for its IPO (initial public offering) at US$28. They reached US$75 at the peak of the first day's trading (Greenstein 2015: 180). Soon Netscape's 25-year-old co-founder, browser designer Marc Andreessen, was on the cover of *Time* magazine, wearing jeans, a T-shirt, and no shoes or socks.[6]

The dot-com bubble quickly spread to other new Web-based enterprises, even those whose business plans were far more tenuous than Netscape's. That in its turn encouraged the rapid growth of Web-display advertising. Mainstream consumer brands embraced the new medium only slowly, although the consumer-goods giant Procter & Gamble, for example, started to spend heavily by the end of the 1990s (Crain 2021: 82, 109). However, the new dot-com companies themselves often advertised intensively as a means of attempting "growth hacking" – speeding up the crucial process of acquiring users – and in the late 1990s, dot-com and other technology companies sometimes accounted for half or more of spending on Web-display advertising (Crain 2021: 81). In a striking form of circularity, advertising revenues were often the crucial anticipated income source for many of the dot-coms that placed those ads. Established print publishers also started to experiment, like *Wired* had, with developing ad-funded Web offshoots (Boczkowski 2005).

Interviewee BZ's depiction of how Web-display ads were sold, at least by established publishers, in the 1990s and the early 2000s as "schmooze and booze" – or BW's "going out to lunch, drinking a martini" – may contain an element of stereotype, but it remained common for deals to be negotiated face to face between an advertiser (or advertising agency acting on its behalf) and a website's publisher. Pricing, too, was initially largely traditional. Instead of HotWired's fixed price for placing an ad on its site for a specific period of time, these website ad slots – i.e., opportunities to show ads – were, and often still are, usually sold according to a price convention directly inherited from print advertising: the CPM, or cost per mille, in other words, the cost of a thousand "impressions." (An "impression" is the showing of one ad to one reader, TV viewer, or Web or app user.)[7]

At its edges, however, this patchwork of direct, face to face, bilateral relationships began to evolve into what was to become display advertising's open marketplace. Even established publishers' sales teams often struggled to find enough direct deals with advertisers to fill the plentiful ad slots on their new websites, leaving them with the problem of "what we call[ed] 'remnant'... the leftovers" (O'Kelley interview). Websites without a basis in the world of print, and so lacking a sales team with established contacts, could find it hard, at least initially, to strike any direct deals, so they could be left with nothing but "remnant" to sell.

"Schmooze and booze" played a smaller role in buying and selling "remnant." Instead of an advertiser or advertising agency and a publisher interacting directly, they typically did so via a new category of firm, "ad networks." These networks occupied a central position in Web-display advertising, especially in its first decade (and, as we will see at the end of this chapter, they continue to do so for advertising within apps). Large numbers of ad networks were set up in the late 1990s or early 2000s. Nearly all were initially small start-ups, and many remained small. They could portray themselves as dot-com firms, but their business model was at its core simple. An ad network bought large blocks of ad slots cheaply from publishers, in the case of less well-established websites, sometimes buying up all of a site's slots, so allowing its owners to concentrate on developing those sites and acquiring users.

The ad network would then fill those slots with ads on behalf of its advertiser clients, charging the latter a substantial mark-up. A direct deal might earn an established publisher dollars, even tens of dollars, per thousand impressions, but an ad network could often buy ad slots for mere "pennies" (interviewee BI) per thousand, and thus a small fraction of a cent per impression. This buying and selling was still done by human beings, but hardly merited a lavish lunch. And, as we shall see below, it soon began to be automated, as buying and selling in the open marketplace moved inside machines.

## Cookies

Before, though, we turn to the move of the market into machines, we need to discuss "cookies," the one part of digital advertising's extensive apparatus of which everyone is aware because browsing the Web now involves endless "cookie consent" banners.[8]

A "cookie" is a string of digits – normally quite short – that is unique to each user, which a website deposits in the user's browser when it first requests access to the site. The cookie is then physically stored in the memory of the device (desktop, laptop, tablet, or smartphone) via which the user is browsing the Web. When the user's browser makes a new request of the same website – e.g., to access a different page on the website, or if the user visits the website again at a later date – their browser sends back to the website the cookie it has deposited. This enables the website to "connect up" the user's different actions and different visits.[9]

Because connecting up different actions by the same human user could potentially be a threat to the user's privacy, cookies have been controversial almost since they were first invented. Netscape, the pioneering browser developer, was where cookies were born. In 1994, the Netscape engineer Lou Montulli and his colleagues altered a fundamental aspect of the Web's original design by giving Netscape's Navigator browser the capacity to deposit and retrieve cookies. With its origins in making documents such as CERN's available, the Web was, in Montulli's words, "designed to be fast and efficient and part of its design was [for a browser] to connect to a website, grab a document and then disconnect." The early Web was therefore, in the terminology of computer science, "stateless," or as Montulli puts it, it lacked "memory": "Each time a user clicked to move to a different page they would become just another random user with no way to associate them with an action they had just done moments ago" (Montulli 2013). Another group within Netscape in 1994 was, however, developing a server for electronic commerce and, Montulli recalls, had been unable to find a way "to build shopping cart functionality" precisely because that required linking separate actions by the same user: adding items to the electronic cart one by one, then paying for all of them in a single transaction. "At some point during the next week the general concept of Web Cookies formed in my head," says Montulli (2013).

There were ways other than cookies to "give the Web a memory" (Schwartz 2001) and different ways in which cookies could be implemented. The latter issue was debated intensely in the informal, international (although in practice usually United States-led), self-regulatory bodies that try to agree the standards that shape the internet and the Web. It also spilled over into the public domain. In 1996, a *Wired* journalist summarized the chief objection to cookies: "they seemed to remove one of the great features (or problems) of the Web: anonymity. Cookies make it possible to track a user's movements on the Web" (Garfinkel 1996).

As in all forms of politics, though, "facts on the ground" can shape material politics. By December 1995, when a subgroup of one of the standard-setting bodies, the Internet Engineering Task Force, began to discuss how to give the Web memory, Netscape's cookies were one of those facts. As Beauvisage (2023) points out, Netscape's way of giving the Web a memory was materially simple, had already been implemented, and worked. Indeed, in late 1995 Netscape's Navigator "dominated the [browser] market," as the subgroup's chair, computer scientist David Kristol, says (2001: 169). Netscape's dominance was temporary: it was soon to be overwhelmed by Microsoft's browser, Internet Explorer. While users had to pay Netscape for Navigator, Explorer was free. Microsoft integrated it with and shipped it along with Microsoft Windows, the operating system of almost all personal computers other than Apple's machines. Microsoft, however, also embraced cookies, giving Internet Explorer, like Navigator, the capacity to deposit cookies in users' browsers.

There thus was, and generally there still is, de facto acceptance not just that the Web needs a memory, but also that cookies are a simple way to provide it. That rough consensus, however, extended – and extends – only to "first-party cookies," those deposited by the site the user is visiting. Largely unresolved was, and is (see chapter 5), an issue identified as early as February 1996 (Kristol 2001: 159): "third-party cookies," in other words, cookies that are deposited and retrieved not by the website being visited but by a different site.

Cookies are specific to websites: only the site that has deposited a cookie in a user's browser can retrieve it.[10] The possibility, despite that, of third-party cookies arises because a "first-party" website – i.e., the site to which the user's browser has requested access – often contains content generated elsewhere on the Web, that is, by "third parties." In particular, if a website works with an ad network, the ads that are shown will normally be generated separately by that network's "ad server," rather than hard-coded into the website itself. That server therefore has its own capacity to deposit a cookie in the user's browser and, crucially, it can then retrieve that cookie when the user is visiting a different website that also employs the same ad network.

Third-party cookies therefore gave ad networks the capacity to track users across websites and build profiles of them. In itself, a cookie is simply an arbitrary string of letters and numbers, but a third-party cookie enables the gradual accrual of information about the user in question, especially if it is present on a website into which the user enters their name, physical address, and perhaps telephone number, as they will usually do when making a purchase. Those additional identifiers can then be used, via datasets accumulated by data brokers, to enrich that information further, for example with the user's occupation, income bracket, age, and so on.[11]

It is important not to exaggerate the completeness or accuracy of the data typically associated with a cookie (an issue to which we will return at the end of chapter 3), but cookies did enable ad networks to promise their advertiser clients not just cheap ads but also targeted ads. Best known among the many ad networks to do this was DoubleClick, set up in 1995 by technologist Kevin O'Connor, his colleague Dwight Merriman, and advertising executive David Carlick.[12] O'Connor and Merriman were based in Atlanta, but chose to set up the firm in New York because, says O'Connor, the city was the home of many of the biggest media companies and traditionally the prime location of the advertising business in the United States.[13] "[B]oth your supply and demand in one spot," is how interviewee CR describes New York's advantage in this respect. Within five years, DoubleClick was placing adverts on around 2,000 websites – many of them then well known, such as AltaVista, Travelocity, and the home page of Netscape's browser – and serving in total over a billion ads a day (Crain 2021: 62, 88; Reese 2002: 7).

DoubleClick was central to what interviewee CR calls New York's "nascent" but "real tech scene," often referred to in the 1990s as Silicon Alley, in an aspirational nod to California's Silicon Valley. In 1998, the firm placed a huge billboard bearing the slogan "DoubleClick Welcomes you to SILICON ALLEY" (Lee 2002) on a rooftop next to Manhattan's iconic Flatiron Building. Silicon Alley's locale was often described – simplistically, says CR – as what Lee (2002) calls the "corridor of industrial lofts" between the Flatiron Building and Union Square.[14] The founders of the big West Coast tech firms were, we shall see in chapter 3, often ambivalent about advertising.[15] Their New York counterparts, and ad networks more generally, wholeheartedly embraced advertising, cookies, and targeting.

Interviewee AD, who was trained in digital advertising by DoubleClick in early 2000, tells us what its and other ad networks' cookies made possible:

> Back then, actually until very recently, browsers were wide open. You could set a cookie and it would last forever. So that was the big benefit of a company like DoubleClick, is they had banner ads on almost every website, they could then get . . . a persistent cookie that would load all over the place and they could see this same person is going to all these different places, and infer a lot of information about you.

That, in its turn, enabled, at least in principle, the delivery of ads to the audience that the advertiser wanted, says AD: "You could pick the publisher, you would go to DoubleClick . . . and they would charge you different rates, depending on the publisher, but also they had targeting, so you could say I want this to run in front of women in the Bay Area at 6pm or something like that . . . you were buying specific audiences."

The DoubleClick system that implemented targeting of this kind was called DART (Dynamic Advertising Reporting and Targeting). As its name suggests, DART sought not just to direct ads to target audiences, but also to provide near real-time reports for advertisers on whether their Web-display advertising campaign seemed to be "working": not just whether ads were being clicked on, but whether those clicks led to sales or downloads (Reese 2002: 3). That is the first appearance in our story of a crucial aspect of digital advertising – the "[c]losing [of] the loop between ads and consumer actions" (Crain 2021: 101) – that is, for example, at the center of the material politics discussed in chapter 5.

Measuring sales and downloads involved DoubleClick not simply in depositing cookies in users' browsers but placing a different technology of tracking on the *advertiser*'s website: tiny, transparent, single-pixel images.[16] Such pixels were crucial in early digital advertising. When a click on an ad took a user to a page on an advertiser's website, their browser would be prompted by the website to render the tiny, invisible image, and in so doing the user's browser would transmit information to the ad network that had placed the pixel. Crucially, a pixel placed on an electronic commerce website's "thank you" page, which is rendered on the user's screen only if they have made a purchase, would record that a sale had occurred (interviewee DM). As a programmer we talked to about pixels told us, "the [pixel's] code runs in the browser to gather as much information as it can and encodes that into the address of the image it requests." What you view, what you buy, what you add to a shopping cart but don't actually buy, information about your browser – all that and more can be transmitted via pixels.

## A market within a machine

DoubleClick's DART had a more basic task than targeting and measuring the efficacy of ads: it also served them, that is, it transmitted them from DoubleClick's servers to the user's screen. It was, in other words, an "ad server." Initially, DART was used only by DoubleClick itself, but in 1997, after "a volcanic in-house debate" (Reese 2002: 7), the firm agreed to allow the *Wall Street Journal* to license the technology. Internal opponents feared that allowing others to use DART would undercut DoubleClick's ad network business, and indeed that may well have happened. However, other major publishers followed the *Journal* in adopting DART, and by 2001 DART licensing fees accounted for 70% of DoubleClick's revenues (Reese 2002: 8). DoubleClick also licensed to advertisers a different version of DART: an advertiser's ad server, which helped them keep track of their advertising campaigns. "It . . . recorded stuff, it was like a counter," says interviewee CR.

As we will see in chapter 4, of the two versions of DART, it was the first, the publisher's ad server, that was to become the crucial machine in Web-display advertising because it is the system that takes the final decision of which ad to show to which user. That, however, was still in the future. For all of the sophistication of the tracking that DoubleClick's DART permitted, it and other early ad servers delivered ads in a relatively inflexible manner. They "were rules-based engines. It was deliver A [an ad for campaign A], then B, then C, then rotate through those" (interviewee BW). "A [publisher's] ad server, all it was doing was mixing and matching the demand that had already been booked," says CR. If, for example, a publisher worked with several ad networks, its ad server would contact them in a fixed, predetermined order, usually according to the average price they paid for ad slots. If the first, typically highest-paying, network chose not to buy a particular slot, "they would send it to the next one [in a fixed 'daisy chain' or 'waterfall'], and the next one, and the next one" (O'Kelley interview).

There was an implicit contradiction between inflexibility of this kind and the growing sophistication of ad targeting. Computer scientist Brian O'Kelley was hired in 2003 by the ad network Right Media, based – like DoubleClick – in New York. O'Kelley soon came to realize that both publishers and ad networks could make more money by what he calls "de-averaging" (O'Kelley interview), building a more flexible ad server that, using machine learning, could in real time allocate ad slots to the campaign or network for which they had the highest value. This new ad server, Right Media's Yield Manager, ran in effect an internal auction, in which these predicted values were treated as equivalent to bids. It was initially only a simulated auction: as O'Kelley says, there were few if any economic actors capable of bidding for individual ad slots in a flood of millions or even billions of them.

Right Media, though, earned additional revenue by letting other ad networks use Yield Manager as their ad server. O'Kelley had the "insight that if you had enough customers using you in the same ad server, you could in real time allow them to be liquid with each other," in other words, to buy ad slots from and sell them to each other (interviewee CR). O'Kelley had previously worked for one of the new electronic stock-trading venues set up in the 1990s (for which see MacKenzie 2021), and began to think of the capability to buy and sell ad slots within Yield Manager as forming the basis for an ad exchange loosely analogous to stock exchanges: Right Media's RMX Direct, launched in August 2006. The networks using it could "input their supply and demand" (interviewee CB), the ad slots they were prepared to sell or wanted to buy. The machine, the ad server, "would do the rest" (CB), allocating slots – in real time (BW) – to the network that would pay the most. In this "federated bidding" (O'Kelley interview), the "market" had moved into the machine, which no longer conducted simply a simulated auction: money was now changing hands.

Right Media's ad exchange was not an immediate threat to DoubleClick, which had far more extensive links to both publishers and advertisers than Right Media had. It was, however, "a big shot across [DoubleClick's] bow," says interviewee CR. "We actually had a meeting about it, we were like, what the f . . . are we doing, we don't have an exchange strategy." That was the start of DoubleClick developing its own (and soon to be Google's) ad exchange, AdX, which we will discuss in chapter 4. Another early exchange was AdECN, set up in 2004, the name of which was an explicit reference to the new stock-trading venues, which were known as ECNs, or electronic communication networks.

As far as we can discover, what was at first bought and sold on all these early ad exchanges were blocks of ad slots, not the individual, real-time opportunity to show an ad to a specific user. That, however, "caus[ed] things [ad opportunities] that were not similar being sold together," as AdECN co-founder Jeff Green told journalist Amit Chowdhry (2017). From 2009–10 onward, therefore, ad exchanges began to break up the blocks and started trading individual ad opportunities: the chance to show an ad to *this* specific user (normally identified by a cookie), *right now*, that is, in roughly a second's time. They launched, in other words, what came to be called "real-time bidding."

## The open marketplace

As Michel Callon's actor-network economic sociology, discussed in chapter 1, emphasizes, economic actors are not given and pre-existing but need to be created. Real-time bidding made possible – and necessitated – those new economic agents. By 2009–10, billions of opportunities to show Web-display ads became available daily. Ingesting this electronic torrent and deciding which opportunities to bid for (and if so, how much) was a task that soon required hundreds of computer servers working simultaneously. Few individual advertisers, however big, felt able to take on this task. It became the job of specialist firms known as "demand-side platforms" or DSPs, which bid on behalf of their multiple advertisers or advertising-agency clients. "[Y]ou'd basically run an . . . analysis that said what . . . each [ad] impression is worth," to each of the advertisers for which the DSP was acting, says interviewee DI, and treat those estimates as bids in a simulated auction, sending the highest bid or bids to the ad exchange. "[S]o you didn't overbid," his DSP's systems also predicted "the likely clearing price of that inventory" on the exchange, reducing the DSP's bids if they seemed unnecessarily high.

The open "programmatic" marketplace in Web-display ads was coming into being. The original ad networks were supplemented, and in many cases displaced, by the emergence of a plethora of new high-tech economic actors: ad exchanges; demand-side platforms bidding on behalf of advertisers; "supply-side platforms," or SSPs, acting on behalf pf publishers by selling their ad slots in what is in effect the SSP's own exchange; and data management platforms, or DMPs, which "enrich" requests for bids by adding to each of them whatever they know about the user in question.

For all its burgeoning diversity and complexity, the open marketplace in Web-display ads was held together materially, albeit imperfectly, by Montulli's 1994 innovation – the cookie – and in particular by the widely circulating third-party cookies discussed above. The presence of such a cookie enables the value of an individual ad opportunity to be estimated. For example, if the cookie is tied to the pixel-generated information that the user has put a product into their online shopping cart, but has not actually purchased it, that is a very valuable opportunity for "retargeting": for showing the user further ads for the product in question, along with links to where they can buy it. Cookies, too, enabled the connection to be drawn between the information held by a data management platform and the user who, right at this moment, was visiting a website that carried ads.

The material tying together of the open marketplace by cookies may now be coming to an end, as we shall touch on in the final section of chapter 5 (see Jones 2024). It was always far from frictionless even in cookies' heyday. Different Web domains deposit different cookies in users' browsers, and, as noted above, a cookie can be retrieved only by the domain that has set it, so cookies are not an Esperanto. In particular, each supply-side platform and each demand-side platform will have a different cookie for the same individual user. For the demand-side platform to know how much to bid for an ad opportunity, it needs to translate, into its own cookie, the cookie it has been sent by the supply-side platform that has requested a bid. The tying together by cookies of the open marketplace thus requires what are in effect giant matching tables, connecting up the different cookies by which you are known to different organizations' systems. The matching is never perfect: our interviewees seem to regard a match rate of 70% as excellent.

And there are yet other imperfections. The apparatus of pixels that records user actions is imperfect, and its results are not usually circulated beyond the organization that has placed the pixel: we are all therefore familiar with being bombarded with ads for a product we have actually already bought. Turning the copious data generated by cookies, pixels, and the rest of digital advertising's measurement apparatus into *knowledge* – is my ad campaign actually cost-effective? – is trickier than it seems because causation is hard to distinguish from mere correlation.

For example, people do indeed often go on to buy a product they have added to an electronic shopping cart but not yet bought. It is hard, however, to be confident that is a retargeting ad that has caused them to make the purchase. Perhaps they were simply mulling the purchase over, or waiting to consult a spouse or family member before buying, and would have bought anyway? Showing an ad for the product in question to them while they are mulling it over can still be very valuable for an advertising platform because measurement systems are likely to credit that ad with the purchase. That was a prime goal of his platform's bidding algorithms, interviewee CM frankly tells us: "We want to be there when it happens and get credit for it." But that, he points out, is quite different from certainty that the ad *caused* the purchase: "whether we drove it or not is very much a second-order concern."

## The different world of apps

The specific form taken by the open marketplace in Web-display apps, with its alphabet soup of participants – ad exchanges, DSPs, SSPs, DMPs, and so on – should not be thought of as inevitable, or as resulting simply from an open market being more efficient than other allocation mechanisms. Display ads are not restricted to the Web: they are also commonplace in smartphone apps. There, however, more traditional participants – ad networks – have kept their hold, and the Web's demand-side and supply-side platforms, although present, are much less prominent. The most successful ad networks in the world of apps have transformed themselves into what are called "mediation platforms," which, for example, perform functions of the kind performed by ad servers on the Web. The "header bidding," discussed in chapter 4, which has become a vital part of buying and selling Web-display ads, is far less prevalent with apps.

Material differences between the Web and apps seem largely to be responsible for these very differently structured markets. On the Web, it is easy for a firm to install or uninstall a pixel on an advertiser's website, or add to a publisher's website the standardized code for "header bidding." Doing the equivalent tasks in the case of an app, via a software development kit or SDK that has to be in effect hard-coded into the app, is much harder, and once an ad network has its SDK in place, replacing it is not simple. When interviewees from Web advertising sought to enter, or considered entering, the world of apps, they encountered what they sometimes considered to be "material micromonopolies" (our words, not theirs): "To unseat an SDK was very hard and they [the ad network/mediation platform] really were the owner of everything that was going to happen within that. It was like a mini-exchange within that closed environment. And again, because the apps are a closed environment, it just functions differently [from the Web's open marketplace]" (interviewee CS).

Even the basic task of programming can be a barrier to those seeking to extend the Web's open marketplace to apps. Much of the apparatus of digital advertising on the Web (for example, the header bidding that we will discuss in chapter 4) is built in JavaScript, a programming language first developed at Netscape to make websites interactive. JavaScript is a widely understood lingua franca, and large numbers of people can program in it. An SDK, in contrast, normally has to be programmed in whatever language the app is written in, and getting the necessary code added to the app is usually a slow process. The engineers responsible for the app or SDK within it "queue you up," says DK. "They put you in a development cycle." As BQ puts it: "The SDKs are unavoidable. . . . [F]or [a] mobile app, [an] SDK has to be packaged together whenever you launch a new version of your app. It's really hard, it's a lot of code you have to drag in, you have to make sure it works, sometimes it doesn't compile. Compared to JavaScript it's a hundred times harder."

We do not, however, have to look at the very different world of apps to realize that the Web's open marketplace for display advertising was not an inevitability. Even as it was coalescing, the open marketplace has coexisted with, competed with, and often lost out to what were to become giant money machines with very different material and economic structures: first, Google Search, and then social media platforms, especially Facebook and Instagram. Those money machines are the topic of the next chapter.

# 3

# Money Machines and the Characteristics of Digital Advertising

Chapter 2 explored the coming into being of digital advertising's open marketplace in Web-display ads, with its multiplicity of small or medium-sized firms. In this chapter, we shift focus to what have become two giant presences in digital advertising: Google, especially Google Search, and Facebook, renamed Meta Platforms, Inc. in October 2021.

We'll begin by discussing an aspect of Google that is under-emphasized in the literature of platform studies: its materiality, which among other things underpins its platform power. Google's engineers built its megamachine not out of expensive, powerful individual computers, but by aggregating huge numbers of fallible, cheap, and individually not particularly powerful machines. In an approach that has come to be called "infrastructure as code" – now widespread, but largely pioneered by Google – its engineers employed software to manage and circumvent those machines' inevitable physical failures, while also maintaining a relentless focus on their system's speed.

Even if you build it with cheap machines, a megamachine is expensive. The necessary money came from selling ads to accompany the results of Google searches. We will discuss how those ads are sold, which has left a near-permanent stamp on digital advertising's economic arrangements, and how their effectiveness was measured – which will provide a first glimpse of what in chapter 1 we called Google's "systematicity." We also emphasize, however, the need to grasp Google's complexities. It is not just an ensemble of machines – the nearly two hundred thousand people it employs play crucial roles – and it is organizationally complex. It is not a corporation in which top managers always take the initiative and make the decisions, and lower-level employees simply implement those decisions.

We will then turn to Facebook. Its platform power, like Google's, has its material roots in a sophisticated, globe-spanning technical system that combines scale and speed. Facebook, however, was not originally an advertising giant. What was most crucial in giving it momentum in that respect, we will argue, was a change forced upon Facebook by a basic material issue: mobile phones' small screens. We will also touch upon a crucial internal battle over whether to integrate Facebook advertising with the open marketplace or keep its electronic walls more intact.

The chapter ends by laying out the way in which the development of digital advertising, especially of the money machines, has given that advertising five characteristics that are quite different from those of advertising's more traditional forms. Those characteristics need emphasizing because collective memory of those traditional forms continues to shape, often quite misleadingly, our instincts about what "advertising" is.

## Building a megamachine

As the Web grew exponentially in the 1990s, those who surfed it – that was the verb often used back then – soon needed a systematic way of finding relevant sites. One option was to consult a directory to the Web, but maintaining an up-to-date, usable directory became harder and harder as the Web increased in size. The main alternative was an automated "search engine," several of which were launched in the 1990s. Their developers deployed a digital "crawler" to ingest webpages, and their systems identified keywords in those pages, indexed them, and matched the user's search query to the index, thus producing an ordered list of hopefully relevant sites.

The matching of the words in a user's query to keywords on websites had, however, the grave disadvantage that early search engines could readily be "spammed." If, for example, the developers of one of the pornographic sites that spread alarmingly fast in the 1990s wanted to appear as often as possible in search results, they would plaster that site with popular search terms, such as "cars," frequently hiding them from human eyes, for instance by rendering them "in small white letters on a white background" (Battelle 2005: 104). Attempts to block spamming of this kind were typically successful only temporarily. As spammers found ways of outwitting them, "the situation is getting worst [sic] and worst," reported search-engine specialist Massimo Marchiori (1997: 1231). By 1998, the year in which Google was founded, it was perfectly possible for "the majority of results matching a search for 'cars'" on a widely used search engine to be links to porn (Battelle 2005: 104).

As Google's co-founders, Sergey Brin and Larry Page, then still Stanford University PhD students, put it, "junk results" of this kind "often wash out any results that a user is interested in" (Brin and Page 1998b: 108). Their crucial conceptual innovation is well known. Google's crawlers ingested not just text but also *links* – "[t]he indexer . . . parses out all the links in every Web page" (Brin and Page 1998b: 111) – and its search algorithm ranked websites according to the number of incoming links to each, the rationale being that website developers were more likely to link to important and useful sites. (Famously, that was analogous to the way in which influential and authoritative scientific articles accrue citations in other articles.) As Fourcade and Healy nicely put it, Google's algorithm, PageRank, "didn't just search *through* the network [constituting the Web]; it searched *with* it [understanding] that the network structure of the Web included information about the reputation and reliability of its content" (2024: 23; emphases in original).

Because Google's search engine thus didn't simply match the words in a user's query to keywords on websites, it was designed to "make it nearly impossible to deliberately mislead the system in order to get a higher ranking" (Brin and Page 1998b: 110). That judgment turned out to be hopelessly optimistic: as Google came increasingly to dominate search, efforts "to deliberately mislead the system" became large scale. A typical technique, described to us by interviewee CJ, was to use a "guestbook spammer" to insert links to one's webpage into the comments sections of other pages.

By common consent, however, the quality of Google's search results substantially improved on those of earlier spam-weakened search engines. A June 2000 deal, in which Google became the search engine for the widely used Web portal Yahoo, greatly increased its number of users: "basically our traffic doubled overnight" (Dean 2010).[1] What Yahoo paid Google provided the latter with much-needed revenue, but, crucially, gaining more users meant more data on their search behavior (Levy 2011: 45). For example, did a user spend time on the first website to which they clicked a link (suggesting that the search result was a useful one), or did they "bounce," immediately returning to the search results page, suggesting the opposite? Applying machine learning to data of this kind soon became as important to Google as its original "PageRank" algorithm.

That scale brings with it data is one reason for its importance to platforms. Scale was Google's founders' ambition from the very beginning, when they were PhD students trying to have their crawlers ingest the entire Web. Their attempting to do that consumed much of the limited bandwidth of Stanford University's entire computer network, and involved Page and Brin volunteering to take delivery of new machines at the Computer Science Department's loading dock, so as to be able to make temporary use of them before they were allocated to other users (Dean 2010). Even the company's name reflected the goal of scale. It invoked "googol," an unimaginably big number: $10^{100}$, which vastly exceeds even the number of subatomic particles in the entire universe (for which see Vopson 2021).

Scale, though, is not just an aspiration; achieving it is enormously demanding materially. Google's start-up funding was relatively generous. Its June 1999 "Series A round" – an important milestone, which if successful brings in a start-up's first substantial financing from venture capitalists – raised US$25 million from Sequoia Capital and Kleiner Perkins (Levy 2011: 74). That money, however, would have drained away quickly if Google had started to buy large numbers of sophisticated, powerful computers. The rise of personal computing, though, had made the component parts of ordinary PCs relatively cheap commodity products, so Google chose to use them instead. It placed them in metal trays, lined with cork to insulate the motherboards from the trays, and stacked the trays far more densely than was standard at the time. Because datacenter owners at that period charged their tenants by the floor area their systems occupied, dense stacking reduced Google's costs (Dean 2010).

Early Google employee Douglas Edwards recalls a visit to the datacenter in Santa Clara in which Google rented space to house its machines:

> Every square inch was crammed with racks bristling with stripped down CPUs [central processing units]. There were twenty-one racks and more than fifteen hundred machines, each sprouting cables like Play-Doh pushed through a spaghetti press. . . . where other [firms'] cages were right-angled and inorganic, Google's swarmed with life, a giant termite mound dense with frenetic activity and intersecting curves. (Edwards 2011: 21)

Despite Google having limited money to spend, using the cheapest possible hardware in an intensive way made scaling materially possible: "for every dollar spent, Google had three times more computing power than its competitors" (Vise and Malseed 2005: 79). Even when Google started to build its own datacenters, it still filled them with huge numbers of cheap machines. Hard drives and power supplies were attached to central processor units with Velcro, making failed components easy and quick to remove, and reducing the number of technicians needed to operate a datacenter.[2]

But inexpensive hardware brings with it vulnerability to the vagaries of the material world. Cheap components of the kind Google bought had high failure rates, and they were vulnerable to memory errors, such as a binary digit flipping from a "0" to a "1," or vice versa. Such errors can be caused by overheating, voltage fluctuations, or even the impact of a cosmic-ray particle. More expensive hardware usually has built-in capacity to detect and correct such errors, but the cheap components Google was buying did not. Between October 1999 and March 2000, as Google began to "scale," processes central to any search engine – "crawling" the Web, ingesting giant quantities of text, links, and so on, and building an index that can be used to respond to search queries – had broken down. Search queries were being answered using a version of the index that was as much as "five months out of date" (Somers 2018: 28), and the Web was growing so fast that Google's efforts to remedy the situation by devoting more and more machines to crawling and indexing kept failing. There were even fears that "Google would *never* build its next index" (Levy 2011: 42; emphasis in original).

The Google engineers most central to its frantic investigation into what was going wrong, Sanjay Ghemawat and Jeff Dean, eventually came to the conclusion that the cause "was not logical but physical": it was the material fallibility of its cheap hardware. So, "[t]o survive, Google would have to unite its computers into a seamless, resilient whole" (Somers 2018: 28–9). Google's engineers started to treat multiple machines, even thousands or tens of thousands of them, as if they were a single computer – a megamachine – and gradually developed the capacity for the automated management of giant assemblages of individually fallible machines.

That capacity was crucial to Google's ability to scale and, therefore, to its platform power. We were first pointed to its importance in 2019 by an interviewee from an earlier project, on ultrafast trading in finance, who told us that "the software they [Google] use to manage their physical infrastructure" was "their edge." Nowadays, that approach, "infrastructure as code," is more widely available, but its first truly large-scale use was in Google's megamachine. Among the Google systems central to this is "Borg," one that again we were first pointed to by another interviewee.

That, at first purely internal, name was a sci-fi joke but well chosen. In the *Star Trek* series, the Borg are part-biological, part-robotic organisms that share a common consciousness or "hive mind." Borg manages huge clusters of machines: in 2010, around five years after its full-scale introduction, a typical Google cluster was 5,000–20,000 machines (Dean 2010). Borg keeps computational jobs, such as the production of search results, running, even if an individual machine crashes or physically fails, by automatically reassigning its work to other machines. It avoids, again automatically, devoting too much of any one task to machines that are in the same datacenter rack or have the same power supply, so reducing the risk of disruption caused by multiple machines failing simultaneously. Borg's workload increased fast – by 2011, Google was deploying perhaps a million machines (Levy 2011: 181) – but it kept pace. "[E]very time we have approached a limit," a group of Google engineers responsible for Borg wrote, "we've managed to eliminate it" (Verma et al. 2015: 5).

Another aspect of the materiality of platform power is speed, which is often a precondition of scale because even small delays in processes can accumulate catastrophically as the scale of a system's operations increases. Google's founders wanted their search engine to be fast, indeed the world's fastest. Co-founder Larry Page, and at least one other early Google employee, developed the almost preternatural capacity to sense time, without the aid of any measurement device, in tenths of a second. (A tenth of a second is generally reckoned the lower threshold of the perceptibility to humans of the passage of time: Canales 2009.) Page told journalist and author Steven Levy that he would sometimes audibly count seconds when a new system was being demonstrated to him: "[o]ne one-thousand, two one-thousand. That tends to get people's attention" (Levy 2011: 185).

The emphasis on speed had important consequences for the materiality of the megamachine's Borg-like hive mind. At first, Google's most crucial data structure – the search index, used to generate the results of users' billions of search queries – had to be stored on spinning hard discs, which had far greater capacity than computer memory built into silicon chips. Retrieving data from a machine's hard disc could, however, take as much as a hundredth of a second, around five hundred times what it would take to retrieve it from the machine's silicon-chip memory.[3] That would have been of little consequence if it had to be done only a handful of times in response to each user query, but as Google's index grew in size, more and more discs had to be accessed, making the process, in the words of Google's Jeff Dean, "more and more problematic" (Dean 2010).

"[Y]ou eventually realize," said Dean, "that if I look at all these machines we are using to serve this index, I could actually hold one copy of the index in [silicon-chip] memory across all those machines." Eliminating delays by doing that, as Google's engineers first did in 2001, multiplied the megamachine's capacity to handle ever-growing volumes of search queries: "you get a really big increase in throughput," Dean reported. Its consequence, however, was that generating even one individual search result could require the simultaneous operation of huge numbers of machines: "the query is now going to touch thousands of machines, not just dozens" (Dean 2010). Even at the level of an individual user's query, Google Search had thus become a megamachine, dependent upon its giant-scale, silicon-chip, "hive mind" memory.

## Money machine

But how was Google going to earn money from its fast-increasing numbers of users? In 2001, "[t]he VCs" – the venture capitalists who had invested in Google – "were screaming bloody murder," reports Levy (2011: 83). The obvious way of making money was to place display ads on Google's uncluttered, pristine white homepage, with its millions of visitors. "[O]ne deal with DoubleClick . . . would probably net the company millions of dollars," says journalist and entrepreneur John Battelle (2005: 123), but Page and Brin did not want to do that deal: "that felt like a sellout." As one of the venture capitalists, Sequoia Capital's Michael Moritz, a member of Google's Board of Directors from 1999 to 2007, put it, its founders "didn't want to turn the Web site into the online version of Forty-second Street" – in other words, into Manhattan's advertising-dominated Times Square (quoted by Battelle 2005: 123).

Even more unacceptable to Brin and Page was the approach apparently taken by at least one 1990s search engine, "to sell 'preferred listings', i.e., assuring a particular entry to stay in the top ten for some time" (Marchiori 1997: 1231). "This business model resulted in an uproar," Brin and Page wrote, and as a result the search engine accused of this practice "has ceased to be viable" (1998a: appendix A). That appendix, omitted from the published version of the scientific article describing Page and Brin's search engine (Brin and Page 1998b), also laid out their reasons for hesitancy about advertising. In response to the search term "cellular phone," the 1998 prototype version of Google Search, driven by the PageRank algorithm, returned, as a top result, an academic paper on the dangers of using a mobile phone while driving:

It is clear that a search engine which was taking money for showing cellular phone ads would have difficulty justifying the page that our system returned to its paying advertisers. . . . [W]e expect that advertising funded search engines will be inherently biased towards the advertisers and away from the needs of the consumers. (Brin and Page 1998a: appendix A)

The most successful way found in the 1990s of combining ads with a search engine was developed by a start-up, GoTo (later renamed Overture), launched in 1997 by the serial entrepreneur Bill Gross. It combined an existing search engine, Inktomi, with ads triggered by commercially relevant search terms such as "Chicago hotel." The first of GoTo's two key innovations was an automated auction in which advertisers bid for the right to have the links to their websites shown in the search results. (Since this was almost a decade before the open marketplace's automated ad exchanges, discussed in the previous chapter, it counts as the first instance of an advertising market moving into a machine.) Second, GoTo's pricing was "pay-per-click": unlike the dominant model in Web display, in which the advertiser paid simply for the ad to be shown, GoTo billed the advertiser for an ad only if the user clicked on it.[4]

For all their ambivalence about ads, Brin and Page knew "that they needed an ad system," but they wanted one that produced ads relevant to search queries, "not fluff that imposed itself on users" (Levy 2011: 78, 84). Google started to show text ads (not the pervasive images of the world of Web display) that it "deemed relevant to the search query that a user typed," placing them above the "organic" search results, but on a yellow background so that they could be distinguished from the latter.[5] Those ads were at first sold quite traditionally by a New York-based sales team that "took customers to dinner, explained what keywords meant, and told advertisers what it would cost to buy ads" (Levy 2011: 84–5).

In October 2000, however, Google launched a different mechanism for the selling of search ads, AdWords, which was to turn search ads into one of the great money machines of human history: it now earns Google around US$175 billion dollars a year (Alphabet Inc. 2024: 35).[6] The development of AdWords was led, ironically enough, by a Google computer scientist Eric Veach, who, as noted in chapter 1, confessed to Steven Levy (2011: 83), "I hate ads." AdWords was a "self-service" system, designed to cater for smaller advertisers whose budgets did not justify a human salesperson's expensive attention. The team that designed AdWords was small, just seven people, and Veach describes it as at first being "a backwater of the company" (Levy 2011: 83, 85).

AdWords ads were smaller than the ads sold person to person by the New York team, and could be bought in a fully automated way. They were placed not above the organic results but to their right, and each was labelled "sponsored link." The pitch was encapsulated in an October 2000 test ad composed by the AdWords team themselves: "Have a credit card and 5 minutes? Get your ad on Google today." AdWords ads could appear within 30 minutes: there was not normally any human scrutiny of an ad. Its price was denominated, as traditionally, as a CPM or cost per mille: that is, the cost for showing the ad a thousand times. With no negotiation between human beings involved, the cost was fixed: US$15 (or 1.5 cents per ad) for "the most desirable position, the top ad on the right," US$12 for the next slot, and so on (Levy 2011: 85–6).

Those late 2000 arrangements, however, were only the early prototype of the money machine. A couple of 2001–2 tweaks made Google's AdWords more like GoTo's system. AdWords' pricing model was changed to pay-per-click, which triggered a lawsuit from GoTo/Overture alleging patent infringement, which Google settled out of court on the eve of the initial public offering of its shares (Battelle 2005: 116). AdWords also began auctioning each advertising opportunity, just as GoTo did. In three crucial respects, though, Google's money machine differed from GoTo's.

First, GoTo ran a separate auction for each slot, with the advertiser having to decide how much to bid for the top slot, how much for the second-to-top, etc. Google reduced this to a simpler, single automated auction, with the best bid winning the top slot, the second-best the next slot, etc.

Second, participants in GoTo's auctions had incentives constantly to change their bids even for the same keyword. The winner paid the full amount of their bid, which would often be considerably greater than the second-best bid, incentivizing "bid shading": an advertiser gradually reducing its bids for a particular keyword, to discover how low a bid would keep winning. There were even automated systems "that would reduce your [GoTo] bids constantly," interviewee AI tells us. Advertisers' spending on these "bidding robots" most likely had the effect of reducing GoTo's revenues (Edelman, Ostrovsky, and Schwarz 2007: 245–6).

"I wanted to avoid that cat-and-mouse game," Google's Veach told Levy (2011: 89). He designed Google's auctions so that, while the highest bidder (with the bid adjusted for "quality," as described below) won the auction, they paid only what the second-highest bidder had offered to pay, plus a single cent. This meant that Google's own system achieved for advertisers the outcome that "bidding robots" were trying to find: the smallest bid that would actually win the auction. "Second-price auctions," as these are called, became a standard feature of digital advertising until they were partially displaced by a revival in Web-display advertising of first-price auctions, driven there by the success of the header bidding discussed in chapter 4.

Second-price auctions ("Vickrey auctions," as they are sometimes called, after the Nobel-Prize-winning economist William Vickrey) are well regarded in economics, and we initially thought that Google's introduction of them might be the result of the influence of economic theory, but it appears that Veach, an engineer not an economist, introduced them quite independently of that. "Economics in the wild" (in the sense of Callon 2007), such as Veach's, is a much broader endeavor than simply the academic discipline.[7]

A third way in which Google's approach to search ads differed from GoTo's was that AdWords bids were automatically adjusted by Google's system's estimate of the "quality" of the ad in question: its relevance to the user's search query. That adjustment meant that a lower bid to show an ad that the system deemed "relevant" to the query could win out over a higher bid to show a less relevant ad. GoTo also sought to ensure relevance, but did so "manually," reports interviewee AI: it "relied 100 per cent on an editorial team to ensure that your [Web] site was relevant to the keywords" on which you were bidding.[8]

Google's automated quality-score adjustment of bids was and is an aspect of its "stacking" of different modes of "economization," in the sense in which we used those terms in chapter 1. To make money, Google needed to "marketize" its users' attention by auctioning access to their screens for advertising. But it also needed to avoid reducing the value of its "gift" to users (free, high-quality search results), which was what had brought them to Google in the first place, by cluttering that gift with irrelevant ads. The quality score was an attempt to square the circle, a rough-and-ready compromise between Google's need for revenue and its founders' fear of gaudy, obtrusive advertising damaging their product.

Google did not and does not disclose how exactly the quality score is calculated, and trying to work that out became something of an obsession for heavy users of AdWords, especially in the system's early years. One such user, interviewee DO, was:

> so curious about it I would call Google all the time and sometimes they would let me speak to an engineer. They were sitting in the same room, they'd be like, you're asking too much, let me get someone. They would call over an engineer or a data scientist to tell me how it really worked. Because I was so early,

I learned that what they called quality score was just predicted click-through rate.

That last sentence is almost certainly an oversimplification, at least nowadays, but the rationale for using click-through rate as an important part of how "ad quality" is measured is clear. That a user clicks on an ad does not prove that the ad is relevant to their query, but it can count as evidence that it is. For Google's systems to take likely click-through rate into account when assessing bids to show ads also makes economic sense. Because advertisers pay Google only for search ads that are clicked on, high bids to show ads that are unlikely to be clicked on can easily result in less revenue for Google than lower bids for ads that will be clicked on more often. "That," says interviewee DO, "was my first beginning to understand how platforms think about things, the economics that they were doing on their side." The quality score wasn't simply "rewarding me for quality," he continues, "it was maximizing their yield."

The centrality of click-through rate to Google's auctions and to its advertising income made *predicting* clicks on ads an enormously important task for the megamachine it was building: quality scores had to be assigned *before* the auction winner was decided and the winning ad shown. It was one of the quintessential early "big data" problems tackled by Google's megamachine. As a Google team working on it wrote, "It is necessary to make predictions many billions of times per day and quickly update the model as new clicks and non-clicks are observed . . . this data rate means that training data sets are enormous [and models have] billions of coefficients" (McMahan et al. 2013: 1–2). Another team of Google engineers worked on the necessary material underpinning of the mass-scale prediction of click-through probabilities, a system that they called "Photon." It made possible the continuous merging of giant streams of data – for example on users' searches and on their clicks on ads – "in real-time with high scalability and low latency [electronic delay] ... process[ing] millions of events per minute." They reported that, among other things, Photon "allows Google to optimize the budget spent for each advertiser on a continuous basis" (Ananthanarayanan et al. 2013: 577). That capacity – big platforms applying machine learning at giant scale to optimize advertisers' spending, rather than the latter trying to control their advertising in fine-grained detail – has turned out to be deeply consequential, as we will discuss in chapter 6.

AdWords was indeed a money machine. It helped Google earn its first profits (around US$100 million) in 2002, and the following year's profits were nearly double that (McCullough 2018: 231). "[W]e just started growing," Google's Sheryl Sandberg told Levy. "It went unbelievably well. And nobody knew just how well until the IPO": Google's 2004 initial public offering of its shares, the event that marked the start of its transformation from high-tech start-up into what, remarkably quickly, became a giant corporation (Levy 2011: 99). And, increasingly bolstered by machine-learning ad optimization of the kind we have just described, the money machine kept growing and growing: Google Search advertising remains to this day the primary foundation of Google/Alphabet's economic success.

## The crucial feedback loop

Central to the optimization of advertising by Google and other major platforms is having a feedback loop between showing an ad to a user and recording any actions the user then takes, such as purchasing the product in question. That feedback loop is crucial in encouraging advertisers to keep spending, or even increase spending, on ads that seem to be "working." Google's creation of that feedback loop is another pivotal aspect of why Google search ads became a money machine.

Interviewee AR, who moved from an advertising agency to Google in the early 2000s, described to us the importance of this feedback loop. In the traditional advertising world, an advertiser would provide its agency with a set budget, perhaps for the coming year. The job of the agency was then to allocate that budget across media channels (TV and radio, newspapers, magazines, etc., and also, e.g., billboards) "to get the most out of it," hopefully not in a self-interested way: AR notes that "most of the advertising agencies have some sort of relationship with different [media], maybe part of their media group, or the people that they know" (see chapter 6). The success of the agency's campaign on behalf of the advertiser would be measured not in real time but retrospectively, perhaps using simple, aggregate indicators (such as an increase in sales following an intensive TV advertising campaign), or perhaps by the more elaborate, but also still aggregate, technique known as "media mix modeling" or "marketing mix modeling."[9]

Advertising digitally, though, makes it possible to measure advertising's effectiveness in real time and to shift measurement from an aggregate to an individual level. That can be done, for example, by using a "pixel": as discussed in chapter 2, a pixel is in essence a snippet of code on the advertiser's website. The pixel can record the online purchases or other relevant actions, if any, that an individual user takes after being shown a specific ad, which can then be linked to the ad to measure its effectiveness. (A major reason why the privacy initiatives discussed in chapter 5 are controversial within digital advertising is precisely because they disrupt this crucial feedback loop by rendering difficult, even impossible, individual-level measurement of this kind.) Google's AdWords came with an evolving measurement apparatus of this type, which eventually gave it the capacity to provide advertisers, in close to real time, with simple measures of the economic return on their ad spending or of their "investment" in ads: their "ROAS" or their "ROI," as those measures are abbreviated in the field.

In leaving his advertising agency to work for Google, interviewee AR thus moved from a world in which advertising's effectiveness could be measured only cloudily, in an aggregate way, and in retrospect, to a world in which, as he puts it, "with Google, if you invest in something [i.e., buy search ads using AdWords] you see the revenue coming with that . . . it was a . . . transformation. [Advertisers] don't limit themselves with [fixed] budgets, because . . . they turn on an investment focus . . . they want to grow." AR recollects even having to dissuade one client who was so impressed by the ROI (return on ad investment) figures that AdWords generated that he proposed massively increasing ad spending: "I want to give you $2 million and bring me that revenue." AR had to tell him that "it doesn't go like that. There is marginal return that goes down."

There was, however, a problem with using only a pixel to measure the effectiveness of ads. An advertiser might well simultaneously be buying Google search ads, display ads bought via one or more of the demand-side platforms touched on in chapter 2, and Facebook ads, at least once Facebook's ad business became large scale (as discussed below). Using all of these channels would mean multiple pixels on the advertiser's website, all of which would "fire" if, say, a purchase was made. Each pixel's owner would then credit the sale to any ads it had shown to the user in question. "So AdWords would say 'we closed it [achieved the sale]' if the person at any point had been through AdWords [i.e., had been shown an AdWords ad]," says interviewee DM. "The same with all the other channels." Multiple credit claiming of this kind could easily make it impossible for the effectiveness of any individual advertising channel to be measured convincingly.

The measurement apparatus that accompanied AdWords was, in addition, initially "rudimentary . . . hard to set up and not very accurate" (Levy 2011: 113). In 2005, therefore, Google bought, for around US$20 million, a small San Diego-based specialist firm, Urchin Software, the first of Google's crucial advertising technology acquisitions. Urchin's software provided website owners with statistics on visitors to their sites, and allowed advertisers to estimate how effective their advertising was.[10] As search marketer Tim Ash told the San Jose *Mercury News* when the acquisition was announced:

> They [Urchin] take data from Overture (or Google) and combine it with what they get from the [advertiser's] site, and they can tell whether a campaign works. . . . They can track things all the way through and say this sale is associated with typing in these keywords. This is completely trackable down to the granular level. (Bazeley 2005)

Google turned Urchin's system into a crucial, underappreciated source of its platform power: Google Analytics, launched in November 2005. The original plan had been to "charge $500 a month to use [Google Analytics], but offer discounts to AdWords customers," but the team working on Google Analytics "had no experience in building a billing system," and feared that would slow the service's launch. So its leader, Wesley Chan, went to see Google's co-founder Larry Page and persuaded him that Google should offer the new service free of charge (Levy 2011: 114). Google Analytics quickly became, and still remains, an essential part of the infrastructure underpinning digital advertising.

Google Analytics, like Urchin, allows an advertiser to resolve the conflict caused by multiple pixels leading to multiple claims from different advertising channels for credit for the same single purchase. "[W]hat Google Analytics did," says interviewee DM, "it gave you the ability to go in and say where in the process was the sale actually generated." There was, however, a material prerequisite, at least in the case of Web-display ads. A member of staff, often junior, of an advertising agency or demand-side platform has to "tag" those ads correctly so that Google Analytics can allocate to the ads the credit for a purchase. As interviewee AO says, tagging is not glamorous or prestigious: "You've got 23-year-olds who are hungover, tired, overworked, not appreciated, someone shouting at them going, why isn't my campaign live? They just grab the tags, stick them in the platform. [There is] human error."

That mundane workplace reality may have contributed to Google's search-ad money machine displacing the open marketplace in Web-display ads, which we discussed in chapter 2, as the economically most successful form of digital advertising. "[W]ith Google Analytics, if you don't tag it properly, then conversion [e.g., purchases] from banners [display ads] will actually not be registered in the system," says interviewee DM:

> Where with AdWords, because it's the same system to the same system, you get all the data in Google Analytics. So when people looking at the budget saying, okay apparently this AdWords thing is showing me a lot of results, and I can't see my banners anywhere. . . . [T]hat helped motivate . . . people to move budget from banners to [search] ads.

It's not clear from our interviews how typical interviewee DM's experience is, but what he says highlights an important component of platform power: material integration or "systematicity."[11] The open marketplace in Web-display ads is materially interconnected, but with different organizations deploying different systems, not seamlessly so. In contrast, as interviewee AV puts it, "a lot of advertisers are working within the Google stack," in other words, using Google systems that communicate with each other "natively." Doing that "make[s] the process a lot more seamless" (interviewee BG).

## The complexities of Google

Big Tech corporations – even Google, which is in some respects relatively open – are frequently opaque to outsiders. It is, in consequence, easy to slip into simplistic, reductionist analyses of them and their actions. Google and Facebook/Meta (which we will discuss shortly) *are* relatively tightly integrated technical systems, which is why we have called this chapter "money *machines*." But, as we suggested in chapter 1, that does not imply that they are *simply* assemblages of machines, or even just ensembles of machines and human programmers. As we noted in that chapter, Google's parent corporation, Alphabet, has almost 200,000 employees, by no means all of them programmers. In addition, Google's temporary employees, interns, and external contractors seem at times to have outnumbered its direct, permanent employees (Wakabayashi 2019), and many play crucial roles. A striking example is what Google says are some 16,000 "search quality raters," employed by external companies, who work to provide it with human feedback on the quality of algorithmic search results (Google LLC n.d.; Meisner, Duffy, and Ziewitz 2024).[12] In research work for our future publications, Caliskan has trained to be one of these workers. Facebook's parent corporation, Meta, employs what seems to be a similar number of human "content moderators," discussed in Gillespie (2018), and until recently it also used "third party" fact checkers, although just before the start of the second Trump Administration Meta decided to discontinue use of the latter.

Google attempts tightly to structure the work of its search quality raters: its guidelines for them total around 170 pages (Meisner, Duffy, and Ziewitz 2024: 1027). Harder to control are the practices of developers of websites worldwide, especially those who seek to improve the search rankings of those sites. Sometimes they do this by making their sites more easily "readable" by Google's crawlers, which Google encourages and will give advice on, but sometimes they employ techniques that Google considers illegitimate and seeks to block, mostly algorithmically but sometimes also by using human monitors (Ziewitz 2019). And whether human users reliably distinguish between "organic" search results and search ads (a distinction central to Google's corporate self-understanding) is not clear-cut: only 1.3% of a sample of 1,000 German users of Google search were reportedly able consistently to do that correctly (Lewandowski et al. 2018).

Another complexity of Google is its organizational structure. It is easy to imagine a major corporation such as Google as being managed "top down," with senior executives deciding what to do, and those beneath them then following instructions. Interviewee CR, for example, found Google to be quite unlike that: "Basically it's run by product managers and engineering managers who want to get promotions. The way to get promotions is you [lead the creation of] products. So everyone wants to innovate, everyone wants to make a big mark and it's totally uncoordinated . . . half the time."

Another interviewee agrees that "overall" Google is indeed "bottom up" in that sense. "If you're a market leader and trying to come up with ideas," she says, "I think it's easier to do bottom up." Areas such as cloud services in which Google was not the market leader are, however, different, she adds. Though it has now caught up technically, and even become a leader in its security features, Google Cloud used to be "behind . . . AWS [Amazon Web Services] and Microsoft's Azure," in the functionalities it provided to its clients:

> so there's a mandate to just fill in the gaps. Oh, they [AWS or Azure] let you use multiple user authentication for this, this, and that. We have to do it too. You can maybe creatively come up with how to solve it, but you don't get to decide what the features are, because we're just trying to keep up. So when you're the laggard, you have less freedom.

Top-down initiatives within Google, however, often have "limited success," says CR. "There have been numerous instances in Google's history where they've freaked out, they put someone on top and they're like, you're the dictator, make this happen." In one example, he says: "they put this guy in charge who was a long time Googler and he had carte blanche to build anything and he ordered everyone around, caused all kinds of problems and then came out with a product nobody wanted."

As we discussed in chapter 1, a large organization such as a major corporation should not be thought of as the equivalent of a person weighing up their options, taking a decision, and implementing it. "Corporations are co-operative systems," wrote the organisational sociologist Tom Burns, but "[t]hey are also social systems within which people compete for advancement," where what Burns called "micropolitics" is prevalent (Burns 1961: 257). What looks like a corporate decision may actually simply be a "micropolitical" outcome, the result of internal conflict or compromise.

Take, for example, Google's decision in 2020 to phase out the depositing by default of third-party cookies (explained in chapter 2) in the browsers of users who have not explicitly opted to allow this. At the conferences that we attended around then, the phase-out was very much seen as a move emanating from the browser designers in Google's Chrome Team. Google's display-ads specialists, one of them told us, were far from unanimously happy, but seem to have been unable to block the move, although (as we will touch on in chapter 5) it was first postponed and now substantially altered.

Although we have no firsthand research data on Google's response to the enormously successful launch of OpenAI's ChatGPT in 2022, Google's organizational structure was said by some to be responsible for it seeming to be outflanked by OpenAI. Two *Financial Times* journalists reported: "Current and former Google executives describe the company as series of fiefdoms. Each product line has its own leader, with workers incentivised to make incremental changes to optimise products, rather than radically innovate or work across teams" (Murgia and Waters 2024). In April 2024, indeed, Google's chief executive decided to reorganize the company, moving all the various teams working on artificial intelligence into a single division, DeepMind, and creating a new "platform and devices" team to encompass the previously separate teams responsible for Search, Chrome, Android, and so on (Morris 2024).

## Facebook

Digital advertising's highest-earning money machine is still Google search ads, which, as noted above, currently bring in around US$175 billion annually. In second place is advertising on Facebook and Instagram, another huge money machine that provided revenues of US$132 billion in 2023 to Meta, those platforms' parent company.

Facebook's and Instagram's overall histories don't need repeated here. Facebook (originally Thefacebook) was launched in February 2004, famously by a Harvard University undergraduate, Mark Zuckerberg. Facebook's early years were portrayed, controversially, in a 2010 Hollywood film, *The Social Network*, and its history has been documented by Kirkpatrick (2011) and Levy (2020). Launched in 2010, Instagram was acquired by Facebook in 2012; for its story, see Frier (2020). Facebook Inc. was, as we've already said, renamed Meta Platforms Inc. in October 2021.

Many of the themes of our discussion of Google, such as scaling and systematicity, also apply to Facebook/Meta. The rapid rise and then eclipse of the pioneering, early social media site, Friendster, founded in March 2003, was an object lesson for Facebook in the importance of the capacity to scale. Just as Facebook was to do, Friendster "integrate[d] . . . online and off-line identities," seeking to connect people who knew each other in real life, and constructing an elaborate graph of the social connections among them (Chafkin 2007). By Fall 2003, Friendster had attracted over two million registered users, large amounts of venture capital funding, and an approach from Google to buy the company for US$30 million. Friendster's system, however, slowed down as the demand upon it grew. "By late 2003, load times regularly clocked in at over a minute and users were beginning to complain in blogs and forums" (Chafkin 2007). As Friendster's founder, Jonathan Abrams, put it, "people could barely log into the website for two years," while its rival sites, MySpace and Facebook, gained momentum: "Friendster ... lost a lot of market share in the US for [system] stability issues" (quoted by Fiegerman 2014).

Facebook's Zuckerberg knew, therefore, that "[m]illiseconds [thousandths of a second] mattered," and he resisted the addition of features that might slow its system (Kirkpatrick 2011: 58). As Facebook's scale grew – by 2013, its system handled "billions of requests per second" and, given the rich information provided to the platform by its then more than a billion users, held "trillions of items" of data (Nishtala et al. 2013: 385) – Facebook's engineers paid careful attention to structuring that system so that its scale did not come at the cost of speed. A key technique that they used was "memcaching": keeping frequently needed items of data in fast, temporary computer memory rather than simply in slower permanent storage, so that they could be retrieved in microseconds – millionths of a second – not milliseconds. By 2013, Facebook system was, its engineers believed, "the largest memcached installation in the world" (Nishtala et al. 2013: 385, 394).

It was always clear that ads were going to need to be the chief revenue source of a social media platform that did not charge its users, but, just as in the case of Google, Facebook's embrace of advertising was initially equivocal. Mark Zuckerberg "didn't want unwelcome advertising to break the spell of his product," and Mark Rabkin, hired from Google in 2007 to develop Facebook's ad serving infrastructure, initially headed a team of only five engineers (Levy 2020: 199, 296). As late as 2012, it seemed to Antonio García Martínez, then a Facebook ads manager, that "the Ads team was held at arm's length, as if it was a pair of sweaty underwear" (García Martínez 2016: 2).

They were internal disagreements within Facebook, despite Zuckerberg remaining a very hands-on chief executive. One disagreement, which turned out to be highly consequential, was about *where* ads should be shown on the user's screen. The central innovation in Facebook's early years was its News Feed, which was algorithmically curated, specific to each user, and designed to pull together in one on-screen location what the user's friends were posting and the changes in their profiles. That centralization provoked opposition from Facebook executives concerned to preserve and increase its then relatively small advertising income, which was based on showing what were essentially conventional display ads: the fewer pages users visited, the fewer ads they would see. Zuckerberg, however, supported the team developing the News Feed, which was launched in 2006. Precisely because it did indeed become the center of most users' attention, the News Feed then seemed to some within Facebook to be the logical place to insert ads, but "[t]he engineers working on the feed" resisted this: they "wanted to keep the stream of stories as pristine as possible" (Levy 2020: 138, 181).

Despite the engineers' opposition, ads did briefly appear in Facebook's News Feed, but were later "purged from Facebook's flagship feature, shunted to their traditional place on the side" of the user's screen (Levy 2020: 295). The trigger of their removal appears to have been the first major privacy controversy to hit Facebook, concerning a system called "Beacon." Like a pixel, Beacon was placed on vendors' websites, and closed the loop between ads and purchases, reporting the latter to Facebook. However, unless the purchaser denied it permission to do so, Beacon also inserted news of those purchases into users' News Feeds, providing a form of "word-of-mouth promotion" of products (Nakashima 2007). Beacon sparked a fierce backlash and even a class-action lawsuit. One user complained bitterly to the *Wall Street Journal* that Beacon had exposed to his full Facebook network the fact that his Christmas present for his wife, a jewelled, white gold "eternity" ring, had been bought on Overstock.com (Nakashima 2007).

The physical separation of ads from the News Feed was mirrored organizationally. Zuckerberg told Levy, "we didn't have to worry about ads in News Feed because we just had this column of ads . . . we had a separate [ads] team that was off to the side; they didn't have to talk to the News Feed team and it was wonderful." What ended those arrangements was the combination of a crisis of a different kind – Facebook's initially faltering response to the shift, rapidly gathering momentum from 2009 onward, from laptops and desktops to smartphones – and an obdurate material consideration: mobile phones' small screens. As Facebook scrambled to secure its place on smartphones, ads *had* to be shown within the News Feed. As Zuckerberg put it: "There's no room for a right-hand column ads on mobile" (Levy 2020: 295–6).

Along with Facebook's rich data on its users, the physical shift of Facebook ads to the center of users' on-screen attention launched the money machine. "[C]lick through rates" for standard display ads "are minimal," interviewee AL tells us. "We're talking about 0.1% and [if you achieve that] then you're like wow, this worked." The re-engineered Facebook performed at least ten times better, she says:

> a team member came to my office . . . the numbers were 1% click through rate, 2% click through rate . . . I was like, there's no way . . . you guys are extrapolating these wrong. . . . I was wrong. Facebook really truly figured it out how to run advertising natively, so it looks like it's not interrupting users' experience within the platform and they really figured it out to the data piece so you're only showing [ads] to people that are truly relevant to what you're trying to sell.

Other advertising practitioners testified similarly:

> [O]n Google you're actively searching . . . On Facebook and Instagram you're just scrolling and looking at [News Feed]

updates that ... are more personal to you and then a certain ad looks like an update and tricks your mind into thinking this might be something I'm interested in. [T]argeting things like relationship [status] and layering interest[s] is really effective because you get the sweet spot, like a Venn diagram, of someone who is married and also likes to go on holiday. You get that sweet spot ... here's a couple's vacation. That you could potentially [be] thinking about. (Interviewee AP)

With Facebook, you don't start with a keyword [as with Google search ads], you're ... advertising to people who fit a certain ... profile. ... Before Cambridge Analytica[13] and GDPR [the European Union's General Data Protection Regulation, in force since 2018], Facebook had thousands of data categories. You could say white women who make $75,000, who are engaged to be married, who studied sociology in college – whatever. (Interviewee AB)

A second, also consequential, internal disagreement concerned how Facebook ads should be sold and whether that selling should be connected to the open marketplace in display ads (discussed in chapter 2). The ads manager quoted above, Antonio García Martínez, who joined Facebook in April 2011, believed that the best way for Facebook to "monetize" its platform and the data provided by its logged-in user base was to allow that data to be connected up anonymously to valuable open-marketplace data, for example on "remarketing" opportunities: the chance, for instance, to show an ad for a product to a user who has added that product to an online shopping cart, but not purchased it.

García Martínez sought, as he puts it, to "bolt ... a real-time ad exchange onto a social media platform with bajillions of users" (2016: 488). He led the building of an exchange similar to those discussed in chapter 2, via which Facebook would send demand-side platforms and other potential bidders a continuous stream of requests to bid for particular opportunities to show an ad on Facebook. However, he faced opposition, he says, from those who wished to preserve the electronic walls of Facebook's walled garden.

Support grew, for example, for a different way of combining Facebook's and external data, in which advertisers would provide Facebook with a list of customers or, for example, website visitors, identified by data such as email addresses, names, or telephone numbers. Facebook would then "hash" (cryptographically scramble) the data, match it with its own internal data, and create a "Custom Audience" of Facebook users that matched the list. Facebook's enormous numbers of logged-in users meant that match rates were "as high as 90%," says García Martínez, far above those typical of the open marketplace's more haphazard cookie matching. "That means for every hundred people marketers target via Custom Audiences, Facebook will find ninety of them, a shockingly high fraction in the fuzzy world of advertising" (2016: 394).

García Martínez was on the losing side of the internal debate he describes. He lost his job in April 2013, and although the open-marketplace-style Facebook Exchange survived him, it did not prosper, and it was closed down in 2016. Among the issues underlying the debate, says García Martínez, was a fundamental divide between "targeting" and "optimization":

> [Targeting] involves advertisers using their knowledge and user data to select which user sees which ad; [optimization] involves the ad network (in this case, Facebook) using its data around user behavior to choose who sees which ad. . . . The network would rather control ad delivery itself via optimization; the advertiser wants the power to control what it spends money on via targeting . . . as well as the ability to build a storehouse of in-house marketing knowledge. (García Martínez 2016: 306)

That tension persists. Today's big-platform advertising systems indeed prioritize machine-learning optimization over human-guided targeting, a fundamental issue to which we will return in chapter 6.

## Five characteristics of digital advertising

Let us now step back from the detail of the open marketplace (discussed in chapter 2) and the "money machines," discussed in this chapter, and sketch five overall features of digital advertising. All are well understood within the sector; some less so outside of it.[14] These are features that are present in the open marketplace but are to be found much more emphatically in, for example, Google's and Meta's systems.

The first of these features, widely known even outside of digital advertising, is individualization: the capacity to select an ad for, and sometimes to tailor it to, the specific user. That capacity was almost entirely lacking in traditional advertising media such as broadcast television, radio, newspapers, magazines, and billboards. At best, an advertiser or advertising agency could choose particular TV shows, or magazines with a specific focus such as interior design, gardening, motor cars, or golf. The implicit promise of digital advertising was to shift communication between the advertiser and the consumer from the "one-to-many" model of traditional media to "one-to-one" messaging.

Real though that promise was, it is important to emphasize that it has by no means always been fully realized. Individualization is variable even within digital advertising. Initially, Google Search ads were originally not individually targeted in any real sense. The words that the user entered into the search engine, advertisers' bids for those words, and Google's systems' calculation of an ad's likely click-through rate were what triggered those ads; little else mattered. Interviewees active in the early years of Google Search advertising report that it could not at first be targeted by age, gender, income bracket, and so on: at most, it was possible to restrict one's advertising to a specific country (e.g., the United

Kingdom: interviewee AI), or specific regions of, for example, Denmark (interviewee DM).[15] Even in 2020, interviewees from one of the world's biggest search advertisers told us that their system entered sociodemographic features and precise location into Google's system as "bid modifiers," which increased or reduced a bid that was still determined primarily by the words the user had entered into the search engine.

For this reason, we think that Zuboff's (2019) famous portrayal of Google as *the* prototype of surveillance capitalism somewhat misses the mark, at least in respect to Google's early years. DoubleClick, the prolific depositor of cookies that we encountered in chapter 2's discussion of Web-display advertising, has a better claim to be that prototype, as Crain (2021) in effect emphasizes.[16] More generally, empirical caution about *actual* targeting capacity is needed. The user data copiously collected within digital advertising, especially in the open marketplace, is often of limited value.

For example, the same individual can appear in the "profiles" that data brokers sell or advertising technology platforms provide in wildly inconsistent ways: sometimes as both female and male, falling into a number of different age and income brackets, and as both unemployed and employed (NOYB 2024). Inconsistencies of that kind should not be imagined as resulting from a commitment to, for example, gender fluidity. It is more likely simply to be an example of what Pink et al. (2018) call "broken data." Resolving inconsistencies in large datasets can be hard, and sometimes incentives to do so may be weak (a "profile" of which the vendor can say it has many instances can be more valuable than one with fewer instances). Another pervasive example of broken data is that the cookies deposited by one organization frequently cannot be "matched" to those deposited by another firm's system.

A large platform with logged-in users is, by contrast, much better placed to collect consistent, "unbroken" data on them, and that is an important aspect of platform power. Even here, though, things are changing in some respects, as we shall see in chapter 5, which discusses powerful, albeit partial, recent, and current, material de-individualizing measures within digital advertising.

The second overall feature of digital advertising, which we have also emphasized in this and the previous chapter, is the capacity for automated measurement of where/how an ad was served, the user's interactions (if any) with it, and any subsequent actions by the user, such as a purchase. In one sense, the importance of this reflects a weakness of digital advertising. If an advertiser buys an ad to run in the commercial breaks of a specific broadcast TV program, they can watch that program and literally see their ad being delivered. Not so with an individualized digital ad. Human senses are no longer adequate: less direct measurement – "mediated" measurement, to use the terminology of chapter 6 – is needed. But the apparatus of that measurement has a strength that often more than counterbalances digital advertising's weakness in this respect: its capacity to provide advertisers with near real-time measures of the cost-effectiveness of their advertising. This, as we have emphasized, is an important resource, especially for the biggest platforms, another crucial aspect of platform power.

Third, small advertisers are much more prevalent in digital advertising (especially on the major platforms) than in at least the higher-profile forms of pre-digital advertising, such as broadcast TV ads. Interviewee DH estimates that "on the order of 10 million advertisers . . . are actively running ads with Meta and Google," which he contrasts with an estimated 10,000 firms globally using the services of the Trade Desk, a leading entry-point to the open marketplace.

"Digital advertising is a big economy of small advertisers" is how app economy analyst Eric Seufert (2024c) puts it. During the protests following the killing of George Floyd by a police officer in Minneapolis in May 2020, a group of anti-racist and other organizations launched a campaign, Stop Hate for Profit, which called for an advertisers' boycott of Facebook, accused of not doing enough to block hate speech. Several dozen major advertisers (including Coca-Cola, Ben & Jerry's, Unilever, and Starbucks) joined the boycott, and spending by the hundred leading advertisers on Facebook dropped by an estimated 12% (Seufert 2024c). Facebook's total advertising revenues, however, continued to rise: cutbacks by leading names were insufficient to outweigh spending by the very much larger number of smaller advertisers, who had fewer alternatives to turn to.

The role of real-time digital measurement and the prevalence of small advertisers are tightly related to a fourth feature of digital advertising: the preponderance in it of "direct-response" advertising. The big corporations that boycotted Facebook were largely "brand" advertisers, seeking, as traditionally, to enhance consumers' views of their products (and typically using traditional media as well to do that, which may be one reason why they were prepared to boycott Facebook). Smaller advertisers, with much more limited budgets, often have a much more immediate goal: a direct response, a "conversion" as it would be called within advertising, such as an immediate purchase of one of their products. Although "brand" advertisers do purchase Google search ads, the majority of those ads seem to be direct response, and that seems generally true of Facebook as well (see the case of games advertising, discussed in chapter 5). The measurement capacities we've discussed provide small advertisers with easily digestible metrics such as Return on Ad Spend. Those metrics do not *prove* that their ad spending is cost-effective (that an ad has been shown to a user and the user then buys the product does not prove that the ad caused the purchase), but they are in practice very reassuring in that respect.

Fifth – and in a sense tying together the above four features – is the large role in digital advertising of automated optimization, in other words of efforts to maximize the cost-effectiveness of advertising in real time. True, for much of the history of digital advertising, automated optimization has coexisted with human-guided targeting, and tensions between the two have generally remained latent and implicit. However, the developments that we will discuss in chapters 5 and 6 (frequently fueled by privacy concerns), which often seek to de-individualize advertising's audiences, are making human-guided targeting less precise and less attractive. Automated optimization, as a result, is becoming ever more important, with consequences, for example, for advertising's human practitioners that we will explore in chapter 6.

# 4

# Hacking the System

Today's Web-display advertising market is a megamachine, conducting around half a trillion near-instantaneous electronic ad auctions per day.[1] That's a rate of electronic activity at least comparable with that of the archetypal digital megamachine, Google Search, indeed dwarfing it in numbers of auctions.[2] As we discussed in chapter 1, though, the Web-display advertising megamachine is quite different from Google Search. It has no single owner, and no overall controlling authority. Its core real-time operations intrinsically involve interaction between multiple machines owned and controlled by many different companies.

How the Web-display megamachine is configured advantages some of those companies and disadvantages others in economically consequential ways. That makes its configuration an issue of material political economy. The crucial aspect of configuration on which we focus in this chapter is the extent to which the megamachine should be centralized. Where should the auctions that determine which ads are shown on your phone or laptop happen? On banks of computer servers in massive datacenters, most likely Google's? Or should your phone or laptop become an active component of the megamachine, acting as an electronic auctioneer and itself gathering bids?

This material-political-economy conflict over centralization interacts with our theme of *stacking*, discussed in chapter 1: the layering in a platform of different "economization" processes, such as the marketization of users' attention to their screens in the form of advertising opportunities, and the gifting in return of "free" services to those users. When it concerns "stacked" platforms, a "horizontal" material-political-economy conflict over a particular process in the stack (such as our focus here, the buying and selling of ads) is unlikely to be self-contained but will be subject to the "vertical" influence of stacking on the process in question.

For example, Google's integrated display-ads system, which is at the center of the megamachine, is in practitioners' terminology "full-stack": it incorporates almost the full range of display advertising's economic processes. That has given Google greater capacity than other market participants to shape ad trading. Stacking, however, was also crucial to the feasibility of the decentralizing challenge to this Google-centered configuration. The challenge is called "header bidding" because it employs webpages' normally invisible "headers" to trigger auctions on your device. The resultant bids for your attention were then "hacked" into a central component of Google's system, its ad server. That was done by the labor-intensive repurposing of the tools of one stacked process – the ad server's targeting of ads to specific audiences – in order to transform another process to which that ad server is also central: the buying and selling of ads.

Two further issues cluster around the material-political-economy conflict between centralized and decentralized configurations of the megamachine. The first is legal. Google's reaction to header bidding's decentralizing challenge has become an important part of the competition-law disputes in which the corporation has become embroiled in the United States and Europe. The second is environmental. Header bidding can boost publishers' advertising revenues, and that is important, for example, to news publishers, which have suffered particularly badly from sharp declines in print revenues (MacKenzie 2022). It comes at the cost, however, of large-scale duplication of ad auctions, which are electricity-consuming computations – with the result that, as we shall see, auctions appear to be the largest component of the carbon footprint of the process of Web-display advertising.

## "A single and complete advertising system"

In May 2010, as Google's integrated display-ads system was being assembled, Terry Kawaja, founder of the influential digitally focused boutique investment bank, LUMA Partners, warned attendees at a sector meeting that display advertising was "an overcrowded marketplace." He illustrated the point with a slide, still being shown in updated form even today, which has come to be called the "Lumascape." Even in its original version it was visually daunting, crowded with the names of the nearly 200 companies whose systems made up Web-display advertising's nascent megamachine. (Unfortunately, we've not been able to get copyright permission to reproduce the Lumascape, but an image search will lead you to multiple examples, and even Kawaja's original can be found in a grainy reproduction in Benes 2017.)[3]

In Kawaja's view, the systems deployed by the many dozens of companies that populated the Lumascape were insufficiently integrated with each other. "[T]here are too many point-solutions here," he said. "[T]hese are all venture-capital-backed companies, and ... venture capitalists like their portfolio companies to focus on doing one thing really well, so that's what they have done. That said, the marketplace needs solution providers, *integrated* solution providers."

"Google is coming to display [advertising] in a big way," Kawaja warned, at that point in his talk suddenly playing a burst of loud, scary music. "Yes, drama is necessary," he explained.

"Google looks at things very holistically." Google's systems were already providing alternatives to many of the functions provided by smaller firms, and those alternatives *were* increasingly integrated with each other. They offered advertisers and publishers, for example, the mundane but attractive convenience of "unified billing," rather than having to transact with multiple providers.

Google's entry into display advertising had begun in 2003, seven years earlier, with the idea of expanding its AdWords system. Through AdWords, advertisers could enter keywords and buy ads that appeared alongside relevant user search results. The new idea was to allow advertisers also to buy display ads on webpages where the content matched those keywords. Google's initial display ads program, called AdSense, matched ads by using the webpage content its crawlers were already gathering for its constantly updated index. Like AdWords, AdSense was an automated, "self-service," system, which advertisers could use, and publishers could join, with a minimum of assistance from Google. That made it possible for Google to recruit large numbers of publishers who wanted to earn money selling ad slots without it having to deploy a huge human salesforce.

In digital advertising, the term "publisher" refers to providers of online content of all kinds, not simply the digital equivalents of newspapers and magazines. Even the smallest, technically unsophisticated publisher could join AdSense by doing little more than pasting into the code of its website a Google-provided line of JavaScript, the programming language used to make websites interactive. "You [Web publishers] do the content and leave the selling of the ads to Google," said AdSense's head, Susan Wojcicki. The resulting ad revenue was split 68% for the publisher and 32% for Google, and, within a year, hundreds of thousands of publishers had signed up for AdSense (Levy 2011: 102, 105, and 107).

Google's AdSense was more than simply an addition to the plethora of ways of buying and selling ads offered by the firms in

Kawaja's Lumascape: it was a stepping stone to a system. In their 2006 annual letter to investors, Google's co-founders wrote, "Our goal is to create a single and complete advertising system" (Page and Brin 2006).[4] Statements of grand corporate ambition need a pinch of salt, but in April 2007 Google announced that it had agreed a takeover of DoubleClick, the best-known participant in Web display's open marketplace, although competition-law scrutiny by the US Federal Trade Commission and European Commission meant that the actual acquisition was concluded only in March 2008.

Buying DoubleClick helped give Google a much more central position in the nascent Web-display megamachine. AdSense was used by big publishers as well as small, but often simply as what interviewee BJ calls a "buyer of last resort" for otherwise unsold ad slots. DoubleClick's then owners, the San Francisco-based private equity firm Hellman and Friedman LLC, had planned to sell it, and remarkably the slide deck used in this survives (Paparo 2024c). It boasted of a client base that included "9 of Top 10 global [advertising] agencies and brands," and "35 of Top 50 Web publishers." Although this is not explicit on the slides, almost certainly the latter were mostly users of DoubleClick's publisher's ad server, "DART for Publishers," or DFP.[5]

As we discussed in chapter 2, a publisher's ad server is a crucial system in the Web-display market. It makes the final decision on which ads are shown on a user's screen, tracks the process, ensures the publisher meets their commitments to advertisers, and allows the advertiser to be billed. A sophisticated publisher, such as one of DoubleClick's major clients, often inputs its content classification and rules into its ad server. For example, as interviewee AA told us, the publisher may have rules about not accepting ads from certain advertisers, such as tobacco companies, and about preventing ads from appearing next to each other or next to specific content. In recent years, ad servers have also needed, for example, to store and implement "consent strings," the digital evidence of a user having consented to tracking.

Importantly, too, Google's purchase of DoubleClick brought with it not just its ad server, DFP, but also its nascent ad exchange, AdX, launched in April 2007.[6] DoubleClick had "the sell side [publishers] and the buy side [advertisers and advertising agencies]," says interviewee CR. "So we could just let our own customers transact and it would be half the digital market." The launch of AdX, covered in a major article in the *New York Times* (Story 2007), fed into what CR calls "bidding wars" in which, for example, Google and Microsoft competed fiercely to buy DoubleClick.

In Google's hands, AdX was to become by a considerable margin the world's largest-volume ad exchange. Crucially, DoubleClick's AdX was integrated with the firm's ad server, DFP, enabling what the slide deck used to sell DoubleClick described as "dynamic allocation." What exactly that materially involved in 2007–8 is not fully clear (our interviewees are far more familiar with Google's re-engineered version of the ad server than with the original), but in Google's version dynamic allocation became a central capacity, highly valued by big and sophisticated publishers. It involves the ad server automatically and "dynamically" (i.e., in real time, not in advance) choosing between the highest bid on its integrated ad exchange and other sources of demand, soon including the direct deals that a publisher has with advertisers. If a bid on the exchange was attractive enough, and if the ad server predicted that the publisher was on its way to fulfilling its obligations under those direct deals, it would accept the bid. That additional flexibility could considerably boost a publisher's advertising revenues, and that helped make Google's ad server attractive to publishers using older, less flexible machines.

In approving Google's acquisition of DoubleClick, European policymakers reasoned that ad-serving fees were a small proportion of advertising's costs, and other ad servers were available (Brockhoff et al. 2008: 58). That economic reasoning, however, hugely underestimated the significance of ad servers' materiality.

The material forms taken by display advertising were changing fast (with, e.g., the rise of video ads and ads on mobiles), so ad-server developers had "to be constantly innovating . . . to support the latest . . . thing" (interviewee BR). Ad servers, though, also needed to be scalable: to serve billions of ads daily, they must run on networks of hundreds, thousands, or tens of thousands of physical machines. Almost all developers of ad servers struggled with the twin challenge. "Building a cutting-edge publisher ad server is a nightmare," says CR.

The exception was the ad server that Google acquired from DoubleClick, to which it devoted two years of intensive development, "rebuil[ding] . . . the entire code base from scratch" (Nolet 2010). Over the previous decade, Google had learned – not without struggles of its own, as we saw in chapter 3 – how to make systems run at giant scale. Google kept DoubleClick's name, calling its ad server DoubleClick for Publishers or DFP, but it was actually thoroughly re-engineered, as was AdX, the ad exchange Google inherited from DoubleClick. Re-engineering DFP was particularly challenging. "It was overdue for a rewrite and . . . Google has its own 'stack' which is very distinct. . . . They entered a rewrite period for DFP . . . and everyone was upset about it but it had to be done, and it was torture. It took years" (interviewee CR). Nevertheless, DFP *was* successfully re-engineered.

Google re-launched AdX in September 2009, also re-engineered from the original DoubleClick version in two ways. First, earlier ad exchanges usually involved the buying and selling of *blocks* of ad slots. In contrast, "AdX 2.0," as Google's version of the ad exchange was sometimes referred to when it was launched, provided full support for "real-time bidding," via which publishers could offer for sale individual ad slots (the opportunity to show an ad to this user, right now . . .), and advertisers, ad agencies, and ad networks could bid for those individual slots.

Second, DoubleClick had seen its exchange as a mechanism via which *big* publishers could sell ad slots, and *big* advertisers, advertising agencies, and ad networks could buy them. "We already have the largest sellers and the largest buyers" as clients, DoubleClick's then chief executive David Rosenblatt told the *New York Times*. "This [AdX] will link them for the first time" (Story 2007). That linkage of big players was also part of the vision for Google's AdX 2.0, as its launch announcement made clear (Google Inc. 2009). Google's ad server, DFP, helped – and still helps – big publishers sell ad slots on AdX, and Google also provides ad agencies with a buying tool, DoubleClick Bid Manager (now called DV360, or Display and Video 360), which they can use to buy those slots on behalf of their mainly large advertiser clients.

Crucial to AdX becoming the world's largest ad exchange, though, is that – as elsewhere in digital advertising – a large number of small advertisers can outweigh a much smaller number of big advertisers. In a PDF attached to Google's electronic announcement of AdX 2.0 (Google Inc. 2009) was a schematic diagram of the new exchange. It showed the exchange's interfaces with AdWords (which even small advertisers could use to buy display ads as well as search ads) and AdSense, which small publishers could use to sell display ads. Of course, a small advertiser could not be expected to grasp the daunting logistics of buying ad slots on a real-time electronic exchange, but they did not need to. AdWords, now called simply Google Ads, did and does the buying for them, in aggregate on a giant scale: "Google Ads is literally the largest single source of unique advertising demand in the world. The company doesn't disclose the number of accounts it has, but it is almost certainly in the tens of millions globally . . . half of small business have accounts, and surely every single large advertiser . . . uses [Google] Ads" (Paparo 2024b). Within three years of the new exchange's establishment, between 65% and 74% of the ad slots that advertisers bought on AdX, measured by price, were being bought via Google Ads (Texas et al. 2022: 53).

Did Google's re-engineering and reassembly of DoubleClick's ad server and ad exchange, along with other advertising technology acquisitions it made in this time period, result in the "single and complete advertising system" its co-founders had envisioned? We are cautious about speculating on internal processes within large corporations without firsthand data. From our previous research (e.g., MacKenzie 1990, 1996), we know that building a large technical system involves many unexpected challenges, so it cannot be seen as just the execution of a pre-set plan, especially one from senior management. Interviewee CR, for example, tell us that in practice what he calls "the impetus to make Google into a leader of a very big business in display advertising" came not from the very top of the corporation, but from two lower-level (although still senior) executives, one of whom joined Google only after it acquired DoubleClick.

What was assembled, though, certainly *was* a system. Its "full-stack" component parts (DFP, AdX, DoubleClick Bid Manager, AdSense, Google Ads, Google Analytics, etc.) worked together, perhaps not always seamlessly, but with much less friction than the looser open-marketplace assemblage, with what Kawaja had warned was its lack of integration. Bids to show ads flowed into AdX in huge volume through Google's "stack," via the algorithmic ad-buying systems Google made available to both small and large advertisers.

AdX rapidly became "by far the largest source of exchange inventory" (McDermott 2014), making Google's integrated system, the core of which is shown in Figure 4.1, a powerful, indeed potentially an overwhelming, rival to the more heterogeneous independent sector. The US Federal Trade Commission had approved Google's merger with DoubleClick, but it began to have competition-law concerns, with one of its lawyers privately contacting independent advertising technology firms (McDermott 2014). Her informal enquiries, though, did not generate a lawsuit. Serious legal challenges to Google's role in the Web-display advertising market were to come, but only after that role had been challenged materially by header bidding.

# Hacking the System

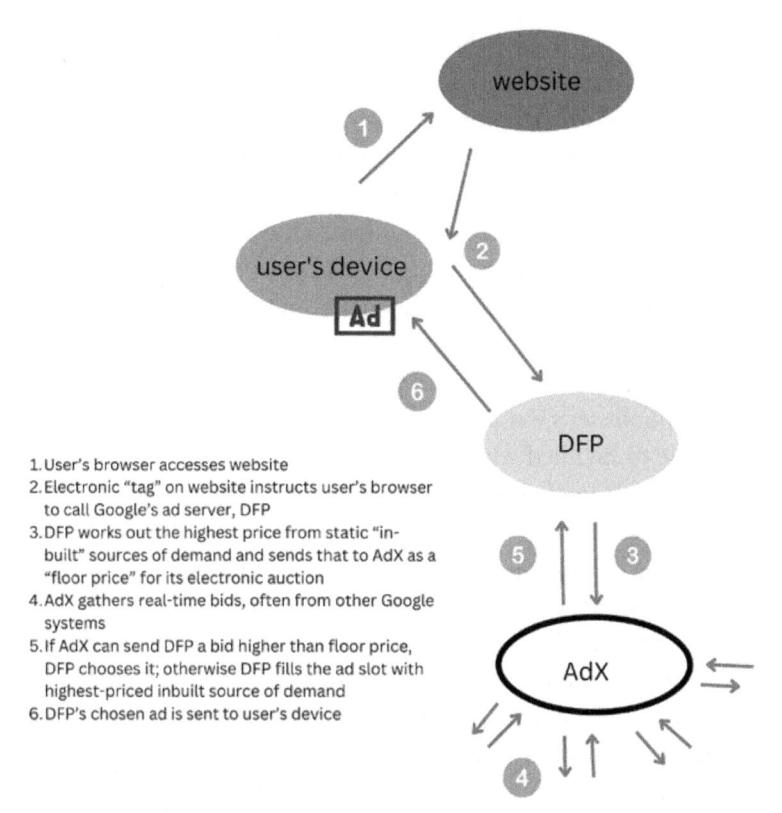

**Figure 4.1** The system that header bidding hacked: how Google's integrated display-advertising system chose the ad to show you

1. User's browser accesses website
2. Electronic "tag" on website instructs user's browser to call Google's ad server, DFP
3. DFP works out the highest price from static "inbuilt" sources of demand and sends that to AdX as a "floor price" for its electronic auction
4. AdX gathers real-time bids, often from other Google systems
5. If AdX can send DFP a bid higher than floor price, DFP chooses it; otherwise DFP fills the ad slot with highest-priced inbuilt source of demand
6. DFP's chosen ad is sent to user's device

This figure shows how the system worked from 2014 to around 2018. "Inbuilt" sources of demand were programmed into DFP by the publisher, and included the publisher's direct deals with advertisers and its estimates of prices that could be obtained by it selling an ad slot via channels other than AdX, e.g. supply-side platforms. How the system operated before 2014 and after 2018 was different: CMA (2020, appendix M, pp. 8–12).

## The rise of header bidding

With the coming together of Google's integrated display-advertising system, the Web-display advertising megamachine gained a center. But when there's a center, there is also a periphery, and those who inhabit it are not always content. That dissatisfaction helped give birth to header bidding, which, as it gathered force, involved a substantial – and as we will see, partially successful – effort to reconfigure the megamachine.

Header bidding gets its name, as we've said, from using the hidden "headers" of webpages to instruct users' browsers to collect bids from sources other than Google's ad exchange, AdX. What gave force to previously ad hoc ways of doing this was dissatisfaction among one particular category of firm in the Web-display open marketplace: supply-side platforms. When a user visits a publisher's webpage, one or more "ad slots" often become available to be filled with ads to show that user. Publishers (i.e., the supply side of display advertising, in other words the providers of advertising opportunities) seldom themselves do the auctioning of those slots: they employ either Google's systems or one or more SSPs to do that.

The publisher's ad server sends the supply-side platform an "ad request," and the SSP turns it into a "bid request," gathering bids for the ad slot by sending the request to the demand-side platforms, discussed in chapter 2, which bid in ad auctions on behalf of advertisers. The SSP sends the best bid or bids back to the publisher's ad server, and if the latter chooses the SSP's bid, that SSP earns a fee from the publisher.[7]

SSPs quickly became significant actors in the marketplace. For example, the Rubicon Project, a Los Angeles-based SSP founded in 2007, helped the United Kingdom's *Guardian* newspaper build its presence in online advertising, enabling it – unusually for a major newspaper – to keep its website accessible globally free of charge. (The relationship later soured, with a legal dispute concerning the fees the *Guardian* was being charged.)

The crucial source of dissatisfaction with Google's integrated system among SSPs was their occupying what many of them perceived to be a peripheral position within Google's DFP (fast becoming the world's dominant publisher's ad server), the system that takes the final decision about which ad to show to which user. Unlike Google's AdX, non-Google SSPs could not send bids in real time into DFP (see Figure 4.1). That mattered because the value of a specific advertising opportunity – this webpage, this user, right now – is highly variable. Most Web-display ad opportunities sell for a fraction of a cent, but a minority are worth a lot more than that, such as an opportunity to retarget a user who has previously shown interest in a product. The arrival of such opportunities is unpredictable, so it is very important to be able to bid directly for individual ad slots as they become available, submitting high bids for particularly valuable slots.

A non-Google SSP's demand for advertising opportunities was represented in DFP only in the form of an essentially static estimate, manually entered into DFP by members of the publisher's staff, of how much the SSP would pay on average for those opportunities. Such an estimate could not realistically be changed in real time as ad slots became available, and SSPs therefore felt they were losing out on valuable opportunities. Publishers too, our interviewees reported, worried that they were missing out on bids from SSPs that might have been higher than a winning AdX bid.

There was therefore a widespread desire among SSPs to find a mechanism that would enable them to bid directly for *every* advertising opportunity, not merely those in which the publisher's estimate of their average bid happened to be higher than the bids available to Google's DFP via AdX. Individual SSPs started to try to persuade publishers to insert code into their webpage headers to instruct users' browsers to request a bid from that SSP prior to electronically calling DFP. The publishers of those webpages, at first often suspicious, began to see header bidding as potentially a useful way of getting higher prices for their ad slots.

As header bidding gained momentum, it faced, but largely overcame, three significant problems. The first was a "general lack of trust . . . across the industry," as BR puts it: "there's a lot of things that can happen where money is potentially lost in the friction of the pipes or whatever" (as we will see in chapter 6, this is a justified fear). Publishers didn't always trust SSPs, and the SSPs themselves didn't trust each other enough to work together. Individual SSPs separately approached each publisher, and the code that each SSP asked the publisher to incorporate into its webpage headers was specific to that SSP and would cause the user's browser to request a bid only from that particular SSP.

The lack of collective action had a potentially disastrous effect on how long it took webpages to load. "There's this terrible publisher's freak-out about this," says BR, "a really bad user experience." The "scripts" containing the code that instructed the user's browser to gather a bid from each SSP could each take around a second to load and, worse, they loaded one after the other, with "every single script ... block[ing] the page [from loading]" (interviewee BQ), until it had finished executing. Nor was there an incentive for individual SSPs to make their scripts faster: "it's to the SSP's advantage to make [load time] really long so that they can collect as many bids as possible [from its demand-side platform clients]," says BQ.

One way to manage the process was to create a software "wrapper" that would load the SSPs' scripts at the same time, excluding from the auction any that were too slow to load. For publishers, though, creating and maintaining such a wrapper would be onerous, says interviewee BV, so in practice it seemed as if an SSP had to do it. That, though, failed to solve the underlying material-politics problem because it raised the question of whether the SSP that wrote the wrapper would give itself a surreptitious advantage, such as more time to gather bids (interviewee BX).

But perhaps trust in a header-bidding wrapper could be built by making its code public as open-source software, so that it could be scrutinized to see if it was doing anything underhand? "Open-sourcing makes a lot of sense ... for political reasons," says interviewee BQ. That, however, meant in practice making the software a gift: freely available, free of charge. The engineers who initiated the open-source project (who worked for the AdTech platform and SSP, AppNexus, co-founded by ad-exchange pioneer Brian O'Kelley) faced internal opposition because of that: "there was a lot of internal friction about why are we spending time on this [the wrapper]," says BR.

They took their case to O'Kelley, AppNexus's CEO. "They're like . . . I know this is our secret sauce, but I think we should open-source it" (O'Kelley interview). "I'm, like, you guys are crazy," he says, but he realized, though, that "if everyone competes on header, it's not going to work very well," and Google might launch a more successful alternative, which he calls a "header-bidding killer": "[S]cenario one, we get some short-term revenue but then we lose to Google. Scenario two, we open-source this, it becomes a platform, and everyone will build around it, then that will beat Google." Only as the meeting ended, recalls O'Kelley, did the engineers reveal to him that they had actually already released an open-source version of the wrapper.

The engineers called their open-source project Prebid, the name signalling that the user's device would gather bids from SSPs before Google's ad server was alerted. Getting support for Prebid from SSPs that competed with AppNexus was, however, initially very hard. There was "a lot of drama in the first year," says BQ, "lots of screaming and yelling." Making the code open source seemed at first to "make the political [problems] even worse, because now everybody can see what you're doing" (BR). The wrapper needed to contain scripts that would seek bids from SSPs other than AppNexus, so the latter's engineers needed to "look at their [other SSPs'] code . . . see how are they doing this," and then rewrite the code (BR). AppNexus's lawyers "gave [the engineers] a green light because the code [they] used is already in the public domain," says BQ, but that did not stop other SSPs "telling . . . publishers they [AppNexus] were stealing our code," in one case even threatening legal action (BR). Publishers,

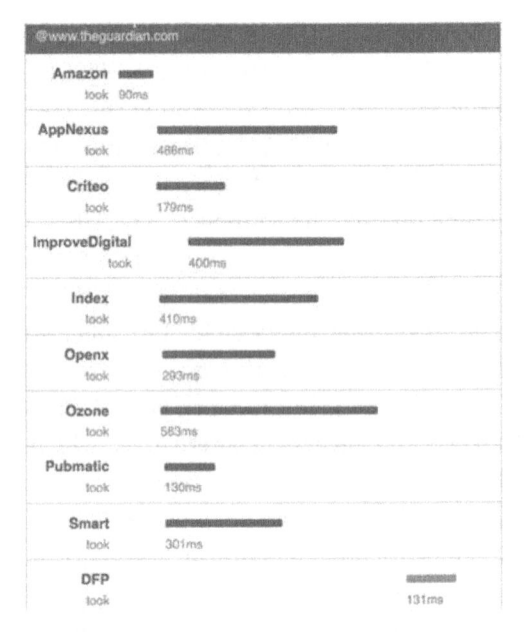

**Figure 4.2  Traces of the megamachine**
Calls for bids prompted by MacKenzie visiting the Guardian's homepage, captured using the Chrome extension, Headerbid Expert. Note that the electronic call to Google's ad server, DFP, is delayed while bids are collected. Times shown are in milliseconds (thousandths of a second). Authors' screenshot.

though, began to accept the gift, adopting the free open-source wrapper: "it was a gradual thing," says BR. "It wasn't overnight."

What became the canonical form of header bidding crystallized around Prebid's open-source software. Examples of the auctioning of opportunities to display ads to MacKenzie are shown in Figures 4.2 and 4.3, and the underlying header-bidding process (which takes around half a second) is sketched in Figure 4.4.[8] Directed by Prebid code in the webpage header, the user's browser requests bids from supply-side platforms with which the website's publisher has a commercial relationship, and the Google Publisher Tag (a snippet of computer code that, among other things, causes the user's browser to alert Google's ad server

## Header Bidding Analysis — BidFilter

| Bidder | Ad | $ CPM | Won | Timing |
|---|---|---|---|---|
| pubmatic | 970x250 | US$3.34 | ✓ | |
| improvedigital | 970x250 | US$0.05 | | |
| oxd | 728x90 | US$2.73 | | |
| and | 970x250 | US$0.09 | | |
| criteo | 970x250 | US$0.09 | | |
| ozone | 970x250 | US$2.14 | | |
| ozone | 728x90 | US$0.43 | | |
| ix | 728x90 | US$2.94 | | |
| ix | 970x250 | US$1.17 | | |
| pubmatic | 970x250 | US$1.04 | | |

**Figure 4.3 Bidding for our attention**

Examples of bids in header bidding, captured using the Chrome extension, BidFilter: authors' screenshot. Although what is being bid for is the right to show one ad, display advertising's convention is to quote the price for a thousand ads (CPM or cost per mille). E.g., the actual ad-slot price corresponding to the winning bid ($3.34 CPM) is 0.334 cents.

Note that most of the bids shown in the figure will themselves be the result of "sub-auctions" conducted by the SSPs involved, such as Pubmatic. Bid Filter detects auctions conducted by the user's device; there are also very likely further auctions of the ad slot in question being conducted elsewhere in the megamachine.

to the advertising opportunity) is wrapped in an electronic timer to delay that alert being sent for around half a second.

In that crucial half second, each of those SSPs conducts a "sub-auction," seeking bids from the demand-side platforms (DSPs) with which it works, and sends the sub-auction's winning bid to the user's browser. The browser forwards the highest of the SSPs' bids to the ad server, and Google's AdX can beat it only if it can produce a higher bid. Hence header bidding's

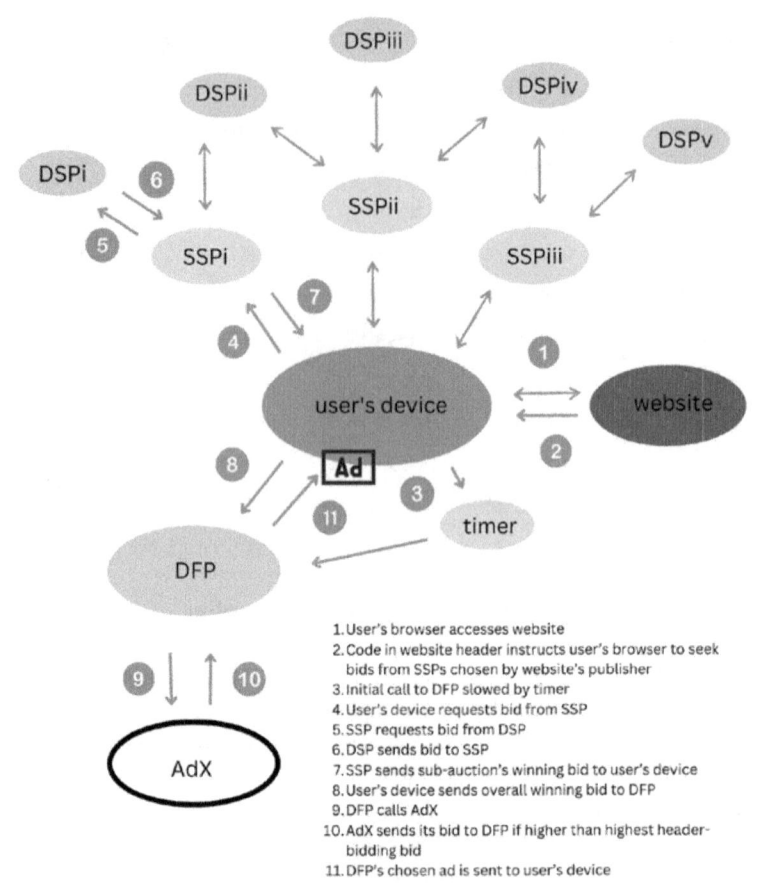

Figure 4.4  How header bidding works (simplified)

1. User's browser accesses website
2. Code in website header instructs user's browser to seek bids from SSPs chosen by website's publisher
3. Initial call to DFP slowed by timer
4. User's device requests bid from SSP
5. SSP requests bid from DSP
6. DSP sends bid to SSP
7. SSP sends sub-auction's winning bid to user's device
8. User's device sends overall winning bid to DFP
9. DFP calls AdX
10. AdX sends its bid to DFP if higher than highest header-bidding bid
11. DFP's chosen ad is sent to user's device

attraction to publishers: the possibility of their receiving higher bids than AdX on its own would produce.

The main source of an SSP's income, as we've said, is the fees it gets from publishers when bids received via that SSP are successful. Adoption of Prebid by publishers therefore gave initially hostile SSPs an incentive to improve how it solicited their bids. "[A] developer from the SSP . . . they'd take a look at it and be like, you know what: you could actually do it this way. And they'd start giving us little tips and tricks to improve it" (interviewee BR). As with other gifts, open-source software such as Prebid can indeed "generate attachments and habits" (Fourcade and Kluttz 2020: 5); power can come not from exclusion or coercion, but from "generosity" and "co-production" (Eyal 2013: 875).

The second problem faced by header bidding is implicitly signalled by the way in which its *proponents* often describe it as a "hack": for example, "a hack of the Google ad server" (interviewee BF); "hack[ing] the [ad server's] priority setting in order for it [header bidding] to work" (BQ); "[t]he whole process is a hack" (BQ); "header bidding is a hack, that's the truth" (BR); "a hack" (BS); "a bit of a hack" (BY). In software engineering's culture, "hack" is a richly polysemic word. On the one hand, it signals expertise: the ability to "accomplish [a] task . . . faster" (Eyal 2013: 869), and thus membership of what Burrell and Fourcade (2021: 217) call "the coding elite." On the other hand, calling something one has done "a hack" is self-deprecating. Prebid's code might have been written quickly and well, but the process it triggered was necessarily inelegant, cumbersome, even ungainly.

At least at first, header bidding required extensive, tediously repetitive work by members of publishers' staff not in the "coding elite." The work was necessary because there was no direct way to represent the highest header-bidding bid in Google's ad server, DFP. So "header bidding tricked the ad server," as interviewee BJ puts it. Header bidding was a "hack" in that sense too. The winning bid is inserted into the ad server by representing bid prices using the mechanism DFP provides to permit ads to be targeted by specifying an intended audience. As mentioned earlier, header bidding involves taking one stacked economic process, targeting, and repurposing it to change another, ad trading. Doing this required the labor-intensive creation of a separate electronic line item – the basic component of an advertising campaign – for every possible bid price, and sometimes repeating the process for every possible bidder. At least thousands of line items were needed, sometimes tens or even hundreds of thousands. Eventually, the process was automated, but until that happened it was a real constraint on the adoption of header bidding.

The third obstacle to header bidding – and one aspect of Google's criticism of the technique – was the delay involved in the user's phone, tablet, or laptop becoming an auctioneer. In 2015, Google executive Jonathan Bellack publicly debated header-bidding advocate Tom Shields.[9] Increased competition for ad slots could better be achieved, Bellack argued, by "using the server-to-server programmatic pipes that work so well," enabling auctions to take only around a tenth of a second. Header bidding, employing a user's device, could, as we have seen, take five times as long.

The objection was serious: delay increases the risk of users leaving a page before ads are visible. Header bidding's proponents responded by developing a second version of the technique, "server-side" header bidding, in which a server designated by the publisher gathers the bids faster than the user's phone or laptop could. The user's device, though, is politically neutral terrain, so to speak – it is not under the control of any SSP – while whatever organization runs the server would have a potential advantage. "It did get a little political on that piece," says BR: "when you move the code to the server . . . You don't really know what's happening." No full solution has yet emerged, so British news publishers from across the political spectrum have taken joint action, establishing a collaborative AdTech effort, the Ozone Project, which has developed and hosts a server-side header-bidding "wrapper."

We confess that we expected this server-side header bidding largely to replace the original "client-side" version in which your device itself gathers bids. That, however, has not yet happened. Interviewees tell us that client-side header bidding retains an important advantage: it involves direct electronic contact between your phone or laptop and SSPs. In the process of your device seeking a bid from an SSP, the latter can retrieve any cookie it has previously placed in your browser. As long as "third-party" cookies of this kind still exist – interviewees say they are becoming less common due to browsers blocking them (see chapter 5) – client-side header bidding has the advantage of potentially providing more information about the user, which is harder to obtain in server-side bidding.

## Conflicts over header bidding

As header bidding – a self-declared "hack" of Google's integrated system – gained momentum, says BR, "we were all curious and wondering what Google's response would be . . . just watching and waiting to see." Interviewees, mainly external to Google, told us that when header bidding emerged, Google's reaction was not enthusiastic. That is consistent with the limited public statements on the topic by Google's members of staff or by the firm itself, such as the debate referred to in the previous section, or Google's 2020 assertion that "[h]eader bidding is characterised by increased latency [electronic delay], reduced transparency and significant user trust and privacy concerns." The last of these was because requests for bids often contain cookies or other identifiers of users, and in header bidding these requests are circulated widely (Google LLC 2020: 10).

Most consequentially, however, Google also developed what is in effect an alternative to header bidding: "Exchange Building," now called "Open Bidding." Like header bidding, Exchange Bidding "give[s] people [publishers' systems] a way to call out to multiple auctions," as an interviewee put it, but without the user's device collecting bids: instead, this happens largely "within the Google ecosystem." The UK Competition and Markets Authority suggests that "a major reason" for Google developing Exchange Bidding "appears to have been to protect Google's revenues from the impact of header bidding" (CMA 2020: appendix

M, 10), but our interviews do not contain direct evidence of this. However, Google's internal name for its Exchange Bidding project, "Jedi," although almost certainly lighthearted (as the names of many projects in tech companies are), did have something of a conflictual, even a "mind-trickster," connotation. The company seems to have worked hard, in an effort that Google called "Jedi Blue" – seemingly a reference to the color of Facebook's logo – to ensure that Facebook, which had flirted with header bidding, embraced Google's Exchange Bidding instead. "We thought we were going to get Facebook in Prebid [header bidding]," interviewee CB told us, but "they . . . went dark."

In assessing Google's reaction to header bidding, though, it is also important to highlight what Google seems largely *not* to have done. As already noted, publishers using header bidding need to create very large numbers of "line items" (the basic electronic components of an advertising campaign) within Google's ad server, DFP, in order to use the mechanisms of one economic process, ad targeting, to reshape another, ad trading. Google could thus have hamstrung header bidding very simply by imposing a tight limit on how many line items a publisher could create. The Texas-led lawsuit against Google that we refer to below does allege that "Google purposefully limits" the number of line items "to foreclose competition from header bidding" (Texas et al. 2022: 134–5), but our header-bidding interviews do not contain firsthand reports of Google doing this.

That is a reminder that material politics may encompass shades of grey, such as gradual accommodation to a perhaps not-entirely welcome material reality, not just out-and-out conflict. Indeed, Google's decisions about the material configuration of its systems are compatible with header-bidding proponent BR's nuanced February 2022 characterization: "[t]hey're not involved [in the Prebid open-source header bidding project]. Google obviously knows about it, and has come to accept it." In 2022, indeed, Google's acceptance of header bidding took material form. In April that year, Google was testing an electronic "bridge" between Prebid and DFP (Sluis 2022), which was in place by that Fall, and made it easier to set up header bidding within DFP.

Header bidding's decentralizing challenge to the existing configuration of the Web-display advertising megamachine has been in many respects successful. All the major publishers to whom we spoke were making heavy use of header bidding, and they seemed to believe that it increased their advertising revenues. (We don't dispute that belief but note that testing it would require quite different research methods from those we have employed.) The decentralizing challenge, however, failed to displace Google's ad server, DFP, from its central position. AppNexus, for which header bidding was, interviewees told us, one aspect of a "full-stack" challenge to Google, did try to do this. It acquired the ad server Open AdStream, and re-engineered it to better support header bidding and operate at global scale. Several Continental European publishers – most prominently Axel Springer – adopted AppNexus's new ad server. We originally hypothesized that this might be explained by particular hostility among those publishers to Google, but BW says that they were still using older ad servers, not DFP, and were thus more open to AppNexus's machine.

Most publishers, though, including all the Anglo-American publishers to whom we spoke, have kept using Google's DFP alongside header building and Prebid. Interviewees identify two main reasons for not shifting away from Google's ad server, even in the case of one publishing group that owned a stake in AppNexus. One is that, as noted, a sophisticated ad server such as Google's exemplifies "stack economization," performing a variety of crucial economic roles that are problematic to disrupt. This makes switching an ad server daunting: Springer's migration to AppNexus, seen as smooth, took three months. The second reason is the material difficulty of representing real-time demand for ad slots from Google's ad exchange AdX – the world's largest source of that demand – in any ad server other than DFP.[10] BJ describes this difficulty as forming a "moat" around DFP, while publisher BY says it was "[t]he big sticking point . . . there was too much revenue risk associated" with a shift away from DFP.

That display advertising's crucial machine remains Google's DFP gives Google continuing influence, and its overall accommodation with header bidding has not precluded moments of sharp conflict. A salient example is "unified pricing" modifications made by Google to DFP in 2019. The modifications materially constrain a publisher using DFP to have the same "floor price" for all sources of demand for ad slots; many publishers previously set a higher floor for Google's AdX, believing it had greater capacity to raise its bids than non-Google SSPs had. Interviewee BY attended an April 2019 New York meeting in which Google staff told publishers about the coming change: "[I]t was a full-on uprising. Americans can be a little bit rude and very, very straightforward . . . there was maybe ten of us [publishers] that were like, you've got to be kidding me . . . we were all just so angry." One Google staff member present was deeply upset, reports BY: "I guess the publishers just really went after him hard." But the change to DFP went ahead. Even BY cannot see a viable alternative to DFP: "we are stuck on this ad server."

## Entangled with the law

Since 2019, a new set of actors – government regulators, especially those responsible for competition law – have come to play important roles in the material politics of the Web-display advertising megamachine, and courtrooms have become an arena for that politics. Jedi Blue, Google's reaction to header bidding more generally, and Google's central position in Web-display advertising are at issue in two lawsuits the company faces. (Those are in addition to the search-advertising lawsuit that we discuss in chapter 7.)

In December 2020, following the fracturing of an originally bipartisan lawsuit, Texas and nine other states with Republican Attorneys General began legal action against Google, accusing it of "unlawfully foreclos[ing] competition" in online advertising and, e.g., "work[ing] tirelessly to stop the innovation of header bidding entirely" (Texas et al. 2022: 84, 128). Those are charges that Google contests vigorously, and at the time of writing, the case has yet to come to trial. Then, in January 2023, the US Justice Department and eight different, predominantly Democratic, states launched a similar lawsuit. It came to trial in September 2024, but at the time of writing there has yet to be a ruling. There are also two competition-law investigations in Europe: one launched by the European Commission in June 2021, the other by the United Kingdom's Competition and Markets Authority in May 2022.

The stakes in these lawsuits and investigations are potentially high, because at least some of the litigants seem to be envisaging a partial breakup of Google's centralized, integrated display-advertising system. The Justice Department suit, for example, demands that, "at minimum," Google divests itself of the two systems on which we have focused, DFP and AdX (US Department of Justice et al. 2023: 140). It is, of course, far from clear that the courts will rule in favor of the complainants, and perfectly possible that, in the changed US political climate that has followed the start of the second Trump presidency, the suits may simply be dropped.

However, a blizzard of litigation, even if it is unsuccessful, can nevertheless affect its target. An interviewee reports telephoning a contact in Google, suggesting a joint initiative to reduce advertising's carbon emissions: "[I said] 'we should work together because I'm pretty sure that you actually are the logically best solution to this.' And they said, 'hang up the phone!' I was like, 'what do you mean? [I]t's just us.'" Our interviewee's contact explained that "every conversation has to have a lawyer in it" if it might possibly lead to legal action against Google. "Google is no longer an innovation threat," says our interviewee, "because they're so constrained by lawyers." Our data does not enable us to tell whether that is the case, but the phone call is of interest because it signals the growing prominence of yet another new component of the material political economy of Web-display advertising: environmental politics.

## The environmental politics of automated auctions

"Now," header bidding is "like it's infrastructure," says one of the technique's chief proponents, Brian O'Kelley. It is, however, fractured infrastructure. Many publishers use both versions of the open-source software, Prebid: the first using the user's device as an auctioneer; the second, "server-side" header bidding, employing a server designated by the publisher. Doing the latter reduces electronic delays, making the trading of ad slots faster, but the "stack" consideration we have already discussed – the desirability for ad targeting purposes of a direct electronic connection between bidders and the user's device – keeps publishers using the first procedure as well. In addition, two further server-side or hybrid equivalents/variants of header bidding are also in widespread use: Google's Exchange/Open Bidding and Amazon's "Transparent Ad Marketplace."[11]

Using and fine-tuning this full four-channel array of ways of gathering bids can bring publishers increased advertising income, as interviewee BH particularly emphasized. Unfortunately, however, it also multiplies auctions many times over. A large publisher will typically work with 21–30 different supply-side partners or SSPs (Jounce Media 2023: 17), and if each SSP triggers an auction in response to ad requests received via all four channels, that could mean as many as 80–120 auctions of the one advertising opportunity.[12] Those figures are increased by the widespread practice of reselling ad opportunities, in which an SSP sends on the ad request to another SSP or ad network. In extreme cases, so Brian O'Kelley tells us, as many as a thousand auctions of a single advertising opportunity can take place. That's how you get to half a trillion Web-display ad auctions per day.

The bidders in those auctions are mainly the demand-side platforms or DSPs that we touched on in chapter 2. At least some of them used to try to have their systems process all available bid requests:

> we had a philosophy like, no [ad] impression left behind. So if you wanted to find the opportunities you had to expose yourself, build full firehose of inventory. So it was absolutely, get plugged in everywhere, see every impression, no filtration, build your systems in order to accommodate full scale because then you could pick and choose in the full universe. That was a great idea until you got to a point where you were taking the full firehose of the internet . . . (interviewee DI)

A big DSP, such as DI's, will want to work across Web display, in-app display, and connected TV/video streaming. Jounce Media's research (reported by Schiff 2024) suggests that that the "full firehose" of all three now involves requests to bid in around 30 million auctions every second.[13] There are, though, only about forty big DSPs globally, Brian O'Kelley tells us, and those are the main bidders in these auctions. It is striking that the proximate endpoint of the megamachine's giant apparatus is this limited number of firms, which suggests that the apparatus may well be unnecessarily large.

Although it would still be technologically feasible for each of those DSPs to build a system big enough to process the entire "firehose," it seems that now none of them judge that to be economically viable. "There is no DSP – not one – that listens to 30 million bid requests per second," says Jounce Media's Chris Kane (Schiff 2024). That, in turn, creates problems for publishers, especially smaller (e.g., minority-owned) publishers, whose ad slots can get submerged in the flood: "Perversely,

**Table 4.1** Ad auctions involve carbon emissions

|  | Average carbon dioxide emissions per impression | Percentage of emissions accounted for by ad selection |
|---|---|---|
| Web-display ads | 0.33 grams | 77% |
| In-app display ads | 0.32 grams | 53% |
| Ads in connected TV/video streaming services | 0.71 grams | 2% |

*Note*: An "impression" is the showing of a single ad, once, to a single user. The relatively low carbon cost of ad selection in connected TV/video streaming most likely reflects the survival of more "traditional" direct advertiser/publisher relations in that sector, which we briefly discuss in chapter 7.

*Source*: Scope3 (2023).

ad tech company initiatives to filter the bidstream accelerate the requirement for publishers to engage in ever-growing auction duplication. Simply ensuring DSPs are aware of the existence of an available impression requires publishers to initiate multiple auctions through multiple ad exchanges" (Jounce Media 2023: 21).

An ad auction, we have emphasized, is a material computation that consumes electricity and typically involves carbon emissions, so the extensive duplication of auctions (a single advertising opportunity being auctioned dozens of times) means greatly increased carbon emissions. Table 4.1 shows the consequence: fully three-quarters of the average emissions associated with Web-display ads is accounted for by the megamachine's electronic auctions. The electronic content of such an ad is typically relatively "light" compared to a connected TV/video streaming ad (which is usually a much larger file), but that lesser intrinsic carbon footprint is greatly increased by the carbon-intensive nature of the ad selection process.

As the influence of environmental politics within digital advertising has grown, environmental wastefulness of this kind has come under increased scrutiny, especially since the establishment in January 2022 of a firm, Scope3, devoted to the measurement of advertising's emissions (co-founded, as it happens, by O'Kelley). Excessive auction duplication is of course also economically wasteful. Handling even a fraction of 30 million bid requests a second requires both supply-side and demand-side platforms to create and maintain a very extensive computational infrastructure.

The fact that auction duplication is environmentally and economically wasteful does not, unfortunately, mean that it is easy to curtail because its curtailment involves "collective action" in the social science sense of the term. That refers to a situation in which there is a course of action that would be to the benefit of all those involved, but where the incentives that each individual actor faces mitigate against taking that action.[14] Situations of that kind are commonplace in political life, and material politics is no exception. The biggest material-political-economy problem of all, climate change, is an example. It is in the interest of all of us to limit global warming as much as possible, but individuals, firms, and countries far too often have incentives not to do that. Any particular transatlantic flight or road trip that I want to take has, set against global emissions, a tiny impact, so I go ahead with it for the benefits it brings me, but if everyone reasons like that (in a way that is individually perfectly rational), then abatement does not happen.

Auction duplication on a giant scale is to the collective disadvantage of almost all publishers: the megamachine's computational infrastructure is very costly, and the firms that build and operate it charge for it in the form of fees that considerably reduce publishers' aggregate revenues (see chapter 6).[15] However, each individual publisher nevertheless has, as we have discussed, an incentive to try to increase its own income by duplicating the auctions of its own ad slots. And that is the classic structure of a collective action problem.

But problems of collective action *can* be solved. As we've discussed, the growth of header bidding required the solution of one such problem: uncoordinated header bidding, which was entirely rational for each individual supply-side platform, but collectively had a potentially disastrous effect on the time it took webpages to load. As we saw, Prebid's open-source software, and the implicit, informal cooperation between SSPs that it facilitated, was crucial to solving that problem and making header bidding successful. Indeed, that cooperation became formal with the establishment of an organization to maintain and develop the necessary bidding infrastructure: Prebid.org. It now has nearly one hundred member firms from across the sector, and those members both fund further software development and exercise governance over it through product management committees.

So let us end this chapter with a speculation: that the two issues we have discussed in its final two sections (Google's competition-law problems and the environmental/economic wastefulness of excessive auction duplication) might have a common solution. Suppose Google divests itself of its publisher's ad server, DFP, and its ad exchange, AdX, either because the courts force it to or it chooses to (DFP and AdX are much less important economically than Google Search to Google's parent corporation, Alphabet, and likely to bring with them persistent competition-law problems).[16] Then perhaps DFP and AdX could be bought not by an individual firm but by an appropriately regulated industry collective akin to Prebid.

As we will discuss in the final chapter, infrastructures – and DFP and AdX are an infrastructure – inevitably give potential power to those who control them, but that power can be limited by regulation, in the way in which regulation constrains how electric, natural gas, and water utilities can behave. Prebid has shown that a collectively owned infrastructure of digital advertising can be successful and innovative. Could that be true of DFP and AdX too? And could both they and the megamachine of which they still form the heart be re-engineered to make it more sustainable, economically and environmentally?

# 5

# Enfolding Your Phone

Mobile phones and the apps that run on them are at the heart of digital economies. There are over a billion iPhones and more than three billion Android phones in use worldwide, around 1.8 million apps in Apple's App Store, and over 2.6 million apps in Google's Play Store, with the latter being downloaded 113 billion times in 2023 (Apple Inc. 2023; Curry 2025; Reichert 2023). Defined narrowly, the app economy has a global turnover of over US$500 billion annually, around two-thirds of which is advertising revenue; the remainder is in-app purchases and other spending via app stores (data.ai 2024). Broaden the definition to include physical goods and services purchased via apps (all those Uber rides . . .), and the numbers get even bigger. In a study funded by Apple, two economists reckon that what they call its "App Store ecosystem" generated economic activity totalling US$1.1 trillion in 2022 (Caminade and Borck 2023).

All this involves your phone being enfolded and inhabited by megamachines. If it's an iPhone – and if you're an American, it probably is – then, most likely, it will be in near-constant contact with one of seven, mostly giant, Apple-owned datacenters worldwide, or one of the unknown number of datacenters in which Apple leases space.[1] If you use Instagram, Facebook, or WhatsApp, then Meta's megamachine inhabits your phone. Even if you don't, it's very likely that almost all the apps on your phone that have a commercial dimension have a Facebook/Meta "software development kit" built into them, which sends data, via Meta's systems, which app developers can use to keep track of events such as app installs and in-app purchases. Google has a roughly analogous measurement apparatus, which is part of the multiple ways in which Android phones and the apps running on them interact with Google's huge datacenters. Google's YouTube is a major mobile-phone presence too.

If you prefer a different social media platform, such as TikTok or Snapchat, there is a sense in which these too inhabit your phone, albeit far less thoroughly so than Meta or Google, and – particularly in the case of Snap – without themselves building a computational infrastructure of comparable scale: they are mesomachines, not megamachines. Ad networks that show ads within a wide range of apps also deploy systems of limited size, but their overall volumes of activity, especially the giant numbers of electronic auctions of your attention that they run, seem now to have reached a scale similar to that of Web-display advertising's open marketplace (Paparo 2024a). In that sense, they too form a megamachine in aggregate, even if not individually.

This set of interacting megamachines and mesomachines is contested ground, and its material political economy – and especially how it has played out on iPhones, which has changed dramatically since 2021 – is the topic of this chapter. (Loosely similar changes may well come to Android phones, but haven't yet.) Because the machine-learning optimization of advertising is crucial to the app economy, we choose mobile-phone games as our entry route into the megamachines. Despite almost always being playable free-of-charge, these games earned an estimated US$107 billion globally from players' in-app purchases in 2023 (data.ai 2024). It is economically crucial for game developers that the advertising of their games is optimized to attract players likely to spend within the game.

Thoroughgoing ad optimization is not simple: it requires something approaching the full power of a megamachine. Platforms such as Facebook and Instagram have traditionally excelled at this, and not just for games but for all forms of advertising on mobile phones (most likely including, at least in the recent past, political advertising). Optimization is made possible by what – borrowing a phrase from an online course taught by the app-economy analyst Eric Seufert – we will call the big platforms' "data icebergs," of which only a small, above-the-waterline part is visible to advertisers.

The construction and use of those icebergs was radically altered by Apple's 2021 changes, made in the name of privacy. Those changes were in effect an experiment in redesigning the operations of the megamachines enfolding your phone, at least if it's an iPhone. They involved changes in how iPhones interact with the systems in Apple's datacenters but had much more dramatic, disruptive effects on the other megamachines, especially those of Facebook/Meta. We will discuss how market participants have reacted to this disruption, and the uneasy stasis that has resulted. The chapter ends by turning, briefly, to Google's ongoing efforts – again in the name of privacy – to redesign another megamachine, that of Web-display advertising. Those efforts are particularly worth attention in that they go beyond the predominantly private-sector material politics discussed in the rest of the chapter to include public bodies.

## Serious games

Let's start with the paradigmatic free-to-play mobile-phone game, Candy Crush Saga, discussed in a classic article by David Nieborg (2015). Playing it involves moving brightly colored sweets around to the sound of cheerful music. Get three or more identical sweets into a line, and they disappear, accompanied by gentle explosions. Your score ticks up, and a cascade of further sweets refills your phone's screen. If all goes well, you'll soon complete a level. A warm, disembodied, male voice offers encouragement: Divine! Sweet!

The iPhone version of Candy Crush was released by the Anglo-Swedish games studio, King, in November 2012, and an Android version a month later. The following December, BBC News reported train carriages in London, New York, and other big cities full of commuters "fixated on one thing only. Getting rows of red jelly beans or orange lozenges to disappear" (Stokel-Walker 2013). You've never had to pay to install Candy Crush, and it has been downloaded more than five billion times in total, which suggests that hundreds of millions of people must have played it; over 200 million reportedly still do (Activision Blizzard 2023). Those players aren't going to exhaust its challenges any time soon: Candy Crush has over 15,000 levels, and dozens more are added weekly. By 2023, Candy Crush had earned over US$20 billion in total for King and Activision Blizzard, the games conglomerate that bought King in 2016 for US$5.9 billion (Activision Blizzard 2023), and Activision Blizzard has now itself been bought by Microsoft for US$69 billion.

How do you make money out of a game – not necessarily big money but at least enough to repay its often high development costs – if it's free? Candy Crush is more difficult than it looks, and you can end up temporarily out of "lives." It's then tempting to spend a modest sum to keep playing without interruption or boost your future chances. When MacKenzie started playing it a couple of years ago, he soon found himself pointed to the on-screen "Candy Shop," in which a variety of deals, priced from 99 pence to £7.99 (US$1.30 – US$10.50), were on offer. He didn't even have to get out his credit card. He tapped, was taken to Apple's App Store, which has his credit card on file, and a thumbprint sealed the deal.

Most players of games such as Candy Crush are less easily tempted to spend than he was. The app-economy analyst Eric Seufert (an interviewee who is kindly allowing us to name him) told us that typically "95 percent, 97 percent of all users who play a game will never monetize." If a game is popular enough, that might still mean tens or hundreds of thousands of players spending within it. Attracting them is therefore a vitally important part of what people in the business unromantically call "user acquisition."

Many of them, like MacKenzie, spend only small sums, and only once in a while. The most valuable players are the bigger spenders, referred to as "whales." Because the basic goal in playing Candy Crush is to get at least three identical digital objects next to each other in a line, it's known in the business as a "match-three" game. There are hundreds, perhaps thousands, of such games. A "match-three whale" – that's the term that's used – is someone who spends tens of dollars monthly in one or more of them. Whales are relative rarities: a participant in a webinar we attended in March 2024 estimated that they typically make up no more than "0.25% of the user base" for a game: i.e., two or three people in a thousand. Whales are, however, potentially very valuable if you can find them and persuade them to try out your game.

Games attract players by word-of-mouth recommendations, charts of ratings and total downloads, endorsements by prominent influencers, general social media buzz, and favorable reviews by games journalists (see, e.g., Nieborg and Foxman 2023). But building a mass user base frequently requires large-scale advertising, often on a social media platform such as TikTok, Snapchat, Facebook, or Instagram.

We will return to Facebook and Instagram later in this chapter, but the most immediately obvious place in which to advertise your game is in another game. MacKenzie was a late convert to the pleasures of mobile-phone games. For many years, someone advertising a game to him, however attractively, would simply have been wasting their money. But if he's already playing a game on his phone, then he's an a priori plausible target. More specifically, if he is playing a match-three game, then a games studio would very likely want to advertise their match-three game to him. It's not going to cost him anything to try it out, and he might find he prefers its slightly different format, images, colors, or soundtrack. Handily, there's a well-established way of making players want to watch a video ad within whatever game they're currently playing, rather than ignore it or be annoyed by it: giving them an in-game boost as a reward for watching the ad.

The lure of trying to acquire new players by advertising within other games is therefore strong. Which ads get to be shown often comes down simply to how much the advertiser is prepared to pay, and, as a games executive points out, the owners of other games "are willing to pay a lot" – more than an advertiser for a different kind of product would – "because that's where they're going to drive their installs" (interviewee CY). As a result, often "the overwhelming majority, 95%, of all ads shown in games, are for other games" (Seufert interview). Sometimes, an ad for a game is itself a game, a brief sample of the real thing, although that's an expensive form of advertising, and Seufert tells us that it has become less popular recently.

"I'm buying users from you, you're buying users from me, a lot of revenue was materialized but actually it all got sort of negated by the fact that we're just buying from each other," says Seufert. Interviewee CY tells us that "fundamental tensions" surround earning money by showing ads for other games: they "can be competitors, which isn't awesome," and can cause "my players to churn out." Most ads in mobile-phone games are sold via automated bidding systems, rather than face-to-face negotiation, so it is not always straightforward to block specific unwanted ads. If a competitor "is determined enough, they can get an ad in your game, no question. These systems are not hard to game" (CY).

It can, however, be hard for a games studio to say no to the revenue stream that advertising provides. Indeed, there's an entire genre of relatively rudimentary "hypercasual" games, which we're told are in effect entirely funded by showing ads for other games. As another experienced games executive puts it, "the justification that the companies make and use is, I'm going to make some ad revenue and then I'm going to spend the ad revenue to create a marketing budget [to acquire users for my game]" (interviewee CZ). A common precaution is to avoid showing ads within a game to players who have made purchases in it. "You're hoping you're giving away your less valuable players," says CZ, "but I'm not sure it's really that scientific."

## Optimizing advertising

"Buying" players – acquiring them by showing them ads – is quintessential "direct-response" advertising. The immediate action it seeks to prompt is usually to get the person shown the ad to install the game or other app being advertised.[2] An install, however, is only the beginning of the story. For a game or other app to be economically viable in the medium term, at least some of its players or users must bring it revenue: via their in-app purchases, their taking out subscriptions, or simply by being there to be advertised to. There is a basic constraint: the average "lifetime value" of a player or user (the total revenue that they bring to the game/app) must exceed the average cost of the advertising that led them to it.[3] That's a matter of economic life or death for a game or app.

After an install, there's therefore potentially a series of other "app events," as they are called, that need to be monitored closely. Does the player finish the "tutorial" with which many games begin? Do they keep playing to at least, let's say, level 5? Crucially, do they make in-game purchases, and if so when, how often, and for how much? If a game or app charges a subscription, it will often begin with a free trial. Does the user install the app, but fail to sign up for the free trial? Does the free trial turn into a paid subscription? As interviewee CW puts it, "you've got these [algorithmic] bidders [for advertising opportunities] with machine learning that are saying this segment is working, bid higher here because there are conversions occurring. [All these] automated feedback loops . . . are running."

What is being optimized for in at least the more sophisticated of those feedback loops is not just installs but subsequent app events as well. Machine-learning optimization is on offer throughout digital advertising, but its doyens are Google and Facebook, which, as we have noted, was renamed Meta in October 2021. For nearly a decade, for example, Facebook has enabled you to specify with surprising precision what you want its advertising systems to optimize on your behalf. In 2016, Facebook introduced "App Event Optimization," which allows fine-tuning by focusing advertising so that it generates installs that its systems predict will be followed by actions of the kind that you want to prioritize, such as in-app purchases. A year later, it added the capacity for "Value Optimization," which involves seeking to maximize the *total* revenue that advertising-acquired players or users will bring.

Advertising that is tailored for Value Optimization can be expensive, but it's the technique you would choose if you are hunting whales. As in most of digital advertising, auctions, in this case internal to Meta, determine which ads get shown to which users, but, as we'll discuss in chapter 6, as an advertiser you don't yourself have to take on the daunting task of working out how much to bid. Specify your goal, your budget, and perhaps the minimum "return on ad spend" that would be acceptable to you, and Meta bids into its own auctions on your behalf.

Particularly useful to us in learning about practicalities such as these was an online course taught by Eric Seufert, the app-economy analyst and user-acquisition specialist we have already mentioned.[4] An entire session of the course was devoted to advertising via Facebook and Instagram, and an especially striking moment was when Seufert described how advertising on Facebook had changed. He talked about meetings, in around

2015, of a computer-game user-acquisition team, in which he and his colleagues would discuss in detail how to target their Facebook advertising: "Maybe we should try car enthusiasts, because . . . we're trying to reach men . . . maybe we should target people that 'like' Bruce Willis's page because he's like an action star . . . That was what you did." Within five years, Facebook's increasingly sophisticated machine learning had made such discussions a waste of time: "Now, Facebook has basically internalized all that and now you're just feeding it with . . . inputs [e.g., multiple variants of your ads so that it can test which are most effective]. None of that stuff you used to do matters." Now, said Seufert, the job of the advertising practitioner is "to feed this experimentation machine."

A major digital-advertising platform, such as Facebook or Google, is like an iceberg, Seufert said in that session. Visible above the waterline are the characteristics of users on which advertisers traditionally focus, such as age, gender, and "interests," like enthusiasm for motorcars. But below the surface, invisible to the advertiser and too copious to make full sense to human beings, is the much larger volume of other data, far more heterogeneous in nature, which the platform possesses.[5] That's the data that can make platforms' machine-learning optimization of advertising considerably more effective than human-guided targeting.

The iceberg's implications go well beyond the advertising of games. One of our interviewees, for example, has a business selling handmade saris and a strong commitment to preserving India's village handicrafts. In our first conversations, he was highly critical of Big Tech. But he has gradually learned that his best market is Tamil Brahmins in India and in the diaspora. There's no list of them for him to work from, and on Facebook or Google "there's no classification saying 'target Tamil Brahmins.'" Yet using data on "customers who've bought . . . from me before, who've interacted with my products, Google and Facebook are able to find them. . . . My clients look for 30-minute recipes. They look for Bollywood news. They look for Tamil cinema news. . . . I have to trust the machine to be more effective than me to do this" (interviewee CF).

It's a useful reminder that, in his words, "machine learning, although it's imperfect, has the potential to amplify the reach of small businesses." But the machine is, of course, amoral. It optimizes for whatever "conversions" it is told to pursue: installs of Angry Birds; sales of saris made by village women; voters signing up for a Donald Trump rally. People whose political predilections resemble ours often like to think that the explanation for Trump's 2016 election or the result of the Brexit referendum was cunning microtargeting by political consultants using platforms such as Facebook, perhaps funded by Russian money or informed by Cambridge Analytica's psychometric data.

Ian Bogost and Alexis Madrigal, writing in the *Atlantic* in April 2020, have a more convincing hypothesis in respect to Facebook: that the Trump campaign's success with it resulted simply from its use of Facebook's standard machine-learning optimization procedures. Trump's ads were banal, but rather than trying to build the case for him they often encouraged a specific action, a conversion: "Buy this hat, sign this petition, RSVP to this rally" (Bogost and Madrigal 2020). Researching the ads for a January 2020 Trump rally in Milwaukee, they found little sign of the targeting of specific demographic groups. Bogost and Madrigal suggest that instead the Trump campaign's use of Facebook began, just like our sari vendor's, by providing its system with a "custom audience", a list of people who have already taken an action, such as providing an email address or phone number, which suggests that they are Trump supporters. Machine learning can then search for "lookalikes": people who resemble the custom audience.[6] But its search for likeness would go well beyond characteristics that a political sociologist might think of as influencing voting preferences. It would use the full power of the submerged portion of the data iceberg.

A "source close to the 2016 Trump campaign" told Bogost and Madrigal (2020) that its use of Facebook was inspired by the successes of the mobile-game studio Machine Zone's machine-learning optimization of user acquisition. But that specific example might not have been needed: by 2016 the practices Bogost and Madrigal report were fast becoming standard among those who realized how machine learning was changing advertising.

## Is it the same phone?

The submerged portion of the iceberg is enormous, but it can't really be used to optimize advertising unless a degree of order can be found in the data it contains. The crucial issue is what practitioners call "identity resolution": the capacity to discern, in an automated way and with at least some degree of accuracy, that two or more often very different data traces involve the same human being.

In advertising on mobile phones, identity resolution largely boils down to something basic and deceptively simple: whether it's the same phone. Megamachines' enfolding of phones can lose much of its economic rationale if which phones are being enfolded is not knowable. In smartphones' early years, it wasn't difficult to tell. Every smartphone, whether Apple or Android, had a unique identifier number, which the phone's owner could not alter or delete, and which was visible to the apps installed on the phone and the ad networks that displayed ads on it, and whose Software Development Kits, or SDKs, were embedded in those apps. Apple told app developers not to "transmit data about a user without obtaining the user's prior permission" (Arthur 2010), but it was a "must not," not the "cannot" of material politics. There was no insurmountable material barrier, and the prohibition seems to have been widely flouted. Mobile-phone apps leaked data, sometimes on a large scale, and that began to become known. "Your Apps Are Watching You," the *Wall Street Journal* warned its readers (Thurm and Kane 2010).

Apple, though, was not yet ready to leave advertisers without a reliable way of answering the question, "Is it the same phone?" By 2010, privacy-conscious people were regularly deleting the "cookies" (as we've discussed, these are strings of digits unique to each user) that websites and Web advertisers had deposited in their browsers. Although cookies are a Web technology not available to mobile-phone apps, Apple decided to give savvy iPhone owners an equivalent to purging cookies. From 2012 onward, it denied apps and ad networks access to phones' permanent identifiers, and instead made available to them a 32-digit IDFA, which uniquely identifies a particular phone but can be changed whenever the phone's owner wants. In 2016, Apple gave iPhone users the additional capacity to "zero out" their IDFAs. If someone has done this, when an app (or an ad network's SDK within it) asks the phone for its IDFA, it receives in response an uninformative string of 32 zeros. Google introduced a similar GAID (Google Advertising Identifier), which owners of Android phones can change or similarly delete.

Most people, though – including us – aren't savvy enough to alter or delete our phone's IDFA or GAID. In practice, therefore, those identifiers weren't so different from the permanent identifiers they replaced, and they quickly became the economic pivot point of the mega and mesomachines enfolding smartphones, the key to finding structure in the data iceberg. When you were shown an ad for a game or other app on your phone, the ad network or social media platform responsible for the ad would capture your phone's IDFA or GAID. If you then installed the game/app, it would immediately ask your phone for its IDFA or GAID, so enabling the install (and any subsequent "app events" such as in-app purchases) to be "attributed" to the ad.

IDFAs or GAIDs thus enabled crucial component parts of the megamachines surrounding mobile phones (social media platforms and other apps, along with ad networks and mobile measurement platforms acting on their behalf) to close the key feedback loop between the showing of ads and users' subsequent actions.[7] That's what made IDFAs and GAIDs the economic pivot points of the ad-optimizing megamachines. They made it possible to measure the efficacy of ads in close to real time, and – using machine learning – to optimize that efficacy. That, indeed, was how an IDFA or a GAID was supposed to work. "Apple created IDFA," says an experienced advertising technology specialist, "so that advertisers could [continue to] 'attribute' marketing campaigns to their app and have a [measurable] return on investment and run effective advertising" (interviewee DD).

There were, however, "scale effects" created by the sheer multitude of the ads, app installs, and app events that flowed through the megamachines. In the case of iPhones, these seem to have been effects that Apple had not fully anticipated. In the ordinary course of showing all those ads and recording all those installs and app events, any large ad network's or social media platform's system would encounter the same, seldom if ever changed, IDFA or GAID multiple times in connection with different games or apps, so linking up the user's behavior across apps. The resultant growth of the data icebergs was further enhanced by two additional ways in which the megamachines operated, ways little known outside the sector but described to us by interviewees, which we outline in a note.[8]

IDFAs and giant-scale data icebergs made possible what interviewee DD calls "effective deterministic [targeting]. They would know that you use Deliveroo to get Chinese or Vietnamese food on a Saturday, they know that you use Tinder . . . They'd have known bloody everything." We were at first puzzled by this use of the word "deterministic" because little in life is that certain, but we now see what he means.[9] First, if the same IDFA (or GAID) is involved with two different data traces, such as a tap on an ad and an install of an app, you can know with some certainty that the phone on which the ad was shown and the phone that installed the app are indeed the same phone. Second, because mobile phones in, for example, North America and Europe typically have only one user, there's a high probability that the same human being was involved. Third, if the IDFA is associated with, say, repeated purchases within a match-three game, and an advertisement for another such game leads the player to take that up instead, it's very likely indeed that they will spend similarly in the new game. Being a whale is repetitive behavior: you are unlikely to stop just because you have switched games.

Interviewees DD and DR reached for the same metaphor to describe the precision of the targeting of ads by the app economy's megamachines when they had unconstrained access to IDFAs: the sniper. An ad network "[u]sed to be able to take a sniper shot with IFDA because certain devices, you could know" that their user was a whale, says DR. A social media platform's algorithm, bidding into the platform's own auctions on behalf of a games studio, could be what DD calls "a $50 sniper because they will bid $50, which is a super high [bid]," but worth it if the target is a whale.[10]

## Redesigning the megamachine

The bombshell landed on the first day of Apple's June 2020 Worldwide Developers Conference, held online because of the pandemic. "We believe tracking should always be transparent and under your control," Apple Privacy Engineering Manager Katie Skinner told the conference. "So, moving forward, App Store policy will require apps to ask before tracking you across apps and websites owned by other companies" (Schiff 2020). Apple materially implemented that new policy, App Tracking Transparency or ATT, in April 2021, when it launched Version 14.5 of its iPhone operating system, iOS.

ATT tightly restricts apps' access to IDFAs, thus blocking crucial aspects of how the megamachines we have just described worked prior to 2021. It is not simply a "must not" prohibition but a material-politics "cannot." Crucial aspects of ATT are implemented in iOS, which materially controls much of what can and cannot happen on iPhones. We have emphasized that a megamachine is a *distributed* machine, and ATT is a quite explicit reconfiguring of that machine: it affects only tracking *across* apps, not an app's tracking of its own users within its digital boundaries.

The internal decision-making process that led to Apple's new privacy measures has not been made public, and (as noted in chapter 1) we lack firsthand fieldwork data on it. Both interviewees and published sources offer hypotheses. "Whoever has the most data wins," says interviewee DD, and the way in which IDFAs were being used to accumulate data and gain capabilities, outside of Apple's control, for prediction, targeting, and ad optimization "pissed Apple off," he says. Seufert (2017) and Levy (2020: 481–5) report a history of tension between Apple and, specifically, Facebook. In 2018, for example, Apple insisted that Facebook remove a Facebook-owned app from the App Store over privacy concerns, or Apple "would ban it," and it even shut down Facebook's access to its "enterprise" program, which allowed companies to make prototype versions of their apps available to their employees (Levy 2020: 483–4).

The "golden fleece" of the app economy "is the capacity of a company to direct app installs and control users' attention," argues Seufert (2017), making who controls that capacity crucial. He implicitly suggests that Apple may have felt that too much of that capacity had leaked away to Facebook. More specifically, DR suggests that Apple's new policy, ATT, boosted the attractiveness to app developers of the App Store search ads that Apple sells, which employ Apple's own first-party data, but he doubts that this was a major motivation.

"I think it was much more risk avoidance," he says – fear of something akin to the Cambridge Analytica data leakage scandal that hit Facebook in 2017–18. An episode of that kind "would be massive for them [Apple]" because of the way the iPhone is positioned by Apple as "being the privacy-focus device" (interviewee DR). All these, however, are speculations. The most

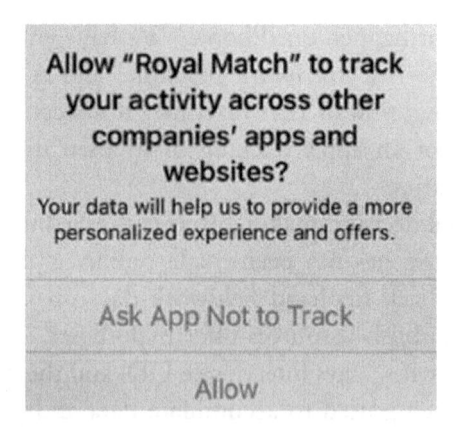

**Figure 5.1** A crucial change in the megamachine: an example of an Apple App Tracking Transparency consent screen. Authors'screenshot.

direct statement we have is from Apple's chief executive, Tim Cook, who said in an October 2021 call to stock analysts that "we believe strongly that privacy is a basic human right. And so that's our motivation there [for ATT]. There's no other motivation" (McGee 2021).

Apple's new policy, ATT, requires any app that wants to track you beyond its own electronic confines to show you a consent screen (such as that shown in Figure 5.1) when you install it. You tap on the screen either to "allow" tracking or to reject it: "Ask app not to track." Crucially, it is just as quick and easy to reject as to accept tracking, and if you choose the former, the app isn't allowed to penalize you by restricting the features available to you. (Apple has, in other words, turned its back on the subtle material politics of consent screens that nudge impatient users to accept tracking.) Your tap is recorded within your phone's operating system.[11] If you reject tracking and the app in question ever asks your phone for its IDFA, iOS ensures that all it gets is the 32 uninformative zeros.

Tapping "Ask app not to track" thus materially removes the app's access to the economic pivot point of the pre-2021 megamachines and mesomachines, and that is what most users tap in most apps. Rates of consent to tracking vary through time and among apps, but in mid-2024 the mobile measurement platform Singular estimated them as averaging just under 14% (Koetsier 2024). But that isn't the end of it. If you want to use IDFAs to connect up an ad for app A shown within app B to an install of app A, the user needs to have consented to tracking in *both* apps A and B.

Without IDFAs, or something to replace them, all that an advertiser or ad network has to work with is a bunch of records of the (probably very large number of) ads it has displayed and a different bunch of records of installs of the game or purchases of the product being advertised. Connecting up the two bunches in order to measure and optimize the effectiveness of advertising is very far from easy. "When you break [the] loop" that used to be closed by being able to match IDFAs, says interviewee CW, "it's much harder."

Facebook protested fiercely against what it called "Apple's forced software update," in December 2020 even taking out full-page adverts in, among others, the *Financial Times* and the *New York Times*. The ad began in huge font: "We're standing up to Apple for small businesses everywhere." It went on to describe the coming changes as "devastating to small businesses" because they endangered their "ability to run personalised ads and reach their customers effectively" (Facebook Inc. 2020).

When, however, Apple implemented those changes, Facebook found itself with no alternative but to comply. For a decade, its users had interacted with it mostly via their phones, so in practice Facebook is a mobile-phone app. Instagram has always been an app, with the additional twist that heavy users of Instagram tend particularly to like iPhones because of their high-quality cameras. So non-compliance would have had effects that couldn't be contemplated. "[W]e have no choice but to show Apple's [tracking consent] prompt," wrote Dan Levy, then a Facebook vice-president, in February 2021. "If we don't, they will block

Facebook from the App Store" (Levy 2020–1). To use a term that we will discuss in chapter 7, Apple has *infrastructural power* in the app economy because it controls systems that others in that economy need to employ, in particular the App Store and iOS.

Facebook's compliance with changes that it anticipated would be highly disruptive is an object lesson in the efficacy of infrastructural power. If the prompt screen has to be shown, and the user taps "Ask app not to track," Facebook became materially unable to access the phone's IDFA. It stumbled, probably losing several billion dollars in ad revenue as it rebuilt its systems to cope with the loss of finely granular data (McGee 2021). As Sheryl Sandberg, then its chief operating officer, described in an "earnings call" on October 25, 2021, "the accuracy of our ads targeting decreased, which increased the cost of driving outcomes for our advertisers. And . . . measuring those outcomes became more difficult" (Seufert 2021). In a further call that day to stock analysts, also quoted by Seufert, Facebook's chief financial officer, David Wehner, told them, "I think just the retooling of . . . all of the targeting and measurement to basically work for aggregated events is just it's difficult especially for smaller advertisers . . . the areas that are hardest impacted . . . I'd probably call out there, online commerce and gaming." Other factors also buffeted tech stocks, and between September 2021 (by which time the effects of Apple's implementation of its new policy had started to become fully evident) and October 2022, Facebook/Meta's stock slid from US$352 to US$93.[12]

Meta's stock has, however, now more than recovered, aided by investor enthusiasm for artificial intelligence and by the "retooling" efforts pointed to by Wehner, which we will discuss in chapter 6. Mobile-phone games were less fortunate. "[W]ithout IDFA, you couldn't take a sniper shot anymore," says interviewee DR: "now you have to use a shotgun." The greater difficulty, and therefore the cost of finding whales and other users who will "monetize," has "increased the obstacle to launching a game," says Seufert. Interviewee DF tells us that launching has become two to three times more expensive. Resultant falls in advertising revenues, Seufert reports, have in their turn badly affected the economics of ad-dependent hypercasual games. Although other factors are again also involved, the previously healthy growth of the computer-game sector as a whole – not just mobile-phone games – has slowed dramatically, with widespread job losses, 10,500 globally in 2023, according to a report on the publishing site Obsidian (Anon. 2023), followed by more than 5,000 in January 2024 alone (Silberling 2024).

## Subterranean material politics

Since 2021, the overt controversy sparked by Apple's privacy policy has gradually been replaced by latent, subterranean conflict between two different ways of configuring the megamachines enfolding iPhones. The first is Apple's preferred arrangement, which, if you have an iPhone, increases the latter's centrality to the megamachine. Data crucial to measurement and ad optimization, such as your taps on ads, is stored not on an external server but in your phone's memory. When you install an app, it can be programmed (by the app's developers, or an ad network whose "software development kit," or SDK, is embedded in the app) to ask your iPhone whether you have been shown an ad for that app, and if so which ad.

It doesn't, however, receive an answer straightaway. No access to the ad data stored on your phone is allowed for 24 hours, plus a randomly varying period of up to a further 24 hours, the rationale of randomization being to stop exact times being used to match up ads and subsequent actions such as purchases or game installs. Once the 24–48 hours is up, the data is sent from your phone to the relevant advertiser or ad network via an Apple server that ensures the preservation of what Apple calls "crowd anonymity." In essence, it means checking that there's nothing about the data that makes your phone distinguishable from at least a moderately large crowd of other phones. For example, at the beginning of an advertising campaign for an app, the number of installs will at first be small, and Apple's systems therefore tightly constrain the information that the advertiser receives until that number grows.[13]

All of that is part of a way of measuring the efficacy of advertising that Apple calls Store Kit Ad Network, or SKAN, and offers free of charge to ad networks and advertisers.[14] It is a material reorganization of the app economy, and it differs from the traditional configuration of the interacting megamachines in that the data it makes available is inherently aggregate, rather than the traditional "that ad was shown on this phone, which then installed the app." As Seufert puts it, in Apple's preferred approach, the ad network or advertiser learns that "this campaign delivered an install" or purchase, but Apple's system in effect says "I won't tell you who the person is" (Seufert interview). Furthermore, the facts that those reports are delayed by at least 24 hours, and the information that is provided on subsequent app events is strictly limited, means that optimizing advertising in anything like real time is much harder than traditionally.

Many other major participants in the app economy are not happy with these constraints, and the second approach to configuring the megamachine tries more fully to preserve existing practices, in particular to continue to tie ads to specific phones and particular installs and to measure and optimize the effectiveness of advertising in real time. There are two main ways of doing this, the first of which – "fingerprinting" – Apple has taken substantial action against.

"Fingerprinting" involves detecting features of a user's phone or other device in the hope of being able to identify it, perhaps not "deterministically" (as when IDFAs were readily available) but at least probabilistically. As interviewee DR points out, some features of a device are necessary for an app to know, such as: "What kind of device am I, because . . . I'm going to send this image in this size at that resolution, so you want to know that. Other things are also quite useful [such as] what [is the] language [setting] of this device?" Other features, however, such as knowledge of the phone's level of battery charge, have fewer legitimate uses: "you start thinking, why does an app need to know that, and the reality is they don't" (DR). Does an app really need to know the total memory space available on your phone, or when you last restarted it?

Even before the operating system update (iOS 14.5) that implemented Apple's privacy changes, it started to crack down on the collection of information for fingerprinting. App developers who submitted updates to their apps for scrutiny by Apple's App Store engineers began to get messages rejecting those updates and telling them, "We found in our review that your app collects user and device information to create a unique identifier for the user's device. Apps that fingerprint the user's device in this way are in violation of the Apple Developer Program License Agreement" (quoted in Koetsier 2021).

The problem with fingerprinting as a substitute for IDFAs as the economic pivot point of a megamachine is that it requires app developers to add code to their apps that asks your iPhone, via an API (application programming interface), for its "battery status," for example, and access to the API is denied unless the app's developers specify in a "Privacy Manifest" supplied to the App Store why their app needs that access. "People are living within the constraints of that, by and large," says DR. "There's no great groundswell of apps being rejected." Some degree of fingerprinting most likely continues – as noted, knowledge of some features of your phone useful for fingerprinting has also got legitimate uses – but Apple's crackdown on it seems broadly to have been successful.

Harder to prevent is use of a second substitute for the IDFA as the mega or mesomachines' pivot: your phone's Internet Protocol, or IP address. It's not a full substitute: when your phone is connected to the internet via a mobile-phone network, it may be sharing the network's local IP address with hundreds or thousands of other phones, and that's a form of crowd anonymity. When, however, your phone's connection is via the WiFi router in your flat or house, its IP address is your router's address. The crowd is then much smaller: it's the devices in your household using the same router. We asked one of our contacts whether whale hunting continues after Apple's changes. It does, he told us, even if it is now less precise. "They used to know that I was a match-three whale," he said, "but my wife wasn't, and my two kids' iPads weren't. But with IP address, they still know my household has one match-three whale in it" (interviewee DD).

For that sort of reason, the use of IP addresses to help measure and optimize advertising's effectiveness is contentious. Four well-informed people have told us that it's widespread, but it's hard for an outsider to determine how important it is relative to other inputs to machine-learning systems, such as data from Apple's SKAN or the behavior of the minority of users who have agreed to tracking. There is, however, a simpler issue: timing. If you use only Apple's SKAN, you have to wait 24–48 hours for data to arrive, and possibly longer if you want information beyond, for example, the simple fact that an install has occurred. But if you can yourself gather the data you need (and IP addresses, for example, can be captured outside of Apple's systems), advertising can continue to be optimized in real time. The megamachine might not work as efficiently as it did when IDFAs were routinely available, but it can still work in roughly the same way.

Is that within Apple's rules? Might it take action against it? The App Store tells app developers that they must not "derive data from a device for the purpose of uniquely identifying it," and among its examples of such data is "the user's network connection" (Apple Inc. n.d.). One of our interviewees who told us about the use of IP addresses to help measure and optimize the efficiency of advertising tells us that those who do this interpret the prohibited "identifying" of a device as "identifying it persistently and specifically," which an IP address does not do.

There are, furthermore, two difficulties more profound than ambiguity in the wording of the rule. First, the use of IP addresses cannot be materially blocked in the relatively straightforward way that fingerprinting can be. IP addresses are the way packets of information are guided through the internet to the correct destination, so denying apps access to them is unrealistic. Second, how could Apple materially detect the problematic use of IP addresses? "Apple is not the internet, and they're not the police officer of the internet. So essentially, Apple could spy on all communications that could come out of your phone, but that would [be] horrifically privacy invasive for the purpose of creating privacy . . ." (interviewee DR).

As far as we can see, the only way in which Apple could plausibly turn the difficult-to-enforce "must not" of the rule into a material-politics "cannot" is by obfuscating IP addresses, that is, encrypting them and routing electronic traffic to and from each iPhone through a relay system of computer servers, so that the endpoint, the phone's IP address, is hidden from external parties. (That's what's done, for both good reasons and to hide from law enforcement, in the "dark Web.") Apple already offers subscribers to its premium iCloud+ service a "private relay" facility of this kind to obfuscate their Web browsing, and it would be technically feasible to extend this to a more thoroughgoing material obfuscation of all the world's billion or so iPhones. That would, however, most likely spark strong government opposition, particularly in China, an important iPhone market. It would also involve extra costs for Apple and/or iPhone owners, and bring with it a great deal of additional processing and electronic traffic, so palpably increasing the internet's already high energy consumption and thus carbon emissions. "Privacy," in other words, is not costless.

## Identity politics

What participants call "identity resolution" – discerning when two or more different data traces involve the same human being – has been central to digital advertising's overall trajectory, which has been to tailor advertising to very specific audiences, and ultimately individuals, rather than, for example, the inherently aggregate viewership of traditional broadcast TV programs. The growing sense that identity resolution can easily violate privacy has led to the search for alternative ways configuring digital advertising's megamachines so that they can operate without relying on identity-resolution devices such as IDFAs. As well as Apple, Google too has been making moves in this direction, albeit more tentatively, by developing "Privacy Sandbox" systems for both Android phones and its Chrome Web browser, the world's most widely used. We will not discuss those changes in detail – as we've suggested, they can be thought of as loosely analogous to Apple's changes – but end this chapter by briefly discussing the very different political-economy relations in which the Chrome changes are being made.

Just as Apple removed default access to the IDFA, the pivot of the distributed machine surrounding iPhones, so Google plans to remove from its Chrome browser the default availability of the equivalent pivot of the megamachine of the open marketplace in Web-display ads: the third-party cookie, which enables users to be tracked across websites, as we discussed in chapter 2. Default settings of other browsers such as Firefox and Safari already block the deposit of third-party cookies, but that has not yet happened with Chrome, the world's most widely used browser. Google's original plan was to have Chrome browsers reject third-party cookies by default unless users explicitly consent to them, but in July 2024 it modified this plan, saying that it was going to offer users "an informed choice" (Chavez 2024) about them. How that choice is going to be materially presented to users is not fully clear at the time of writing in February 2025, but if it is similar to Apple's App Tracking Transparency consent screen, it is likely de facto largely to phase out third-party cookies.

Similar, too, is a widespread concern of smaller market participants about measures that reduce or eliminate their capacity for "third-party" data gathering via IDFAs or cookies. Their concern is that those measures implicitly increase the power of Big Tech corporations, such as Apple or Google, which possess extensive "first-party" data gathered directly from users with their explicit or implicit consent. The crucial difference, however, between the cases of Apple and Google is that the antitrust/competition law conflicts concerning the latter (which we discuss in chapters 4 and 7) have been sharper for longer than the equivalent conflicts concerning Apple.

Google announced its decision to phase out third-party cookies in January 2020, provoking a storm of controversy within digital advertising, prominent in the sector meetings we attended that year. That Fall, a number of UK market participants, including the pressure group Marketers for an Open Web, complained to the UK regulator, the Competition and Markets Authority (which had just completed a major study of market power within digital advertising: CMA 2020), alleging that "Google was abusing its dominant position" (CMA 2021: 8). In January 2021, the CMA launched a competition-law investigation, and Google then offered it a number of commitments to address its concerns, for example a promise not to employ its first-party data on Chrome users' browsing (data that is not accessible to other market participants) to inform its display-advertising systems, which we discussed in chapter 4. Those commitments became legally binding when the CMA finally accepted them in February 2022.[15]

Whether those commitments are sufficient to avoid smaller market participants being disadvantaged relative to Google remains contentious – we witnessed a particularly lively face-to-face meeting about this in late 2023 – and, at the time of writing, the final design of, for example, the Chrome Privacy Sandbox is not yet fully settled. But the differences from the political economy of the Apple changes on which this chapter has focused could not be sharper. Apple was able to make those changes without any public regulatory body needing to scrutinize and approve them; the controversy about them was almost entirely a private-sector conflict. In contrast, the dispute over third-party cookies and the Privacy Sandbox involved a public regulator, the CMA, in scrutinizing design decisions crucial to the megamachine of the open marketplace in Web-display ads, and that regulator was impressively active in seeking the views of market participants at large on those decisions.

To have a public regulator in effect involved in redesigning one of digital advertising's megamachines is an intriguing policy experiment, albeit not an easy one. The Privacy Sandbox is a complicated set of mechanisms; the CMA's team is small; and resolving the underlying tension between preserving privacy and fostering competition is always difficult. But tensions, astutely handled, can be positive and creative (Caliskan, MacKenzie, and Rommerskirchen 2024). Instead of a regulatory turf war breaking out between the CMA, whose remit is competition, and the United Kingdom's Information Commissioner's Office, whose remit is data protection, the two regulators collaborated on the case, as far as we can tell productively. It's too early to write off the possibility that public policy could be a beneficial influence on the design of systems crucial to digital advertising.

# 6

# Digital Advertising's Tensions

If you've stuck with us this far, you don't need us to tell you that digital advertising is pretty darn complicated. Advertising practitioners working for advertisers or advertising agencies have to navigate this complex world, and in this chapter we discuss some prominent tensions they encounter as they attempt this. Some of these tensions are explicit and publicly discussed, for example by Hwang (2020): they are "matters of concern" in the sense of, for example, Callon (2021).[1] The tension with which we ended the previous chapter, between preserving privacy and fostering competition, is an example.

Other tensions, though, are more private. They include ambivalences, for example about systems that a practitioner feels simultaneously attracted to and diffusely suspicious of, and also difficulties: things that they accept that they need to do but find hard, such as demonstrating to clients that advertising "works," which can provoke subjectively felt, sharp anxieties. Tensions can take the form of conflicts between different groups of practitioners. And tensions can also be opportunities, for example, for "moral entrepreneurship," in the sense of Becker (1973), highlighting an unease and making it an explicit matter of concern, perhaps selling a system or service to assuage it.

After a discussion of a conceptual distinction (between intermediaries and mediators) that helps make sense of digital advertising's tensions, we will examine the quite different forms that those tensions take in the open marketplace (which we discussed in chapters 2 and 4) and in what practitioners often call "walled gardens," such as the systems discussed in chapters 3 and 5.[2] The final part of the chapter will focus on the tensions surrounding two interlinked current developments: the loss of agency by advertising's practitioners; and the de-individualization of advertising's audiences.

## Intermediaries and mediators

The distinction that we'll use was drawn by Bruno Latour in a book, *Reassembling the Social*, which lays out how his theoretical position differs from more traditional approaches in sociology: "An *intermediary* . . . transports meaning or force without transformation . . . *Mediators* . . . transform, translate, distort, and modify the meaning or the elements they are supposed to carry" (Latour 2005: 39; emphases in original). Latour argued that what he called "'conventional' sociology" posits "society or other social aggregates" as preexisting, and "draws maps of the world" that consist of these aggregates, "followed by trails of consequences which are never much more than effects, expressions, or reflections of something else" – trails that involve the effects of "the social" being "transported without deformation through a chain of intermediaries." His actor-network theory, in contrast, "pictures a world made of concatenations of mediators where each point can be said to fully act" (Latour 2005: 8, 23, 59, 60).

That, we know, sounds very abstract, so let us draw a more concrete contrast between Latour's position and that of Shoshana Zuboff's influential *Age of Surveillance Capitalism*, in which "economic imperatives" play the fundamental socially causal role, and technical systems are treated as if they are intermediaries: "[W]e *hunt the puppet master, not the puppet* . . . surveillance capitalism is a logic in action and not a technology . . . . Surveillance capitalism's unique economic imperatives are the puppet masters that hide behind the curtain orienting the machines and summoning them to action" (Zuboff 2019: 14–16; emphasis in original).

Latour, however, explicitly queers the "puppet master" metaphor: "[P]uppeteers will rarely behave as having total control over their puppets. They will say queer things like 'their marionettes suggest them to do things they will never have thought possible by themselves.' . . . So who is pulling the strings? Well, the puppets do in addition to their puppeteers" (Latour 2005: 59–60). Technical systems, for example, are not reducible to human intentions. Sometimes they thwart what humans want to do; at other times they helpfully "suggest them to do things" – as mobile phones' small screens helped prompt the move of ads into users' news feeds, crucial to Facebook becoming an advertising leviathan (see chapter 3).

Advertising's practitioners have long been thought of as "cultural intermediaries" (e.g., Cronin 2004), indeed as "the emblematic intermediary occupation" (McFall 2014: 45). The many dozens of advertising technology firms that populate the Lumascape discussed in chapter 4, similarly, are often referred to by practitioners as "intermediaries." Nevertheless, we want to follow Latour and switch the terminology. The people and organizations found in digital advertising are nearly all better thought of in his terms as mediators, not intermediaries – and so are the technical systems that populate the field: Latour clearly intended the intermediary/mediator distinction to apply to things, technologies, "non-humans," and human/non-human hybrids, not just to human beings.

Despite the word "distort" in Latour's formulation of the distinction, to call someone or something a mediator is not a criticism. Indeed, in the intellectual context in which Latour was working, the term often carried a positive connotation. "J'ai besoin de mes intercesseurs . . . la gauche a besoin d'intercesseurs

[I need my mediators; the left needs mediators]" said the hugely influential philosopher Gilles Deleuze (1985: 13, 17), and those mediators need to be, as he put it, "indirect or free," not "direct" or "directly dependent": in other words, not Latourian intermediaries.[3] What is to our knowledge the first article to apply the notion of mediation to advertising (Hennion and Méadel 1989) had a title that many advertising practitioners would embrace as a self-identity: "The Artisans of Desire."[4]

If everything is, or can be, a mediator (as Latour posits), why do we also need the notion of intermediary? Despite the empirical rarity of intermediaries, they have a central place in high-modern imaginaries. In digital advertising, for instance, the *idea* that mediators should be made into intermediaries is often influential. For example, the single most pervasive criticism within digital advertising of the firms and systems that populate the open marketplace is that they are opaque mediators, not "transparent" intermediaries.[5]

One topic on which the intermediary/mediator distinction throws light is data and knowledge. Is unmediated access to "raw truth" and "objective" data possible, via technical devices that can be considered intermediaries (or, indeed, via trustworthy human senses), or does knowing always involve mediators?[6] While that issue sounds abstract, even "philosophical," it is an important everyday matter in digital advertising. Knowledge of the extent to which advertising is cost-effective is a crucial issue for most advertising practitioners. Are the "pixels" and other devices that generate the relevant data, along with the systems that process it, transparent intermediaries, or are they opaque mediators? That is an issue that underpins several of the tensions we have found.

The crucial issue to which the intermediary/mediator distinction applies is, however, the interaction of (or, better, the co-creation of) supply and demand because here high-modern "intermediary" imaginaries of markets are deeply rooted. "Arm's-length" views of supply and demand, common in at least elementary economics, implicitly conceive of supply and demand as pre-formed, and thus as simply "brought together" to facilitate market exchange. In these imaginaries (influential far beyond academic economics), the people, organizations, or technical systems that do the bringing together are – or, at least, should be – intermediaries: they do not, or should not, alter supply and demand. All that intermediaries should do is "transparently" facilitate the "discovery" of a market-clearing price, and "transparency" and "discovery" are metaphors that belong firmly to a world of intermediaries rather than mediators.

That view of supply and demand is, however, sharply criticized by Latour's actor-network theory colleague Michel Callon as an over-abstract, fundamentally misleading, "interface" model: "Supply is not a given, preconstituted block that faces an equally set block, that of a demand. Supply and demand emerge and express themselves over the course of a continuous process. They are constantly in motion" (Callon 2021: 22).

Empirically, for example, Caliskan has shown that market price is not the singular, mathematical "coming together of the two lines of supply and demand," but takes multiple, concrete forms generated by diverse tools and framings (Caliskan 2009: 241). Instead of the impoverished interface model, Callon's approach is to view sellers, buyers, and goods as fluid and co-created in ever-changing, complex ways in concrete, material "market encounters."[7] Although Callon has touched explicitly on the point only briefly (in joint work with Caliskan), his implicit view is that these encounters are shaped by mediators, not intermediaries.[8]

## Tensions in the open marketplace

Let us begin our discussion of intermediaries, mediators, and digital advertising's tensions with the open marketplace. It looks like – indeed, is – a market. Large numbers of publishers (i.e., providers of electronic content of all kinds, not just news publishers) bring to the open marketplace a "supply" of advertising opportunities. It encounters "demand" from advertisers, small as well as large, and numbered in the millions. That encounter happens in good part in "ad exchanges" that have a degree of resemblance to finance's stock exchanges, but it is an entangled, often opaque, form of mediated co-creation, rather than arm's-length interaction via transparent intermediaries. As we shall see in this section, however, there are influential efforts to turn the encounter's mediators into intermediaries.

Tensions in the open marketplace are of two main kinds. The first concerns what is being bought and sold. For example, will an ad actually be viewable by a human being? Or will it be transmitted to the user's device, but not in view on-screen, perhaps because it is "below the fold," that is, in a part of a page in view only if the user scrolls down? The efforts, insightfully described by Cluley (2018), to develop an industry-standard definition of "viewability" met resistance: one of our interviewees, who occupied a mediatory role, admits that "we didn't want people [clients] to measure viewability because it was an expense to us." Ad "exchanges were selling things that were not viewable," he says, and buying only viewable ads was more expensive.

The eventually agreed standard definition of viewability involves "a minimum of 50% of pixels" of a standard display ad being "in view of a minimum of one second" for it to be judged viewable (IAB 2014), or two seconds in the case of a video ad. Tension around the issue remains, however. "It's not a solved problem," says interviewee AE. The "standards are to be honest . . . a joke to me. We, as advertisers, I feel like we've been paying for ads that have not been served, or have not been viewed, for years."

Indeed, will the viewer be a human being or an automated "bot" simulating humans? "[T]here's been such a problem with fraud in this industry," says BJ. "[T]here's a history of [mediator platforms] knowingly looking the other way and letting it [fraud] persist on their platform because it creates lots of revenue." Again, there is an influential industry initiative, Ads.txt, in which publishers create electronic files listing the mediators permitted to sell advertising opportunities on their behalf. These files enable advertisers to reduce the risk of paying for a "bot" viewership or for ads on a low-quality, fraudulent website impersonating a reputable publisher.

Tensions can, however, still arise, even within platforms themselves, for example about how much of what interviewee CS calls "crappy traffic" to sell on: "you're going to get away with some of it, how much do you want to do, what is that threshold?" (An example of "crappy traffic" that is not actually fraudulent is advertising opportunities that have been bought and sold more than once, with the consequence that the user may well have left the page in question before the ad is shown.) Her platform had a "traffic-quality team," but what it did was not always welcome: "[o]n the business-development side, we called it the deal blockers" (CS). Another interviewee, DK, experienced the same tension at a different platform, but from the traffic-quality side: "if we say no, sorry, we've evaluated that site and they are fraudulent, they're going to be, like, come on, we'll take you out for drinks, let's go hang out. They'll do everything they can to on-board that publisher."

Another source of tension of the first kind (over what is bought and sold) is "brand safety" or "brand suitability." For a brand's ad to appear alongside salacious, hateful, pro-terrorist, or otherwise inappropriate content "can be massively damaging," says BB, especially if "someone, somewhere . . . take[s] a screengrab" and shares it on social media. "Worst-case scenario," notes AV, "you lose a client." Advertisers sometimes suspect, he says, that agencies find it "financially interesting to run [ads] on not-brand-safe spots because they're a lot cheaper and you [an agency] can earn way more money" by buying ads for considerably less than the advertiser is paying the agency to show them. "This is," AV adds, "one of the reasons why we see the in-house trends," in which advertisers themselves directly initiate their purchases of ads, so that they can "have actually an overview themselves on where . . . their ads . . . are being shown."

Tensions around viewability, fraud, and brand safety/suitability have fueled the growth, especially since around 2014, of companies that specialize in ad "verification." Their role is to monitor the process of the buying and display of ads so that, again to quote Latour, it "transports meaning or force without transformation" (2005: 39), and the advertiser or advertising agency can therefore gain a degree of confidence that it is buying ads of the kind it intends to buy. Typically, the verification company provides the advertiser or agency with a software "wrapper" to enfold the electronic files of each of their ads, or at least a sample of them. Code in the wrapper "check[s] the URL before they download the ad," blocking the ad if the verification provider's system "[doesn't] like the content of the page" (interviewee AO). The wrapper also determines whether the viewer seems to be a human being, and whether enough of an ad was in view for long enough for it to count as "viewable."

Transforming mediators into intermediaries is not easy: it is "a *rare* exception[,] that has to be accounted for by some extra work – usually by the mobilization of even more mediators!" (Latour 2005: 40; emphasis in original). The extra work of "verification" costs money: around 5–7 cents per 1,000 ad impressions, says AQ, but "if you multiply it with the billions of impressions, it's . . . a lot of money." And our news-publisher interviewees do indeed report experiencing verification as mediation, not intermediation, especially in respect to brand-safety/suitability concerns. That was, for example, particularly the case in the early months of the coronavirus pandemic, when brand-safety/suitability systems often stopped ads appearing alongside news coverage of the pandemic, even in the homepage bannerhead ad slots of outlets such as the *New York Times* or *Wall Street Journal*, reducing publishers' revenues considerably (MacKenzie 2022).

Almost certainly, advertisers and agencies did not intend to ad-block these prestigious homepages, but the blocklists they provided to verification companies seem to have contained pandemic-related keywords that triggered this blocking. Ad-blocking, and anger about it among some of our publisher interviewees, continued post pandemic. Even in 2024, the *Washington Post* reported that at times over 40% of the ad slots accompanying its new stories were being blocked, and *Newsweek*'s chief executive Dev Pragad said that "as much as half of our inventory is being marked as unsafe by a few of the largest brand safety companies" (Pragad 2024; Vargas 2024b).

One side effect of advertisers' and agencies' concerns about viewability and brand safety/suitability has been a particularly direct form of supply–demand co-creation: the rise of "made-for-advertising" sites. These carefully avoid controversial topics likely to trigger ad-blocking, and perform well on automated measures of viewability. As DH tells us, the sites attract users by buying cheap social media ads, which they fill with what CH calls "clickbait: 'you won't believe how much weight these five celebrities have gained.'" When a user clicks on one of these ads, they get taken to the made-for-advertising site, which will have little content but is stuffed with multiple ads (often including video ads that the user cannot skip). The site's goal is arbitrage: to earn more money by showing users these ads than it has paid for the ads that attract them. That is not fraud – the ads are viewable by human beings – but "ads that run on MFA [made-for-advertising] sites are very ineffective at driving sales for marketers" (DH), with "no returns for brands in terms of business results" (CH). Advertisers can, again almost certainly inadvertently, spend large amounts of money on ads on these sites: in June 2023, a study for the US Association of National Advertisers estimated this as around 15% of open-marketplace expenditure (ANA 2023).

A second type of tension in the open marketplace concerns not what is being bought and sold but the processes of buying and selling and whether they are characterized by intermediary-like transparency. MacKenzie encountered this tension in the first sector meeting he attended, in December 2019, at which participants more than once quoted a description of open-marketplace economic relations as "murky at best and fraudulent at worst," which turned out to be a quote from a speech by Marc Pritchard, Chief Brand Officer of Procter & Gamble, then the world's largest advertiser (Pritchard 2017).

In 2018, the Incorporated Society of British Advertisers commissioned auditors PwC to trace the spending of 15 big UK advertisers on ads on websites of members of the United Kingdom's Association of Online Publishers. The PwC team found that on average only 51% of what the advertisers spent reached the publishers. Two-thirds of the remaining 49% was absorbed by fees charged by agencies, platforms, and advertising technology firms. Most strikingly, however, the PwC team found that on average around 15% of advertisers' spending was untraceable (ISBA 2020).

Money seemed to be vanishing at exactly the point at which, in standard economic imaginaries, "supply" and "demand" should be being transparently brought together. "[M]oney was disappearing between DSP and SSP," says interviewee BM: as we have described, DSPs are demand-side platforms, which bid, on behalf of advertisers, for the supply of ad slots brought to market by SSPs, or supply-side platforms. Even experienced practitioners were taken aback: "that was genuinely new for everyone," says BM. That the heart of the open marketplace had been found to be economically opaque remained a frequent talking point in the industry meetings we attended in 2021.

Subsequent efforts to turn economically "murky" mediation into "transparent" intermediation have been led in the United Kingdom by an industry task force, again convened by the Incorporated Society of British Advertisers, which has developed a toolkit for financially auditing buyer–seller interactions in digital advertising. A second study conducted by

PwC found that 65% of advertisers' spending was now reaching publishers, and only 3% of spending could not be traced (PwC 2023). Again, though, the work needed to create intermediary-like transparency needs emphasizing. Tracing the money took nine months, even in a "curated" sector of the open marketplace that had consciously adopted tools to facilitate that tracing.[9]

What is, however, perhaps most striking about open-marketplace tensions of this second kind, concerning transparency of economic relations, is that some aspects of those relations are long established, predating digital advertising. Advertising's traditional mediator organizations, agencies, made much, often most, of their money not from fees charged to their clients (the advertisers that formed the *demand* for advertising) but from payments known as "rebates" from *suppliers* of advertising opportunities, such as TV channels and newspapers. There were even conventions about how much of what an agency's clients had spent should be rebated to the agency: in the United States and the United Kingdom, for example, the traditional rebate was 15% (see, e.g., Tunstall 1964: 29–30).

Crucially, agencies kept these rebates rather than returning the money to their advertiser clients. That was well known in the sector: "everybody was aware" of such arrangements, says interviewee CD, "but it was something like an unspoken thing" – perhaps the source of some embarrassment, but a de facto accepted mediators' practice. Even today, though, the open marketplace often involves complex fee and rebate arrangements that are hard to document and disentangle. Money seeming to "disappear" (as in the 2020 ISBA/PwC study) may not be "nefarious ... stealing money from advertisers," says DH, but what he calls "esoteric" fees, which compensate those involved for loss of revenue in intricacies of mediation opaque to outsiders, such as the frequent discrepancies between the publisher's and the advertiser's systems' counts of how many ads have actually been shown. "[W]e have the hidden fees because we've created this economic model that only works in some cases with these things layered in" (interviewee DI).

If, though, intermediaries are preferred to mediators, interviewee CD's "unspoken" rebate arrangements and DH's "esoteric" mediation-related fees can nevertheless lose legitimacy dramatically. As the main revenue source for advertising agencies became the explicit fees they charged their clients, the latter seem often to have assumed that agencies no longer received rebates from the suppliers of advertising opportunities. However, the Association of National Advertisers (the US equivalent of the Incorporated Society of British Advertisers) commissioned a study that reported in 2016 that rebates were still "pervasive," condemning them as "non-transparent business practices" (K2 Intelligence 2016: 1). Just as striking as this conclusion was who the Association engaged to conduct the study: the celebrated corporate fraud investigators Kroll and Kroll. Rebates, once accepted practice, have become seen by some as an illegitimate "kickback" (interviewee CE), even "systemic fraudulent behavior" (AC).

## Walled gardens

The term "walled garden," as applied to the digital world, was first popularized by the Web pioneer Tim Berners-Lee, who used it to criticize "silo[s]" such as social media sites that are "walled off" from each other and from the wider Web (2010: 82). We, however, do not intend the term to be a criticism: we employ it simply descriptively. A walled garden is a digital environment separated from the broader digital world by a deliberately constructed boundary, and in respect to advertising a walled garden differs from the open marketplace in two main ways.

First, instead of the garden's owner sending ad requests out to ad exchanges and supply-side platforms (as happens in the open marketplace, as described in chapter 4), advertisers or advertising agencies must come to the garden: they can bid to show ads only via the bidding apparatus that the garden provides. Second, walled gardens do not provide advertisers with identifiers of their users: there is no equivalent of the widespread circulation of cookies that was characteristic of the open marketplace, at least until the recent privacy initiatives discussed at the end of chapter 5. To gain entry to a walled garden, a user needs to register with it and provide an email address and often a phone number. So walled gardens normally possess identifiers of their users that are stronger and more permanent than cookies, but they do not circulate those identifiers. Walled gardens typically ingest data at large scale, but only carefully curated data flows out through the doors in their walls.

Those twin features are something of an ideal type since platform policies in those respects have varied through time, for example, in relation to whether it is possible to buy ads on YouTube via buying platforms other than Google's. Nevertheless, the classic examples of walled gardens are indeed big social media platforms, including Facebook, Instagram, TikTok, Twitter (now X), and Snap.[10] Google Search is an ambiguous case. It is not a classic walled garden, in that you can use it without logging in to Google, and the search results it provides include links that will take you outside Google's electronic domain into the wider Web. The advertising apparatus that accompanies Google Search, however, largely has the two characteristics mentioned above, so we include it too in our discussion of walled gardens.

There are tensions around walled gardens, but they are quite different from those in the open marketplace. It is, for example, not normally possible to "follow the money" through a walled garden's internal processes, as the auditors PwC did in the open marketplace, but its taken-for-granted impossibility means that it does not appear to be a source of tension. "You pay the platform for a combination of service, technology, media placement, but you don't know how it breaks down" (interviewee CH). Some of the other open-marketplace anxieties outlined in the previous section have become evident sporadically in the case of walled gardens, but are usually assuaged by the greater degree of control that gardens can exercise. "[I]n the open Web you run into a lot more fraudulent robot traffic" than in a walled garden, says AK. "Google does a pretty good job of suppressing bot charges" (AE). "Facebook, for all its faults . . . because of the way the ad [is] served [in the user's] News Feed [is] very definitive" in regards to viewability (CO).

Walled gardens' automation of the advertising process and straightforward, self-service interfaces mean that they can accommodate not just large advertisers but huge numbers of small advertisers. (In chapter 3, we quoted interviewee DH's estimate that "on the order of 10 million advertisers . . . are actively running ads with Meta and Google.") Walled gardens, especially Google's and Meta's, have also been seen as generally excelling at "attribution," in other words measuring whether ads are "working" cost-effectively. This service, which is fully automated, is typically provided free of charge, and the resultant easily digested, quantitative evidence of cost-effectiveness can greatly help practitioners in the crucial, anxiety-provoking task of convincing clients and managers of the effectiveness of their advertising. Google and Meta have indeed often been treated as, in the words of one practitioner quoted in Hercher (2022), "sources of truth": in our terms as intermediaries, in this respect.

But for a system to be an intermediary, not simply a mediator, is, as we have emphasized, not straightforward, and perceived "truth" needs to be materially produced, often elaborately. The crucial issue is that measuring success in advertising on Google, Meta, or another walled garden typically involves recording events *outside* of the platform, such as purchases or app installs. On the Web, that involves the platform getting its "pixels" (snippets of code) installed in very large numbers of webpages, especially those via which purchases are made or other "conversions," such as signups, take place.[11] To measure purchases, and so on, "we install the Facebook pixel" on the "landing page" to which the ad leads the user, interviewee AK told us. The pixel then "shoots ... back to Facebook" the information that the user "converted," in other words took the action the advertiser desired, and the platform's system can then connect up the conversion and the ad or ads that the user was shown. In apps, an embedded Meta or Google SDK ("software development kit") traditionally performed a role equivalent to that of a pixel on the Web, although that has become more problematic after Apple's privacy changes discussed in chapter 5. Advertising technology firms in the open marketplace also attempt similar measurement, but they lack the sheer scale of deployment of Meta's and Google's pixels and SDKs.

The walled gardens "first ask you," reports advertiser AH, "hey, put this pixel on your site. Send me all the data." The latter sentence, signalling the copious data that flows from advertisers' sites to the walled gardens, *does* indicate a tension. It is easy "literally [to give] every piece of information to Google," says AH, rather than trying to "take control of your business and your destiny and how you operate." His firm, however, is one of the world's leading advertisers, which makes "tak[ing] control" seem conceivable. And even he would acknowledge that there is a trade-off here: installing Meta's and Google's pixels and SDKs in an advertiser's websites or apps generates data on purchases and other conversion events that is well regarded and highly prized. One participant in an industry meeting we attended even talked of "the raw truth that a pixel provides."

That role as an intermediary is, however, the exception. In other respects, walled gardens are predominantly mediators and are generally seen – and accepted – as such. Take, for example, the automated auctions via which opportunities for Google Search, Facebook, and Instagram advertising are sold. These auctions are not the arm's-length bringing together of supply and demand. Typically, algorithms written and operated by the garden (i.e., by the *supplier* of advertising opportunities) decide, hundreds of millions or billions of times daily, whether an advertiser should bid to show an ad to a particular user in a particular digital context and, if so, how much – an arrangement, as already noted, entirely at odds with standard "separate bloc" conceptualizations of supply and demand. For example, Google Search advertising campaigns, as described by multiple interviewees, typically begin with the advertiser giving Google's system the URL that will be the "destination" of the campaign: the site to which users who click on the campaign's ads will be taken. Google's system then generates a list of suggested keywords on which to bid, and the recommended level of bid that would likely be successful often enough to meet the advertiser's goals.

Advertisers or advertising agencies *can* then amend the list of keywords and suggested bids, but our interviews suggest that extensive delegation to Google's system is common. For example, interviewee AI, whose agency specializes in search ads, had long believed that its experienced staff could make more cost-effective bids than Google's system. Now, however, "[t]hey [Google] have finally reached a point where they are better than the [human] bid managers," says AI. "It's all being done by machines now," he reports: "you say [i.e. enter into Google's system] 'I am prepared to pay this amount for a sale.'" Google's algorithms then determine which opportunities the advertiser bids for and how much.

Advertisers retain the capacity to shape Google Search bids in specific ways, for example, temporarily to increase them to make it too expensive for a competitor to win auctions, but use of that capacity seems increasingly to be the exception. Similarly with Meta's platforms, Facebook and Instagram, on which the advertiser or advertising agency enters the goal, for example for sales, app installs, or brand awareness, that it is trying to achieve and the budget it is giving Meta. Meta's systems, using machine learning, then "identify how you are going to best achieve [that] end goal" (interviewee AF). "[Y]ou can't influence Facebook's algo," he says. "You're not in control of that."

The decisions as to which item will next get inserted into a Meta user's feed is taken in real time by automated auctions.[12] Those auctions shape supply and demand, rather than simply bringing them together. Not only is whether an advertiser (i.e., a source of "demand") bids, and if so how much, decided by Meta's (i.e., the "supplier's") algorithms, but the user's friends' posts also bid, as do system messages that originate ultimately from, for example, Facebook's internally powerful Growth Team (messages such as "people you may know"), in both cases with quasi-monetary values assigned by Meta's systems.

Meta's auctions thus determine whether the next item in a user's feed will be an ad, a friend's post, or a system message, and the bids take into account, among other things, that seeing too many ads and too few friends' posts or other "organic" content is likely to alienate users. *There is therefore no predetermined "supply" of Facebook/Instagram advertising opportunities.* In the terminology we introduced in chapter 1, Meta's auctions *stack* processes of "economization," balancing – in real time – the marketization of users' attention by selling advertising opportunities and the need to keep the platform's gifted/bartered "free" service attractive.

Meta's auctions employ the "Vickrey–Clarke–Groves" mechanism from the theoretical economics of auction design. That mechanism, however, remains in practice opaque to practitioners as well as to the social science literature on Facebook.[13] Advertisers on Meta's platforms are in practice separated from Meta's auctions by an algorithmic wall. Advertisers *can* set a maximum bid, but Meta generally advises against that, and the UK Competition and Markets Authority reports that "[o]ver 90% of UK advertisers on Facebook use the default automated bidding feature, which does not allow advertisers to specify a maximum bid" (CMA 2020: 17). Interviewee AF, working for a leading global advertiser, expressed some dissatisfaction with lack of direct control over its Facebook bids: "Even the biggest advertisers are hamstrung by the fact that your bidding algo is pretty much dictated as opposed to invented." More common, however, seems to be AP's acceptance: "Essentially, you can't do anything, you don't have control over your bids at all. That's just a thing."

## "Machines need room to work": de-agencing and de-individualization

In this section, we turn to how walled gardens' role as mediators is currently changing the relationship of advertising practitioners to walled gardens' systems, and the connection between that issue and moves to de-individualize advertising's audiences. Let us begin with the question of practitioners' agency. When we began this research in 2019–21, even interviewees such as AP, who de facto accept lack of control over the size of their bids, seemed to regard the *targeting* of ads as something that human practitioners should control. There were, however, already difficulties in that. As noted, normal practice is for the practitioner to input into the walled garden's system parameters such as their goal (e.g., "conversions" such as purchases) and total budget, and the platform's bidding algorithm then seeks to spend that budget as cost-effectively as possible. This can have the effect that ads are preferentially delivered to those to whom it is cheaper to deliver them, rather than their audience being as the practitioner intended. For example, Lambrecht and Tucker (2018) found that a gender-neutral Facebook ad for scientific careers was differentially shown to men, who are typically lower-cost advertising targets than women.

It is common to assume that advertising on platforms such as Facebook is "microtargeted" by human practitioners (including political advertisers) to very specific audiences. That practice, however, is coming under increasing pressure. Meta, for example, explicitly warns against it, arguing that its machine-learning systems outperform human practitioners. "To reach your goals," it says to practitioners, "machines need room to work":

"[Practitioners] accustomed to running campaigns may be wary of trusting machines with their work. But automated systems enhanced by machine learning work best when parameters are broad. Teams working within these systems are advised to embrace a certain agnosticism toward placement, platforms and yes, even audience."[14]

Meta's argument/injunction – that human practitioners should not attempt to control in detail the targeting of advertising but should delegate it to walled gardens' machine-learning systems – is shared by Google and other major platforms. Google, for example, also often advises practitioners to "take your hands off the wheel" (interviewee AC). Practitioners' attitudes to that advice vary. For DE, for example, human-guided targeting "was a very early way of doing things," which should be abandoned. Walled gardens, such as Meta's, have rich information on users' behavior, and these "actual behavioral histories," as he calls them, make possible much more effective advertising than advertisers' possibly quite mistaken intuitions about particular sociodemographic groups.

Other interviewees have misgivings. AL is uneasy about a relationship with walled gardens in which "we get surprises all the time" about what the platform does: "I don't think we go deep enough to understand if the difference is coming from the [platform's] system or it's coming from the audience [that the platform is targeting]" (AL). AM acknowledges the difficulty of keeping human control over targeting: "the more niche you want to get, the harder it is." But, she says, "I don't trust [the platform] because Facebook is kind of like [an opaque] box." So instead of running a single integrated campaign with "one big audience group," and leaving targeting to the platform's machine-learning systems, she will sometimes try to keep control by splitting a campaign into separate campaigns, for example for specific genders, age groups, or user devices (e.g., Apple versus Android phones). That reduces the walled garden's ad-delivery optimization, but gives her, she believes, "a better understanding of what really works . . . it's better if you have a little bit more control" (AM).

AP reported to us in 2021 a case in which individual resistance of this kind to perceived de-agencing of the human practitioner became more widespread. (As we discussed in chapter 1, by "de-agencing" we mean the stripping from practitioners of previously important capacities for action and control.) AP's example was Facebook's Campaign Budget Optimization (CBO), introduced in November 2017. As AP puts it, "[y]ou turn [CBO] on and Facebook spends the budget for you on [the] ad sets[15] or the audiences that it deems . . . best within that campaign." In 2019, says AP, Facebook proposed making its use mandatory, but "[t]here was so much backlash over it that they decided not to make it compulsory."

Since 2021, however, the issue of the human practitioner's agency has become interwoven with the second issue discussed in this section: moves to de-individualize advertising's audiences. As we described in chapter 5, the two crucial such moves so far have been browser designers' moves to restrict the deposit in users' browsers of the "third-party" cookies used to track users across websites, and Apple's decision that from April 2021's iOS14.5 onward, every app in its App Store needs a user's explicit permission to track them beyond the app's electronic boundaries, for example via their phone's IDFA.

Those twin restrictions make it more difficult to assemble the crucial "behavioral histories" referred to by interviewee DE and harder to measure and optimize the efficacy of advertising in real time. All the major social media platforms, such as Facebook, Instagram, TikTok, and Snapchat, face the difficulties we discussed in chapter 5 because in practice they all almost always take the form of mobile-phone apps. The measurement apparatus is still there – Meta's pixels and SDKs, for example, are still present on the Web and in apps – but the privacy changes have rendered partially inaccessible the "raw truth" that the apparatus used to generate. Specifically, it is now much harder, indeed sometimes impossible, directly to connect the ads you may have been shown to the purchases that you may have made or the apps you may have chosen to install on your phone.

The loss of intermediary-like, SDK- or pixel-generated, deterministic "raw truth" about an individual's actions has led to further reinforcement of walled gardens' mediator roles because walled gardens have had to intensify their use of humanly opaque machine-learning systems to draw aggregate, "probabilistic" rather than individual/"deterministic," connections between the showing of ads and users' subsequent actions. Social media platforms now encourage advertisers to have their own servers (not the user's browser or a system controlled by Apple) send data on purchases and so on to the platform's systems, which seek to correlate this data with the ads the platform has shown users, using machine learning. In the words of interviewee AP, this "basically models people's behaviors and uses that . . . to track conversions [e.g., purchases] rather than tracking conversions directly . . . via the pixel."

This partially "de-individualized" modeling of the behavior of aggregates of users has both direct and indirect links to the de-agencing of advertising's human practitioners. The direct link is that because the modeling is inherently probabilistic, it must pass tests of statistical significance to achieve confidence that its results are not spurious. That requires larger samples than typically needed when deterministic data on individuals' actions is available (Hercher 2021), which is most likely one reason why walled gardens now strongly advise practitioners against, or even prevent (see below), human-guided microtargeting.

The indirect link to de-agencing is that the loss of individual-level data has given further impetus to walled gardens' construction of ambitious machine-learning systems that increasingly automate all aspects of the advertising process, not just bidding and targeting. The two paradigmatic such systems are Google's Performance Max, launched at full scale in November 2021, and Meta's March 2022 Advantage+ (Seufert 2024b). In them, as well as the walled garden's system bidding on behalf of the advertiser and, to an increasing extent, selecting the audience for the advertiser's ads, it also chooses the platform on which the ads are shown, for example in the case of Performance Max choosing among, for instance, Google Search, YouTube, Google Maps, and the Google Display Network, via which display ads are placed on non-Google websites and apps. Both Performance Max and Advantage+ are capable of automatically reformatting the advertiser's ads for the demands of these different channels, and they are increasingly employing generative AI capabilities to turn text and images provided by the advertiser into ads.

A probable reason for walled gardens' managers and engineers seeking to dissuade or even prevent human practitioners from trying to exercise detailed control over their advertising campaigns is the desire to compensate for their systems' loss of individual-level behavior data. Fast, extensive, and fully automated experimentation with showing different ads to different audiences via different channels – even if it yields only aggregate data – can be a very useful real-time input into the machine-learning optimization of advertising. Human "interference" could easily slow down this machine learning, even undermine it. App economy analyst Eric Seufert views experimentation-based machine learning, very plausibly, as a key factor in Meta's recovery from the disruption caused by Apple's 2021 App Tracking Transparency measures: "Meta's Advantage+ product automates most aspects of campaign optimization, allowing for more rapid and exhaustive experimentation and faster implementation of campaign improvements" (Seufert 2024a).

Thoroughgoing use of machine learning to automate large swathes of advertising work is a source of ambivalence among practitioners. The greatest degree of enthusiasm was manifested by advertising technology specialist AC: "I've seen companies where they had sixty people in their marketing function. I would replace all of them with one algorithm." Other practitioners employ walled-garden affordances of the kind just described for pragmatic reasons but without wanting to see them displace humans. Using these affordances "sav[es] time" (interviewee AI), and therefore money, so making an agency's services more attractive to clients, and it minimizes tediously repetitive work, such as creating multiple versions of an ad, with for instance differently placed and differently colored components, and testing which is most effective. But saving time, money, and work intrinsically involves passing responsibility for decisions – for example, about which ad to show to whom – to the walled garden's system. Practitioners accept that, at the very least, they must "give time for the machine to purr" (AH) before trying to intervene: CC's "at least one good week" seems to be a typical non-intervention period. Similarly, there seems to be acceptance that asking Facebook's advertising system to optimize for "conversions" such as purchases requires the practitioner not to intervene until at least fifty conversions have occurred.

"[W]e're going to do what works," says CJ, "which by the way, generally speaking, [Google's automated affordances] work ... great." Eventually, though, the human practitioner *should* intervene, he says, and "do more of what works and less of what doesn't work." An online practitioner panel on walled gardens' automated affordances that we attended exemplified such ambivalences. There was much talk of the "exciting stuff that you can now do," but occasional bleaker formulations: as one speaker put it, these affordances can feel like "the last bricks of the wall around us," and learning how best to use them might simply be learning "how you can feed the monster [the walled garden's system] best." DG, interviewed in February 2024, "doesn't trust it [machine learning] yet ... I don't like the lack of control, but it's done well for some [advertising campaigns] ... maybe I don't have a job in two years." That last phrase was a joke, but, like many jokes, it seemed to touch on an issue that she took seriously.

We expect our interpretation – that in some respects advertising's human practitioners are being *de-agenced* – to be controversial. It would, for instance, be rejected by platforms themselves. At the center, quite literally, of a sector meeting we attended in 2023 was a large, elaborate, amply staffed Google installation, which was an extended material riff on the notion of the advertising practitioner as racing driver. At the installation's core was an actual McLaren Formula One racing car (see Figure 6.1). A giant nearby billboard urged attendees, "Go from spectator to driver with Google AI." The more powerful tools that Google was placing in the hands of the human practitioner were intermediaries, not mediators; it was agencing the practitioner, not de-agencing her.

Yet spending considerable amounts of money and effort to evoke "agencing" may itself signal a tension: the fear that the opposite interpretation may be taking hold among advertising practitioners, and needs to be combatted. Our academic colleagues in market studies and related fields might also, we have found, prefer a more hedged interpretation, such as "distributing agency differently." In our view, though, it would be a mistake for sociological research on markets to conceptualize only how "devices . . . contribute to and augment the agency of humans as a result of processes of agencing" (Fuentes and Sörum 2019: 135). The opposite effect is perfectly possible and needs identifying explicitly. That is what the notion of "de-agencing" does.

Highly automated advertising systems such as Google's Performance Max and Meta's Advantage+ are – so far at least – offered to practitioners as optional, not compulsory. Here, though, is where Beuscart and Mellet's (2013) distinction between direct-response advertising (which, as noted, seeks to prompt an immediate action, such as purchase of a product or installation of a game) and longer-term brand building is significant. As Beauvisage and colleagues argue, advertising agency staff who work on brand building need targeting to be humanly "intelligible" to clients and see it as a valuable skill firmly "under their professional jurisdiction." "[A]utomated targeting," therefore, "is still frowned upon" (Beauvisage at al. 2023: 14).

**Figure 6.1 An icon of agencing**

McLaren Formula One racing car inside the Google booth at an advertising sector conference, 2023.

Authors' fieldwork photograph.

In direct response, though, the goal is not the enhancement of a brand but immediately measurable outcomes, achieved at minimum cost. In a small digital agency, each individual advertising practitioner may have dozens of client accounts to service and thus dozens of advertising campaigns to run. Or if a games studio's user-acquisition specialist's "boss is yelling at them, I need more installs, get me more installs at this price . . . they'll do anything to get those installs at that price" (interviewee CR), and if automated rather than human-guided targeting helps, there is a considerable incentive to adopt it. Furthermore, brand building can easily morph into direct response, at least in the case of small and mid-sized advertisers without large amounts of money to spend. Walled gardens' automatically produced metrics of the immediate or near-term monetary return on advertising spending can quickly become very prominent to advertisers with limited budgets. If what it is for advertising to "work" is measured in this way, use of machine-learning systems designed to optimize for it, such as Performance Max and Advantage+, can cease to be genuinely optional.

And once an "option" is embraced, constraints that are no longer optional follow. If, for example, an advertising practitioner at a games studio or firm seeking to acquire users for its apps adopts the powerful affordances of Meta's "Advantage+ app campaigns," s/he retains almost no capacity for traditional human-guided targeting. So that "the system has more flexibility," Meta tells her, "[y]ou can't add additional targeting options including demographics, interests and behaviours. . . . You can't target your audience based on gender. . . . You can't target your audience based on their relationship status." Even "age" is available to her only in the form of a minimum age threshold to meet legal requirements.[16]

It might seem as if our analysis is drifting toward the monolithic, Zuboffian view of platform power that we have disavowed, albeit with the advertising practitioner, rather than the everyday user of the platform, as its subject, so it is important to emphasize the continuing possibility, and sometimes actuality, of contestation. Human beings are resourceful and can often find ways of circumventing constraints. Controversy can erupt unexpectedly. It did so, for example, in November 2023, when the specialist analysis firm Adalytics publicly attacked automatic ad placement by Google's systems, in particular the placing of search ads not within Google Search itself but on "Google Search Partner" sites that included, Adalytics alleged, pornographic and extreme right-wing sites, and sites subject to US government sanctions.[17] Google responded that only a tiny proportion of sites were problematic, but it has given advertisers, at first temporarily and then from March 2024 more permanently, the capacity to opt out of automatic placement of their ads on specific Search Partner sites.

Advertisers, furthermore, still have an alternative to walled gardens: the open marketplace. Advertising there can be cheaper and therefore more cost-effective, at least for a large, brand-oriented advertiser sophisticated enough to navigate its tensions: "if you're at the scale of Procter & Gamble, you can staff a full-time team to be good at this" (DH). The triumph of walled gardens over the open marketplace is not inevitable, and the continued health of the latter can have wider benefits: for example, as we noted in chapter 4, news journalism is often dependent on open-marketplace ad revenue. And as chapter 5 showed, the impressive optimizing power of walled-garden advertising systems rests on material foundations that were shaken by Apple's 2021 App Tracking Transparency measures, and may be shaken again in the future. There are, and will continue to be, implicit tensions even at the heart of platform capitalism, and power is indeed still contestable, not monolithic.

# 7

# Conclusion

Our overall argument in this book is threefold. First, digital advertising's main systems should be thought of as "megamachines": computational processes that inhabit huge arrays of physical machines. This highlights their scale, their environmental impact, and the fact that – like any machine – they can be designed differently. Second, digital advertising is in consequence a domain of what we call "material political economy." There are sharp conflicts over how the crucial megamachines should be configured, conflicts that are economically consequential. In digital advertising, "politics," in a very broad political-economy sense of the term, is often pursued by material means – by making some things materially hard/impossible to do, and other things easy to do.

Our third argument has so far been largely implicit and will be fleshed out in this chapter. It is that platform power structures the field of digital advertising, and it has multiple, mutually reinforcing components. Those include the "money power" of the big platforms, and, currently, the latter's direct access (in the United States at least) to government. Other components of platform power, however, are more directly material. These include what we call platforms' "systematicity" (the degree of integration of their component parts, including the "stacking" of different economization processes), the capacity to scale up massively and to generate credible knowledge, and the "infrastructural power" that accrues to systems that enable others to do things they need to do. We do not, however, want to exaggerate platform power because we also emphasize that resistance to it is possible. Platform power *can* successfully be contested. That is the lesson we draw from the case of header bidding (chapter 4), and even that of the tracking of mobile-phone users (chapter 5), although the latter case is different in that the challenge to the status quo came from a corporation, Apple, amply endowed with its own platform power.

The next section of this chapter recaps what we've discussed in the book so far. We then briefly discuss two forms of advertising that we haven't examined in the previous chapters: advertising on connected TV/video-streaming services, and "retail media" such as Amazon. Next, we turn to aspects of digital advertising that many practitioners would like to see changed, touching on what they themselves can do to alter them, and what they can't realistically change – sometimes because of platform power. We then focus directly on the latter, examining the main components of it that emerge from our research, and the potential role of regulation and regulators in constraining it. We end by briefly discussing three issues – harmful online content and conduct, privacy/surveillance, advertising's environmental impact – that point to the need to redesign digital megamachines.

## What we've covered in the previous chapters

In chapter 2, we examined the origins in the 1990s of digital advertising and its best-known tool: the cookie, especially third-party "tracking" cookies, which are deposited in users' browsers by a system other than the website the user is visiting, and which have for many years been the source of controversy concerning user privacy. Chapter 2 also shows how the originally ad hoc digital advertising market, often reliant on face-to-face negotiation between human beings, began to move into machines in the form of automated ad exchanges, providing the foundation of today's "open marketplace" in Web-display ads.

Chapter 3 began with the building of the archetypal digital megamachine, Google Search, before turning to the ads infrastructure that made it digital advertising's preeminent money machine, and then to Google's systematicity: the relatively seamless integration, in what practitioners call Google's "AdTech [advertising technology] stack," of what in the open marketplace are often separate aspects of the advertising process. We also examined the sometimes happenstance process by which Facebook/Meta, which also deploys a giant-scale, tightly integrated system, became digital advertising's other most prominent presence.

As we've already said, systematicity is an important source of platform power, but even powerful platforms can successfully be challenged. The decentralized "header bidding" discussed in chapter 4 succeeded in partially circumventing Google's integrated system, "hacking" one of its central components, Google's "ad server." Header bidding – at least in its original, still canonical form – materially changed *where* the crucial process of gathering bids for the user's attention takes place, shifting it from Google's servers to the user's own device.

The challenge to the material status quo discussed in chapter 5 concerns an apparently tiny part of the megamachine enfolding your iPhone (if that's the kind of phone you have): your iPhone's 32-digit IDFA. IDFAs had become pivotal to the optimization of advertising on iPhones, and therefore central to the operations of big digital platforms, such as Facebook and Instagram, that in everyday life take the material form of mobile-phone apps. The change that Apple made, in 2021, tightly restricted apps' access to IDFAs, and so doing substantially de-individualized advertising's audiences. Those apps' developers were often deeply unhappy, with Facebook protesting particularly vigorously, but had no option but to comply. It was a vivid demonstration of the efficacy of infrastructural power: Apple's control of iPhones' operating systems and of the App Store (in most cases, the only way via which an app can find its way into a user's phone) gives Apple power over apps, even those deployed by other giant corporations.

In chapter 6, we turned to the experiences of advertising's human practitioners when navigating the complex, contested terrain sketched in the previous chapters. We touched upon aspects of digital advertising that are tacitly taken for granted, such as "demand" (i.e., advertisers or agencies acting on their behalf) surrendering to "supply" (the big platforms' algorithms) the decisions about which advertising opportunities to bid for, and how much to bid. We focused more strongly, however, on tensions within digital advertising. Some tensions are explicit, public matters of concern, such as ad fraud and ads that are not viewable. Others take the form of more private ambivalences, for example concerning two linked developments. The first is the de-agencing of advertising's human practitioners: the partial stripping from them, by big platforms' machine-learning optimization of advertising, of previously valued capacities, such as to guide and control in detail the targeting of their ads. The second, discussed also in chapter 5, is the partial de-individualizing of advertising's audiences.

## Other areas of digital advertising

We haven't tried to give a comprehensive account of digital advertising, which would have needed a dauntingly long book. Social media influencers, for example, are an important marketing channel, but the "influencer economy" raises different issues – such as the precarity and vulnerability of influencers (see, e.g., Duffy, Ononye, and Sawey 2024) – from those salient in the types of advertising on which we have focused. It is, however, worth briefly discussing two important forms of digital advertising that are closer to those we have examined.

The first is advertising within connected TV/video-streaming services such as Netflix or Amazon Prime Video. There's a sharp, implicit clash in connected TV advertising, we have found, between the apparatuses of digital advertising of the kind discussed in the previous chapters and the quite different apparatuses that developed to buy, sell, and keep track of the advertising that accompanies traditional, prescheduled, "linear" television. In the terminology of the theorist discussed in chapter 1, Michel Callon, two *agencements* clash within connected-TV advertising. (The notion of an *agencement* is a rich one; briefly, it is a specific combination of human beings and non-human entities that is endowed with the capacity to act.)[1]

The traditional world of the buying and selling of linear TV ads – stereotypically associated with Bloody Marys, "smoky swagger," and relationship-reinforcing rounds of golf on elite courses such as Shinnecock Hills in the Hamptons (Crupi 2011) – seems largely to have vanished. What, however, remains influential, and at the core of the older of the two clashing *agencements*, are buying, selling, and measurement conventions inherited from linear TV, conventions which were the subject of a sophisticated academic literature.[2] The underlying measurement problem was the absence of any direct mechanism that could be deployed at scale to detect the presence of viewers of traditional broadcast television. Instead, measurement relied upon selecting panels of viewers designed to be nationally representative, incentivizing panel members with regular modest payments, and equipping them or their homes with measurement equipment, sometimes quite intrusive, such as infrared scanners installed in their living rooms (Hessler 2021). As Hessler documents, and interviewee CX described to us, the current main form of this measurement relies on small "people meters," triggered by humanly inaudible audio signals encoded into TV programs, that panel members are meant to wear or carry with them at all times.

That traditional form of audience measurement, in which the dominant firm is Nielsen Holdings, remains important. US television's traditional, glamorous "upfronts" are also still prominent. Face-to-face gatherings, they are held in New York in May each year, still bringing together TV executives, big advertisers, and advertising agencies, even if the deals they discuss are now more diverse than those that gave the "upfronts" their name: advertisers' "tentative, but fairly reliable commitments" to buy ads in shows scheduled for broadcast in the coming Fall (Lotz 2007: 549). All of this may yet entirely succumb to the already clear encroachment of the competing *agencement*: digital advertising's very different apparatuses for buying, selling, and measuring advertising. What seems, however, at least equally likely is the emergence of hybrid forms, incorporating material and organizational elements from both the competing worlds.[3]

The second sector of digital advertising that needs highlighting is what is called "retail media." Here we find "walled gardens" in the terminology of chapter 6, operated not by social media corporations but by companies of other kinds that offer advertisers the chance to advertise directly to their customers. Uber, for example, does this, but the most important examples are the big retailers, such as Walmart, Tesco, and, above all, Amazon. Because the products that are advertised can readily be bought on the platform in question, it can offer a particularly tight form of the crucial feedback loop between the showing of an ad and a subsequent purchase. Retail media platforms have plentiful rich data on their customers' previous purchases that can be used to optimize advertising, and, crucially, it is "first party" data, gathered and owned by the platform, and therefore not subject to the increasing privacy restrictions discussed in chapter 5.

The combination of a tight feedback loop and extensive first-party data makes these retail media platforms, especially Amazon, a potent threat in the medium term to digital advertising's leviathans, Google and Meta. If you have a commercially relevant search query, it is now quite common to begin by entering it into Amazon's system rather than Google's, and, while Meta is working hard to build its own e-commerce sales capacity (so avoiding the difficulties of closing the loop that we discussed in chapter 5), rivaling Amazon in this respect is plainly very difficult.

A basic material-politics issue – what is easy to find or do on-screen, and what is more awkward – is particularly crucial in retail media. (It is important, perhaps especially for public-service broadcasters, in the case of TV/streaming too, in which a television's operating system gives the system's owner control over how easily channels and programs can be found, a potentially vital form of the "infrastructural power" discussed below.)[4] Which products can you immediately see and, with a single click, buy or add to your shopping cart; and which require further navigating and more clicks? In e-commerce, too, prices are often set algorithmically, and that can involve large-scale Web crawling to discover and respond to competitors' prices. Such matters can be consequential, raising, for example, competition-law issues, as is revealed by the fiercely contested lawsuit launched by the Federal Trade Commission in 2023 against Amazon (Federal Trade Commission 2023; Zapolsky 2023).

## Reforming advertising, and what practitioners can and can't do

Our research hasn't been normative: we didn't set out to discover whether digital advertising needs to change, and if so how. We simply don't, for example, have evidence on whether advertising encourages excessive consumption, except to say that its doing so would, ironically, be evidence of advertising "working," even if undesirably, and we have emphasized the difficulty of determining whether advertising does work. Nor are we hostile to advertising. One of us, Caliskan, founded MaMame, a social enterprise in Turkey selling meals cooked by women at home, and he understands only too well start-ups' need to attract customers and the usefulness of digital advertising for this.

Advertising practitioners themselves, however, raised normatively relevant issues with us. Again, we cannot deal with all of these, but let us give three examples (we will turn to more, privacy/surveillance and advertising's carbon emissions, at the end of the chapter). The first is quite specific. The most disturbing thing we were told in our fieldwork was by an interviewee who had worked for an agency that had, as a client, a UK subprime lender. Devising advertising to find new customers for the lender, he discovered that there are websites:

> that seem quite nice, they allow you to check your credit score or to see what credit cards you could get. . . . They would sell segments, audiences of people who are in deep financial trouble . . . you can . . . go and target them, sell them more crap [loans with very high interest rates], put them deeper into trouble. (interviewee CH)

It was a career-transforming moment for this interviewee: "all of a sudden I wasn't sitting behind a computer screen playing a game anymore." What he reports is of course an issue of the ethics and legality of data collection, targeting, and lending, but it also raises an intriguing, important hypothesis: that there are forms of advertising that "work" disproportionately when users are psychologically vulnerable, disadvantaged socioeconomically, suffer discrimination, and so on. Our research was not designed to test that hypothesis, but there are intriguing clues in the literature and our fieldwork that it is worth taking seriously.[5]

A second normatively relevant issue is the prevalence of economic waste in digital advertising. The "made-for-advertising" sites discussed in chapter 6, whose minimal, low-quality content is overwhelmed by multiple ads, are a prime example of where wasteful spending happens. Advertisers are unlikely to benefit economically from placing ads on such sites, but that placement is cheap, and can generate attractive metrics, such as a high rate of video ads apparently being viewed to completion. Even advertising on "brand-name websites ... you feel good about" can involve waste of this kind, reports ad consultant DH. There's "an ad product that lives in the comment section of lots of websites," inserting video ads that "autop ... when ... out of view." He told the staff of one advertising agency that this product was "gobbling up a lot of budget" for a specific campaign's video ads. Their response, he reports, was "Who are we to judge the quality of media? Our job is to achieve the metric that this marketer wants." There are, says DH, "so many steps in the telephone tag to the actual hands-on-keyboard buyer [of advertising opportunities] who is tasked with hitting [a] KPI [key performance indicator] that they wind up buying obviously wasteful inventory. Versions of that story, I think, play out for a lot of brands."

Wasteful spending of this kind is closely related to a third issue: the placement of ads alongside salacious, hateful, violent, or illegal content, and the inadvertent funding of hate speech and misinformation, or even of sites alleged to facilitate the circulation of images of child sexual abuse. The analysis firm Adalytics, for example, has found ads for mainstream advertisers accompanying alarming webpages, articles, and blogs, the titles of which include "No Cock Like Horse Cock," "Big Black N***a Dicks, "Super Mario 3 Masturbation," and "Lynch All Black People," that last item appearing alongside US Navy recruitment ads (Adalytics 2024). It also found, accompanying those ads, what appear to be the electronic traces of "verification" systems of the kind discussed in chapter 6, although those systems may not have been being employed by the advertisers in question to block ads appearing alongside content damaging to them.

The alternative to advertisers relying upon an automated system to try to avoid outcomes that are damaging to their brands, or harmful in wider ways, would be for them to exercise conscious control over where their ads appear. That inherently involves being more selective: advertising on a smaller number of sites. Trying to maintain an "exclusion list" of sites not to advertise on is "playing Whac-A-Mole," says Bill Duggan of the US Association of National Advertisers, because such sites reinvent themselves endlessly. Instead, he argues, advertisers should construct an *inclusion* list of sites on which they actively want to advertise, constantly update that list, and provide it to the advertising agencies and demand-side platforms buying ads on their behalf (Vargas 2024a).

Unfortunately, for an advertiser to exercise conscious control over where their ads appear has in some respects become less straightforward than it might seem, as evidenced by the fate of the Global Alliance for Responsible Media (GARM), set up in 2019 by the World Federation of Advertisers. It was attacked fiercely in July 2024 in an interim report by the staff of the House of Representatives Judiciary Committee, entitled "GARM's Harm: How the World's Biggest Brands Seek to Control Online Speech." GARM, the Judiciary Committee report alleged, "told its members to boycott advertising on Twitter after Mr [Elon] Musk's purchase of the platform" (Judiciary Committee 2024: 12). The following month, Twitter (now called X) sued GARM and its member corporations – including, for example, Unilever and Mars – accusing them of breaking competition law. In response, the World Federation of Advertisers decided to close down GARM, saying that "recent allegations ... have ... significantly drained its resources and finances" (World Federation of Advertisers 2024). Republican successes in the 2024 elections almost certainly mean even stronger political constraints on US advertisers' capacity to control where their ads appear.

A more mundane constraint on advertisers arises from the divide that we have emphasized repeatedly between advertising, designed to build the reputation of a brand, and direct-response advertising, which seeks a near-immediate "conversion," such as a purchase or an app install. There are multiple channels that brand advertisers can choose among, making exercising control by stopping advertising on one of them conceivable. In contrast, direct-response advertisers need to use a sophisticated apparatus of the kind Google and Meta have developed, leaving those advertisers with much less choice of platform, and they are often quite small firms, which can make it daunting to leave the big platforms for the less easily navigable open marketplace. Twitter, now X, is an interesting case in this respect in that brand advertising on its platform seems to have outweighed direct response (Seufert 2022), which until recently seemed to leave it potentially vulnerable to brands turning their back on it. Currently, however, brands that had appeared to have done so seem to be returning to X: Musk's central position in the Trump Administration may be playing a part in their decisions to do that.

What practitioners can and can't do, will and won't do, to reform advertising is, in summary, at least in part an issue of power. A large brand advertiser potentially has considerable influence in the open marketplace, if it chooses to use it, but much less power vis-à-vis the big platforms because even the largest single advertiser's budget is dwarfed by the aggregate spending of often small but very numerous direct-response advertisers. In chapter 3, we touched on the resultant failure of 2020's big-advertiser boycott of Facebook to dent its revenues significantly, and interviewees from one of the world's biggest advertisers clearly did not think that spending around US$1 billion annually on Google ads gave them power over Google. For that kind of reason, where big platforms are concerned we are skeptical of conclusions such as Joseph and Bishop's argument that "YouTube's business model is *governed* by advertisers" (2024: 14; emphasis in the original).

## Platform power

What, then, does platform power consist in? "Power" is a conceptually tricky notion, an issue that we touch on below, but let us begin close to our empirical material by identifying five aspects of the power of platforms that emerge from our research, along with a sixth, direct access to government, that is newly salient as we finish writing this book in February 2025.

The first aspect of platform power is the capacity to scale. Achieving scale – in particular, attracting very large numbers of users – can bring a platform both power-enhancing network effects (very likely, e.g., an important determinant of the attractiveness and "stickiness" of a social media platform is the number of your friends that are on it) and also enhanced data power.[6] As we saw in chapter 3, the impressive capabilities of Google's search engine – crucial to its platform power – were by no means simply the result of the sophistication of its algorithms. As Google's scale increased and the number of searches using it grew, the more data it acquired to keep refining that search engine. That process made it increasingly hard for other search engines, which lacked Google's scale, successfully to compete with it. By 2020, 89.2% of general search engine queries in the United States were on Google; for search on mobile devices, its share was 94.9% (Mehta 2024: 156).

Scale can generate a particularly strong form of platform power: technological lock-in, in which the more that a system is adopted and used, the more it improves, and the harder it becomes to displace it.[7] That was also the case, to at least some degree, with Facebook/Meta, in which adoption by direct-response advertisers brought Meta's platforms more and more data linked by identifiers such as an iPhone's IDFA, so making those platforms ever more indispensable for such advertisers. Lock-in *can* end – Apple's blocking of access to IDFAs briefly seemed to endanger Meta's powerful capacity to support direct-response advertising, and AI's large language models may undermine the dominance of Google Search – but while lock-in persists, it is crucial to the material political economy of digital systems.

Successful scaling involves more than simply achieving a large user base. It necessitates a material system – potentially a megamachine – capable of handling huge volumes of digital activity without slowing down or becoming unstable. Chapter 3 gave the example of the difficulties in this respect faced by the pioneering, fast-growing social media platform Friendster, which seem to have contributed to its eclipse by later platforms such as Facebook. Even Google, though ultimately successful, encountered substantial problems on its path to scale. Achieving scale is a daunting, expensive, material task, and lock-in can therefore be reinforced by the difficulties faced by a new entrant trying to gain scale.

Today, cloud providers such as Amazon Web Services enable what is in effect the renting of infrastructure akin to what Google and Facebook built from scratch. That, however, has limitations as a way for a new entrant to achieve scale. Over the long run, renting computational capacity "is more expensive," says interviewee DI: "your unit economics are higher." Building your own digital infrastructure has crucial advantages, he says: "you owned your own bare metal and it was just faster, you could tune it to the needs of AdTech, you could code it in C++, you could basically configure each box exactly the way you wanted it." That, however, needs upfront capital investment, is more demanding ("less turnkey," says DI), and requires careful planning to avoid sudden increases in scale of operations overwhelming your system: "you can't just burst into whatever you want."

A second, also deeply material, aspect of platform power that we have identified is systematicity. We emphasized, in particular, the importance of Google's systematicity: the integration within Google, and therefore relatively seamless cooperation, of what in digital advertising's open marketplace were and are usually separate mechanisms, owned by different firms, which interact only with a degree of friction (such as the difficulty of matching one firm's cookies with another's). Google's systematicity was, for example, critical to it becoming a central, indeed a dominant, presence in the market for Web-display ads, and it has been a real constraint on the otherwise successful effort by header bidding to displace Google from that position, described in chapter 4.

Closely related to systematicity is a third aspect of platform power, successful "stacking." As discussed in chapter 1, platforms layer together economization processes of different kinds. In the case of platforms of the kind discussed in this book, the two most important processes are the gifting or bartering of the platform's "free" services (with users in return consciously or unconsciously giving data to the platform) and the marketization of users' attention by selling advertisers opportunities to show ads to them. That conjunction is easily enough grasped in the abstract, but concretely getting this stacking right is, as Tim Wu says, an issue of "existential importance" for the developers of an ad-funded platform. Intrusive ads can all too easily ruin the experience of using a website or a platform's services, "slowing them down, taking up screen space, and diverting the user's attention from what she really wanted to do" (Wu 2016: 262, 296).

There was, and is, no simple formula for how to stack economization processes, and the innovations that turned Google and Facebook into money machines had an element of accident to them. As we described in chapter 3, the mechanism crucial to Google's success was developed by an engineer who hated ads, while Facebook's key design decision – to place ads directly in users' news feeds, rather than in their previously separate, easily ignorable on-screen location – was forced on it by a simple material consideration: mobile phones' small screens. Nor should successful stacking be seen as achieved once and for all by an overall design decision such as that. Stacking is a continuous process that goes on in real time, for example via the auction mechanism, discussed in chapter 6, at the heart of Meta's platforms, Facebook and Instagram.

A fourth aspect to platform power is epistemic power: the capacity to generate believable knowledge claims. Although that is an important resource for any platform, our topic, advertising, brings it into particular focus. As we've discussed, a vital component of stacking is for a platform that sells ads to be able to provide plausible evidence that those ads are working cost-effectively, ideally evidence that is easily portable: that advertising agencies can show to their clients and advertisers' marketing departments show to their senior managers, and so on. Chapter 4 discussed the importance of Google's capacity to provide evidence of this kind, and chapter 5 demonstrated how serious it was for Facebook/Meta when Apple's changes disrupted its evidence-generating capacity.

If scale is achieved, marketization and other modes of economization are successfully stacked, and epistemic power attained, a platform can earn money – lots of it. A fifth facet of platform power is therefore "money power": the financial resources that accrue to a successful platform.[8] Those resources give a big platform the ability to hire and retain the best engineers in sufficiently large numbers to successfully tackle difficult problems, thus enhancing a platform's capacities and protecting it from potential rivals – a process that may well be playing out currently in research and development in machine learning and artificial intelligence. As we described in chapter 4, for example, having those engineers enabled Google to succeed where others were failing: designing an ad server that continued to work robustly in the face of increasing scale of use and the emergence of new ad formats. That ad server has become indispensable to publishers of all kinds, which has helped keep Google in a central position in the market for Web-display ads, despite the challenge from header bidding.

Having large amounts of money, though, does not automatically bring with it platform power. What interviewee BI calls two "dominant players," the Web portals Yahoo and America Online (AOL), earned very large revenues in digital advertising's early years. By 2000, AOL's market capitalization was US$160 billion, three times that of General Motors (Wu 2016: 212). The duo had ample capacity to buy emergent advertising technology firms: Yahoo, for example, tried to buy Google in 2002 and went on to buy other firms, including ad-exchange pioneer Right Media. However, Yahoo and AOL found it hard, says BI, to fuse their purchases into a fully successful, integrated advertising business, ending up themselves being bought by telecoms company Verizon, which, "after incurring significant losses," eventually sold them to private equity firm Apollo in 2021 for US$5 billion (Thomas 2023). After competing unsuccessfully with Google to buy DoubleClick (we discussed the latter's US$3.1 billion acquisition by Google in chapter 4), another giant of the digital economy, Microsoft, paid US$6.3 billion for the AdTech firm, aQuantive. Five years later, though, Microsoft "wrote off almost the entire value of the acquisition, taking a US$6.2 billion writedown" (Goldman 2012).

Google did deploy its money power to buy other businesses, for example acquiring YouTube in 2006 for US$1.65 billion, but often preferred "to build rather than to buy" (interviewee BI). In chapter 4, for example, we described Google's extensive post-acquisition re-engineering of DoubleClick's systems. Many of such purchases that Google did make (e.g., the acquisition of Urchin, discussed in chapter 3) seem to have been chosen because they brought capabilities that helped integrate and strengthen Google's evolving advertising system, says BI: "Google benefited from looking at their business as being Search, DoubleClick, YouTube and looking at how they could really leverage the three of those into one unified marketplace, if you will, [a] one-stop shop."

This points to an important characteristic of the five aspects of platform power just discussed: scaling, systematicity, stacking, epistemic power, and money power. They, and the other forms of power that they bring with them, such as data power and technological lock-in, are not separate dimensions. They operate in concert and reinforce each other and can be transformed into each other, as when money power is used to make a corporate acquisition that increases systematicity.

Those five aspects of platform power are long-standing, present within digital advertising from the late 1990s and early 2000s. The sixth aspect, direct access to government and political power, is newer. Google, for example, was initially "disdainful of lobbying," and it did not open a Washington DC office – with initially just a single member of staff – until seven years after its foundation (Hamburger and Gold 2014). Tech sector lobbying subsequently grew in scale considerably (Duhigg 2024) but was far from universally successful, as US Federal, state-led, and European Commission antitrust lawsuits against Big Tech demonstrate. However, the early weeks of the second Trump Administration in 2025 seem to signal a sea change. Not only is Elon Musk playing a central role in that administration, but Trump's previously fractious relationship with Big Tech more generally has been replaced by visible rapprochement.

As with many other aspects of the new administration's policies, it would be foolish to try to predict whether Big Tech's direct access to government and political power will continue: the technology sector, or particular companies within it, may fall out of favor. If, however, the current rapprochement proves durable, the analysis of platform power will need to take full account of this sixth component. For example, the regulatory constraints on platform power that we discuss below are likely to erode over the medium term, not just in the United States but elsewhere as well. In particular, the European Union, which has up to now taken a leading role in the regulation and policing of not just European but also US-based platforms, may face retribution (in the form of tariffs, or even withdrawal of US collaboration on issues of national security) if it continues to do so vigorously.

## Infrastructural power

"Power," we noted above, is conceptually tricky. A long-standing divide in its analysis by sociologists is between "power over" and "power to." The great German sociologist Max Weber offered what has become the classic "power over" definition: "'Power' [*Macht*] is the probability that one actor within a social relationship will be in a position to carry out his own will despite resistance, regardless of the basis on which this probability rests" (Weber 1947: 152). "Power to" was, in contrast, the focus of the twentieth century's most influential American sociologist, Talcott Parsons, for whom power was the "capacity to get things done . . . the capacity of a social system to mobilize resources to attain collective goals" (Parsons 1967: 225).

We are deliberately not aligning ourselves with either pole of this dichotomy. Scalability, systematicity, stacking, epistemic power, and money power, especially in conjunction, give a platform "power to," but that readily translates itself into "power over" – over ordinary users, content creators, news publishers (Nielsen and Ganter 2022; Poell, Nieborg, and Duffy 2023), and advertisers, our focus in this book.

More generally, "power to" – the capacity to get things done – is at the heart of how we conceive of material political economy, although Parsons's definition needs to be stripped of the overlay of his conservatively oriented functionalist sociology, such as the notion that a social system can have collective goals. *Which* things need to get done, and *how*, are typically the subject of conflict, and we would always want to emphasize the point made in chapter 1: that material political economy (its real-world practice, rather than its conceptual discussion) often involves making it hard, even impossible, to do some things.

The crucial way in which the notion of "power to" has implicitly made its way into discussion of platform power is via a reframed version of sociologist Michael Mann's concept of *infrastructural power* (Mann 1984): for its adoption, see, for example, van Dijck, Nieborg, and Poell (2019: 9, 12) and Flensburg and Lai (2023). Mann formulated the concept while investigating "the autonomous power of the state," as distinct from, for example, simplistic versions of Marxism that saw the state as the tool of the capitalist class,

Mann distinguishes between the state's "despotic" and "infrastructural" power. Despotic power, in Mann's formulation, refers to actions that the state elite can "undertake without routine, institutionalised negotiation with civil society groups." Invoking traditional empires and absolute monarchies, but also *Alice in Wonderland*, Mann epitomizes despotic power as "the ability of all these Red Queens to shout 'off with his head' and have their whim gratified without further ado – provided the person is at hand" (Mann 1984: 188–9). That last phrase is Mann's pointer to infrastructural power: "the capacity of the state to actually penetrate civil society." This, he notes, "was comparatively weak in the historical societies just mentioned – once you were out of sight of the Red Queen, she had difficulty in getting at you" (Mann 1984: 189).

The reframing twist to Mann's notion of "infrastructural power" comes, for example, in the work of the political economist Benjamin Braun. State bodies such as central banks often "seek to maximize their economic steering capacity" (Braun 2020: 396) – in Mann's sense, their infrastructural power – by operating via financial markets and private bodies such as banks. That, however, gives those private bodies a subtly different (in the case discussed by Braun, a countervailing) form of infrastructural power: the power that comes from doing something that is essential to what someone or something else wants or needs to do.

Digital platforms of all kinds (not just those discussed in this book) have often become essential to other people, organizations, or technical systems in precisely that way: without the platform, crucial tasks become harder or impossible. That is the form of infrastructural power – often largely invisible, except in cases of disruption, such as that examined in chapter 5 – that is most relevant to digital advertising and to platforms more generally.[9] It forms a crucial bridge between "platform studies" and the literature in science and technology studies on infrastructures, a literature that we haven't addressed explicitly in order to avoid overcomplicating this book.[10]

The infrastructural power of digital platforms takes multiple forms. One that is relatively visible is in the relationship between platforms and news publishers. As journalist and journalism professor Emily Bell puts it, "they [platforms] are at the core of our business, but we are not at the core of theirs" (2021: 295).[11] Often less easily visible, because it can be deeply "technical," is the infrastructural power in the relationship between a platform and an app running on that platform. The case of this most prominent in this book is that discussed in chapter 5, where the platform was the operating system of iPhones, Apple's iOS (along with Apple's App Store), and the apps in question included both Instagram and Facebook. The duo seemed to be – and in many respects are – powerful platforms, but, as we have emphasized, their presence in everyday life is in the form of mobile-phone apps, and that gives Apple infrastructural power over them.

Deeply technical as they may be, platform/app relations are often also political in a broad sense of the word. For example, as well as being an app, Facebook was – and is – itself a platform. Facebook's becoming a platform, on which other developers could build their own apps, was crucial to its transformation from promising social media site to giant corporation (Levy 2020). Facebook's history is in good part a story of its relationship to apps running on its platform – a story of material political economy. The material interconnections between apps and a platform (such as the application programming interfaces (APIs) that the platform provides to app developers) are "*governance arrangement[s]*," not neutral technical links: "Because APIs facilitate and govern the material conditions of app development and the social and economic processes they sustain, powerful platforms influence the evolution of their larger ecosystems. As such, the technicity of Facebook's API governance represents a major source of the platform's 'infrastructural power'" (van der Vlist, Helmond, Burkhardt, and Seitz 2022: 1; emphasis in original). Indeed, Anne Helmond and colleagues, in that article and other work, have shown how Facebook's history can be traced via those APIs and what they reveal about Facebook's place in this economically, politically, and technologically contested terrain.

The details of that history are intricate and demanding so let us give two simpler examples of the material political economy of platform-app relations. The first is the way in which Facebook and Twitter tightly restricted the data available via their APIs following the Cambridge Analytica controversy touched on in chapter 3. Those restrictions are fiercely contested by researcher Axel Bruns, who points out that as well as limiting the activities of commercial apps, those changes also "frustrate critical, independent, public interest scrutiny by scholars" (2019: 1544).

The second example of the politics of platform-app relations was inadvertently highlighted by the global digital chaos of July 2024, which followed a faulty update to CrowdStrike security software running on Microsoft's Windows operating system. The entirely explicit politics in the background to this was a 2009 agreement that Microsoft reached with the European Commission, following competition-law pressure from the latter. Microsoft seems to have interpreted the agreement as requiring it to provide external developers of security systems with the same API access that Microsoft's own products enjoyed.[12] This includes access to Windows's "kernel," its very core, which was what made a fault in third-party software so disruptive. In contrast, for example, Apple's desktop/laptop operating system, MacOS, prevents non-Apple programs accessing its kernel, "forcing them to operate in the more limited 'user mode'" (Stacey and Waters 2024). Security specialist Josephine Wolff (2024) comments:

Perhaps we are willing to sacrifice some security in the name of competition, but we should never, under any circumstances, sacrifice our computer kernels.

Whether that is the right trade-off is contestable, but that is exactly the point: that apparently "technical" issues of platform/app relations can also be issues of material political economy.

## Constraining platform power

The notion of "infrastructural power" helps make sense of the power that platforms possess. Power, however, does not *always* accrue to people or systems that are essential to what other people or systems need to do. The systems that supply water and electricity are paradigmatic examples of infrastructure, and fundamental to any industrial society, but utility companies such as water and electricity suppliers are not normally the most powerful of all corporations. Depriving households or companies of water or electricity would be a potent threat, but suppliers can't arbitrarily do that – if they did, they would rapidly face legal action and government intervention. The supply of water and electricity is a source of power – it is crucial to the "capacity to get things done" – but their suppliers have only limited discretion over its provision, greatly limiting the extent to which they *possess* that power.[13]

In a word, the supply of water and electricity is legally *regulated*, at least in the kind of societies discussed in this book. It would be quite mistaken to imply that digital advertising and the platform economy are unregulated. At least three areas of law bear upon them: privacy and data protection; consumer protection; and competition or antitrust law.[14] (The US term "antitrust" owes its origins to cartels often having taken the legal form of trusts when US competition law, notably the Sherman Act of 1890, was first being formulated.)

Of the three forms of law, competition/antitrust law has had the most direct bearing on platform power in the years since we began this research in 2019. In a reversal of the situation at the end of the twentieth century, when competition regulators in the United States were more activist than their European counterparts (Philippon 2019), the European Union has led in this respect, with its regulators successfully wielding its Digital Markets Act, which came into force in 2022, for example to get Apple to loosen some of the constraints that the rules of its App Store place on apps and to give external developers access to the silicon chip in iPhones that enables contactless payments.

The Digital Markets Act involves a crucial step in the direction advocated by Lawrence and Laybourn-Langton (2018: 27–9) and van Dijck, Nieborg, and Poell (2019): to regulate the infrastructurally most deeply embedded platforms *as utilities*. The Act defines "[a] small number of large undertakings providing core platform services . . . with considerable economic power" as being "gatekeeper" platforms, and it subjects them to a body of obligations and restrictions well beyond those to which all EU enterprises are subject (European Parliament and Council 2022: 2). By May 2024, the European Commission had designated 24 platforms (ranging from Google Search to the travel site Booking.com) as gatekeepers. Distinguishing gatekeepers from other platforms, implicitly viewing them as infrastructures, and beginning to regulate them as utilities are important regulatory innovations because trying to curb platform power with regulation that applies to all digital platforms could easily end up enhancing the power of the biggest of them by imposing undue burdens on new enterprises. The EU's GDPR (General Data Protection Regulation) has, for example, been criticized on exactly those grounds.

That matters because another constraint, in addition to regulation, on a platform's infrastructural power is the presence of competing platforms. Interviewee CY, from a games-development firm, contrasts the situation in mobile gaming (where there are two platforms, Apple and Android, but only limited genuine competition between them because of the loyalty of Apple's often more affluent customers to the firm's devices) to that in game consoles. "Consoles are competitive," he says. Three big firms, Microsoft (Xbox), Sony (Playstation), and Nintendo, offer competing platforms: "[All three console-providers] want as many games as possible on there. They're definitely incentivized to play nicer with developers because it makes their core products more attractive (CY)."

European Union regulators have, as noted, taken the lead in seeking to limit gatekeeper platforms' discretion in how they deploy their platform power. US regulators, however, potentially have more direct sway over Big Tech platforms, most of which are headquartered in the United States. The Biden Administration appointed to senior positions antitrust specialists – notably Lina Khan to chair the Federal Trade Commission and Jonathan Kanter to head the Justice Department's unit responsible for antitrust litigation – whose views of market power are broader than the narrow, price-oriented orthodoxy that had come to prevail in US law. Federal regulators have launched antitrust suits against Facebook, Apple, and Amazon, and two suits against Google (one focusing on Google Search, the other on its role in display advertising, discussed in chapter 4).

The Google Search case was launched during the first Trump presidency; whether it will survive the second remains to be seen. At the time of writing, it is the only one of these Federal antitrust suits to have reached the point of a legal judgment, a "memorandum opinion" by Judge Amit P. Mehta, sitting in the District Court for the District of Columbia, one of the 94 district courts in the United States that hear Federal cases (Mehta 2024).[15] The central issue in that case is Google's payments to other companies to ensure that its search engine is the "preloaded default," in particular on Apple devices. Google has, for example, a revenue-sharing arrangement with Apple, under which it pays the latter an agreed proportion of the resultant advertising revenues. The size of that share is redacted in Mehta's findings, but an expert witness for Google gave the figure of 36% in his testimony, amounting to around US$20 billion in 2022 (Mehta 2024: 103; Nylen 2023).

Default position is a quintessential issue of material politics: it is easy for a user to stick with the default option, slightly more awkward and/or time-consuming to switch to something else. That in its turn affects one of the aspects of platform power discussed above, scaling. Default position, argues Judge Mehta, helps maintain and grow the number of Google searches, and scale – as we have pointed out – can bring with it data power. "Google derives extraordinary volumes of user data," from those searches, writes Mehta, and "uses that information to improve search quality" (2024: 2).

If Mehta's reasoning is correct, users get better search results, but the barrier to another search engine effectively competing with Google becomes higher. His overall conclusion is stark: "Google is a monopolist, and it has acted as one to maintain its monopoly. It has violated Section 2 of the Sherman Act," which as noted above is the foundation stone of US antitrust law. The agreements that Google entered into to secure default position for its search engine "have anticompetitive effects," he writes (Mehta 2024: 4, 275). He has not ruled, however, that Google *intended* those agreements to have those effects. On that issue, he quotes the 2001 judgment on appeal of the antitrust suit against Microsoft, touched on below: "our focus is upon the effect of that conduct, not upon the intent behind it" (Mehta 2024: 275).

Google is appealing against Mehta's judgment, which could be overturned, in full or in part, and the Trump Administration could instruct the Department of Justice not to proceed with the case. Nor is it clear what the courts will demand from Google if the case continues and the judgment is upheld. That could include Google having to divest itself of its Chrome browser (which has been demanded by the Department of Justice) or insisting that payments to secure default position be stopped.

The latter could have significant consequences. It might create a powerful rival to Google Search by incentivizing Apple to launch a search engine of its own and incorporate it into its devices. Apple's "crawlers" have been active on the Web for some time, potentially giving Apple the material capacity quickly to generate a full search index.

The most dramatic outcome of this, or other pending antitrust suits, would be a breakup of one of the major platform corporations. There are precedents. The paradigmatic "trust" that gave antitrust law its name, John D. Rockefeller's Standard Oil, was broken up by a 1911 Supreme Court judgment.[16] In 1984, following antitrust litigation by the Department of Justice, "Ma Bell" (the Bell System), the United States' regulated telephone monopoly, was voluntary broken up by its owner, AT&T (the American Telephone and Telegraph Company). In 2000, the District Court for the District of Columbia (which heard the Google Search case) ordered that Microsoft be broken up, although the relevant Appeal Court then overturned that order.

### Redesigning megamachines

At the time of writing, early in 2025, it is however difficult to envisage – at least in the near future – competition law being employed to break up Google or any other Big Tech corporation. Even in the United Kingdom, whose Competition and Markets Authority (CMA) has been impressively activist in respect to digital advertising, "softer" interpretations and implementation of competition law seem likely to prevail in the short term. The Labour government appears to have decided, in our view mistakenly, that the CMA is an obstacle to its pursuit of economic growth, and has removed its chairperson.

Competition law, however, is only one of the ways in which platform power can be constrained. Given our focus in this book, we take particular interest in initiatives that involve potential redesign of megamachines. Three issues are of particular interest in this respect, and at least the first two of them have aspects that potentially cross today's sharp political divides, so progress can perhaps be made on them even in otherwise unfavorable political circumstances. The first issue is online conduct and content that may not violate existing law but is nevertheless harmful. This issue has helped prompt new legislation such as the United Kingdom's 2023 Online Safety Act and the European Union's 2022 Digital Services Act (complementary to, but distinct from, its Digital Markets Act).

That issue is intrinsically sociotechnical and takes a wide variety of forms, too many to review here. Some involve the balance between allowing free speech and inhibiting hate speech, and preventing, for example, "revenge porn" and technologically enabled misogyny, such as use of "nudification" software. Others, such as preventing harms to children, involve difficult issues of technical redesign, such as building robust age-verification procedures. There is, however, at least a degree of potential political consensus in favor of intervening in the design of digital systems to minimize their harmful effects on children (Angel and boyd 2024).

It is, of course, wrong to be naively optimistic about the effects of design interventions. We share Angel and boyd's caution about naive "technolegal solutionism," for example in respect to protecting children from harm: "Children face violence at home, in church, and at school . . . [T]echnology is rarely the cause of teen's issues, but it is certainly the place they turn to when they are struggling . . . social media makes youth mental health problems *visible*." As Angel and boyd argue, therefore, "technological fixes often fail because of ecological dynamics," and so, "attention must be first and foremost given to the *social* problems of abuse, addiction, poverty, social inequality, etc. that sit at the root of many of the negative outcomes that legislators want to prevent" (Angel and boyd 2024: 93–4: emphases in original). Nevertheless, some of the specific "redesign" measures that are being proposed, such as forcing platforms to restrict their autoplaying of video content to children, seem well motivated and unlikely to have major drawbacks.

The second issue in which the design of megamachines is at stake is privacy and surveillance. This is again a potentially bipartisan issue, and one on which Big Tech is divided and commercial interests clash. It is, for example, hard to imagine Apple voluntairly reversing the material-politics move discussed in chapter 5 by allowing social media platforms, other apps, and advertising networks unrestricted access to iPhones' IDFAs: the potential damage to consumers' image of the iPhone would be too great. True, it is equally difficult to imagine, in the near term, a major new US Federal privacy-oriented regulation akin to the European Union's GDPR. Privacy initiatives by individual states can, however, also change platforms' incentives. For a platform to have to detect where in the United States a user is based, and alter its procedures accordingly, is complicated, so platforms may find it simplest to comply with the rules of the strictest jurisdiction, especially if that is a prosperous state with a large population, such as California.

The single most prominent specific privacy/surveillance issue in digital advertising that remains unresolved at the time of writing is the status of third-party "tracking" cookies in Google's Chrome, the world's most widely used browser. As we noted in chapter 5, Google initially planned simply to end websites' default capacity to deposit these cookies in users' browsers but will now instead offer users a choice about this. The crucial material-politics issue, however, is the precise mechanism of that choice. It will, hopefully, be a "global" choice (i.e., one that holds for all websites, rather than having cumbersomely to be made each time you visit a new site), and framed neutrally, with it being just as quick and easy to reject default third-party cookies as to accept them. If, however, the latter is not the case, there is a major opportunity for both privacy activists and regulators to intervene on the issue.

A third issue that definitely requires redesign of the digital economy's megamachines is the latter's environmental impact, in particular their carbon footprint and the water consumption required to cool datacenters packed with vast numbers of heat-generating computer servers. Alas, achieving political consensus to match the scientific consensus on the reality of anthropogenic climate change is likely to remain elusive in the near term. It is, however, worth emphasizing that environmental wastefulness in digital advertising – in particular, unnecessary carbon emissions – is often simultaneously economically wasteful (such as unproductively showing huge numbers of ads on ad-saturated made-for-advertising sites) and thus commercially damaging too.

Advertising practitioners can help reduce wasteful emissions in some relatively simple ways, such as shrinking the digital files containing their ads to "the highest quality that can be perceived by the human eye," ensuring that the only "data sent is . . . what is actually consumed," and making "sure ads stop loading when they're out of view" (Johansson 2024). By cutting the number of SSPs with which they work, practitioners can also help cut the number of duplicate auctions for which they are responsible. That should also have the beneficial effect of reducing their exposure to made-for-advertising sites because "it's easier for [such sites] to sneak into convoluted supply chains which are heavy on reselling," in which a publisher's ad requests go to multiple SSPs, some of which forward them on to yet more SSPs if they cannot fulfill them themselves (Vargas 2024a).

Clearly, though, more systematic measures to reduce emissions are needed, too. In June 2024, the Global Alliance for Responsible Media, which we touched on above, and Ad Net Zero, set up in 2020 by UK advertising-industry bodies, launched a Global Media Sustainability Framework. The locale for the launch was in a sense ironic: it was advertising's prestigious, heavily attended, but (because of many participants' transatlantic air travel) carbon-intensive annual Cannes Lions Festival. The framework's goal is, however, important: to standardize emissions measurement and give publishers a benchmark for reporting to advertisers the emissions involved in buying their ad slots (Joseph 2024). That is potentially of considerable significance because if those measurements start to affect advertisers' spending patterns, they will give publishers a financial incentive to rein in excessive auction duplication.

Whether that initiative will be successful in a more hostile political context, however, remains to be seen. Nor should one be naive about the measurement and reporting of emissions. It is itself a major sphere of material political economy, and different ways of doing it can have very different results, financial and reputational. Divides over this are not simply between environmental activists and major corporations but sometimes between those corporations. A crucial divisive topic, for example, is how to measure the emissions for which datacenters are responsible. One flashpoint is the renewable energy certificates issued by "clean power" electricity suppliers. Currently, a company can buy these certificates and set them against its emissions, even if the supplier involved is not providing electricity to its datacenters. Google is seeking to tighten those rules and "only match energy consumption with clean energy and certificates from the grids where power is consumed." Its Big Tech opponents see that as too costly, even "utopian," arguing that instead companies "should be able to use certificates in a more flexible way with no restrictions at all on geographical origin" (Bryan, Hodgson, and Tauschinski 2024).

Whatever the outcome of disputes about measurement, it seems very likely that datacenters, and especially proposals to build new ones, will increasingly be the source of material-politics conflicts, in particular in energy- or water-constrained regions or countries. In electricity-constrained Ireland, for example, the consumption of datacenters is already 21% of total electricity supply, greater than that of all the households in its towns and cities (Webber and Moore 2024). As described in chapter 1, there is a current vogue for commissioning nuclear reactors to provide energy to datacenters, as the latter power up even further to support computationally intensive artificial intelligence systems, especially the large language models that underpin systems such as ChatGPT. The nuclear vogue strikes us as a dangerous distraction. It remains to be demonstrated that the small modular nuclear reactors that are being commissioned will actually be proportionately cheaper and quicker to build than their earlier, bigger brethren, notoriously plagued by delays and cost overruns (Schlissel and Wamsted 2024). Furthermore, adding to volumes of nuclear waste, when there is currently no entirely safe long-term way of storing it, seems irresponsible.

Far better, then, to use renewable energy sources such as wind and sunshine, and for public authorities to integrate decisions about granting permission to build or expand datacenters with the planning of the electricity grid and water-supply networks. That might, for example, create opportunities for imaginative thinking, such as using the huge quantities of heat generated by datacenters (currently nearly always treated simply as a waste product to be dissipated into the atmosphere) to heat other buildings and homes. The Danish energy multinational, Danfoss, whose systems are used to cool datacenters, calculates that the aggregate heat generated by the datacenters surrounding Frankfurt, a major financial center and internet hub, could meet the heating needs of that entire city (Milne 2024).

Just as we are going to have to fly less, though, it's also possible that we are going to have to compute less, or at least less wastefully, until the shift to renewable energy is far more advanced than currently. Wasteful computation is, however, often invisible: we were three years into our research before the extraordinary extent of ad auction duplication started to become clear to us. Finding opportunities to reduce computational waste could be an important practical aspect of the research on the material political economy of digital megamachines that we would like to foster. Large language models, the currently most prominent form of artificial intelligence, are a case in point. The biggest such models are already megamachines: training them consumes large quantities of electricity, and thus often involves substantial carbon emissions. This makes the development of smaller, more "frugal," computationally more efficient models urgent (Bender et al. 2021), and that may turn out to have commercial as well as environmental advantages.

The research that we wish to encourage should not restrict itself to the environmental impact of megamachines. The material-political-economy conflicts on which we have focused have other dimensions as well: in the case of header bidding, discussed in chapter 4, the balance of power among publishers, Google, and smaller ad market participants; in chapter 5's case (the design of the megamachine enfolding Apple phones), both users' privacy and the balance of power in that market too.

Digital megamachines have become central not just to today's environmental politics but to economic, social, and political life. Researching them in depth, understanding how they underpin platform power, examining the often-subterranean material-political-economy conflicts that both shape them and that they themselves shape – all those are urgent tasks for the social sciences. And they should not be lonely tasks. We very much hope that other scholars will find the welcoming colleagues and willing, generous informants who have made our research for this book so enjoyable and so stimulating.

# Notes

## Chapter 1 Introduction

1 See chapter 4 for why there are more auctions than ads. Kotila (2021) gives what he calls an "expert opinion" estimate that 146 trillion digital ads are displayed globally each year, which equates to 4.6 million per second or 400 billion daily. That is perfectly conceivable, but we take it to be an upper-bound estimate. The International Telecommunication Union estimates 5.4 billion internet users worldwide in 2023: https://www.itu.int/en/ITU-D/Statistics/pages/stat/default.aspx. One hundred billion ads shown daily would therefore mean an average of fewer than twenty ads per person per day, which therefore seems a plausible lower bound. Our estimate of the total number of auctions is based on Jounce Media's approximate but data-based upper-bound estimate, reported by Schiff (2024), of 30 million Web-display, in-app display, and connected TV auctions per second. That implies 2.6 trillion auctions a day, a figure that would increase somewhat if search ads, social media ads, and so on, were included too (we have no fully reliable estimate of those). The order of magnitude of Jounce's estimate is consistent with reports from individual ad platforms. In 2023, a single supply-side platform, Pubmatic, reported processing – i.e., sending out to auction –

56 trillion ad requests in three months, which equates to around seven million per second (Pubmatic 2023), and Pubmatic told *Ad Exchanger* that its systems rejected many further requests. In 2021, interviewee AO told us that her demand-side platform was receiving "[t]ens of millions of queries [bid requests] per second." As long ago as 2017, the Trade Desk, one of the world's two leading demand-side platforms, told *Forbes*, "We are considering over 9 million ad opportunities every single second" (Chowdhry 2017).

2 We owe the reference to Crain and Nadler (2019: 371).

3 Combining Kotila's (2021) estimate of 146 trillion ads shown annually and our estimate (derived from Lebow 2024) of total digital advertising revenue in 2023 of US$612 billion suggests that revenue per ad averages just over 0.4 cents. In the standard convention of display advertising, that is a CPM or cost per mille (per thousand ads) of a little over US$4, which seems plausible.

4 Drawing upon Pärssinen et al. (2018), Kotila (2021) estimates the average $CO_2$ emissions associated with each ad impression (showing one ad once, to just one user) as 0.08–1.09 grams, which is the estimate we use for our "puff size." We know no more recent aggregate global estimate that can be directly compared with Pärssinen et al. (2018), but Kotila's per impression estimate is consistent with more recent work, notably Scope3 (2023).

5 In 2023, the total advertising revenues of Google's parent company, Alphabet, were US$238 billion (Alphabet Inc. 2024: 35) and Meta's US$132 billion (Meta Platforms Inc. 2024: 103).

6 For performativity more generally, including extensive references to the literature on it, see Unal et al. (forthcoming).

7 Dourish (2017) is a now classic counterargument, emphasizing the materiality of the digital.

8 For a sympathetic treatment of Mumford and similar critics of technological society, see Winner (1977).

9 Alphabet Inc. (2024: 35).

10 See Somers (2018) and the account of MapReduce in Dourish (2017: 120–8).

11 For a satellite image of the Apple datacenter near Reno, Nevada, see: https://commons.wikimedia.org/wiki/File:Apple_datacenter_Reno_satellite_view.jpg
12 For a set of readings on this, see MacKenzie and Wajcman (1999).
13 For a critique of the application of the metaphor of "organic" in this context, see Jobin and Ziewitz (2018). Because the distinctions between gifts, barter, and commodity exchange are complex and negotiable (Humphrey and Hugh-Jones 1992), we do not try to address here the question of whether to conceptualize as gift or as barter the relationship between a platform that provides services that don't have to be paid for and unremunerated users who provide data.
14 Another vital written source, although one with a single author, the analyst Eric Seufert, is the weekly *Mobile Dev Memo*.
15 Customer relationship management includes, e.g., the maintenance of loyalty programs and of lists of customers and the organization of firms' communications with customers. On the relationship between advertising and other aspects of marketing, see Mellet (2025).
16 The distinction between "brand advertising and "direct response" has pre-digital roots, as documented by Turow (2006: ch. 3).
17 The most sophisticated contributions to the literature, such as Cheney-Lippold (2017), Prey (2018), and Fisher and Mehozay (2019), do capture ways in which algorithmically constructed identities have de-individualizing aspects. Our point, however, is that measures such as Apple's have potentially stronger de-individualizing effects.
18 McGuigan has also critically scrutinized digital advertising's "pivot to privacy" (see, e.g., McGuigan, Myers West, Sivan-Sevilla, and Parham 2023).
19 As an anonymous referee for Polity Press emphasized to us, Smythe's work helped inspire a sophisticated body of literature in the 1980s, 1990s, and early 2000s. See chapter 7, note 2.

## Chapter 2 Display Ads, Cookies, and the Open Marketplace

1. Berners-Lee (1989–90). For a fine sociology-of-science study of CERN (the Conseil Européen pour la Recherche Nucléaire) in those years, see Knorr Cetina (1999).
2. The numbers of websites given in this paragraph are taken from https://www.mit.edu/people/mkgray/net/web-growth-summary.html, which reports data collected contemporaneously by Matthew Gray's Worldwide Web Wanderer, a pioneering "Web crawler." ISP numbers (taken come from Greenstein 2015: 139) are based on *Boardwatch Magazine*'s directories of ISPs.
3. Andrew Anker, interviewed by Brian McCullough, for Internet History Podcast, 2014: https://www.internethistorypodcast.com/2014/10/the-webs-first-banner-ads/ . McCullough's extensive series of interviews forms the basis of his book, *How the Internet Happened* (McCullough 2018).
4. The AT&T Campaign is described by Bill Clausen, the AT&T advertising manager who worked with Modern Media, again in an interview with Brian McCullough. See https://www.internethistorypodcast.com/2014/10/the-webs-first-banner-ads/, which also contains reproductions of the banner ad and the "landing page" with the map.
5. Anker, interviewed by McCullough: https://www.internethistorypodcast.com/2014/10/the-webs-first-banner-ads/
6. The cover image, from *Time*'s February 19, 1996 issue, is available at https://content.time.com/time/covers/0,16641,19960219,00.html
7. On pricing conventions in digital advertising, see Beuscart and Mellet (2013).
8. As noted in chapter 1, cookies have been the single most prominent focus so far of research, for example in "market studies," on digital advertising. See, especially, Mellet and Beauvisage (2020), Jones (2020, 2024), Crain (2021), and Beauvisage (2023).
9. To keep things simple, our account in this paragraph sets aside a variety of complications. We are ignoring, for example, cookies'

expiry dates and devices that have more than one human user. In the case of the latter, the connecting up is not specific to a particular user. If a different human being is using the same browser on the same device on a later visit to the website, what the latter will send back to the website is the original cookie, set when a different human being was using the device.

10  That is an aspect of the Web's long-standing "same origin policy," implemented in all Web browsers and designed to limit the damage that a malicious website can do by limiting its interactions with other sites.

11  There is a good description of this process in its heyday by advertising practitioner Antonio García Martínez (2016: 386–94).

12  As well as the insightful discussion of DoubleClick in Crain (2021) another very useful source on the company, involving contemporaneous interviews, is Reese (2002).

13  Kevin O'Connor, interviewed by Brian McCullough for Internet History Podcast, 2014: https://www.internethistorypodcast.com/tag/kevin-oconnor/

14  On Silicon Alley, see Indergaard (2004) and Stark (2009: 81–117).

15  "[A]dvertising is the price you pay for having an unremarkable product or service," said Amazon's Jeff Bezos in 2009 (Johnson and Rittenhouse 2022). Apple's Steve Jobs told journalist Walter Isaacson that an emphasis on marketing was often a cause of corporate decline: "[w]hen the sales guys run the company, the product guys don't matter so much, and a lot of them just turn off" (Isaacson 2012: 97). See chapter 3 for Google's and Facebook's founders' reservations about advertising.

16  Crain (2021: 101) is not fully explicit on the nature of the "invisible tracking codes" involved, but contemporaneous evidence suggests that in the case of DoubleClick they indeed took the form of pixels.

## Chapter 3  Money Machines and the Characteristics of Digital Advertising

1 Dean (2010) is a YouTube recording of a November 2010 talk by Google's Jeff Dean at Stanford University, discussing systems development at Google in its first decade.
2 Markoff and Hansell (2006). Google hardware designer Will Whitted told Edwards that "[t]he average in the US is one tech[nician] per thirty machines. Google was running three thousand machines per tech" (Edwards 2011: 111).
3 The magnetic "heads" that read data from a hard disk and write data to it are carried by an actuator arm that often needs physically to move to get the heads into the correct position. In around 2000, a hard drive "disk seek" took around 10 milliseconds (thousandths of a second); an equivalent "read" from silicon memory was about 18 microseconds (millionths of a seconds). We draw these figures from https://colin-scott.github.io/personal_website/research/interactive_latency.html
4 On the significance of these different pricing conventions, see Beuscart and Mellet (2013).
5 As noted in chapter 1, Jobin and Ziewitz (2018) provide a critique of the notion of "organic" in this context.
6 References to Google and/or search ads as a "money machine" go back to at least 2005 (Vise and Malseed 2005: 259). See also, e.g., Auletta (2009: 90).
7 Google was and is auctioning multiple objects (multiple ad slots) simultaneously, and in that setting its simple second-price auctions are not in fact theoretically optimal, as we touch on in chapter 6.
8 Interviewee AI tells us that GoTo's system "was very much built with [the idea that] you bid for two or three keywords. Or maybe ten or fifteen," which made manual checking of ads' relevance to those keywords feasible.
9 Media mix modeling is a form of multiple regression, typically with the value or volume of aggregate sales as the dependent variable, and independent variables, including amounts of advertising spending or activity via different media channels, along with

additional variables designed to make it possible to take account of confounding factors such as products' price changes. Running a regression analysis of this kind produces at least "correlational" measures of the effectiveness of different channels while controlling for other sources of variation in sales such as seasonality.

10  Urchin itself is long forgotten, but its traces persist in the form of the "UTM [Urchin Tracking Module] parameters" that advertisers add to the URLs to which a click on an ad takes the user. Those allow a purchase, for example, to be connected back to that ad, and that forms a different way (in addition to pixels) of measuring the effectiveness of ads. If you click on a Web ad, and then look at the full URL of the site to which you are taken, you will usually find a question mark after the final slash, and what follows it are sometimes still UTM parameters. The fact that UTM parameters are not available to track installs of mobile-phone apps back to the ad that may have led the user to install the app is one reason why the Apple privacy changes discussed in chapter 5 had such tumultuous effects.

11  For Google viewed as a large technical system, see Rieder (2022).

12  Meisner, Duffy, and Ziewitz (2024: 1019) give a much higher estimate – 380,000 – of the number of Google's search quality raters.

13  In the 2017–18 scandal surrounding the political consultancy Cambridge Analytica, it became clear that access had been gained to information on tens of millions of Facebook users without their knowledge.

14  Although we did not have McGuigan's (2023) discussion of the affordances of digital advertising in mind when we first wrote this section, and we frame things somewhat differently, his discussion is an important precursor, as we acknowledge in chapter 1.

15  Interviewee DM suggests that the launch of Gmail in 2004 began to provide Google with the data needed for demographic targeting.

16  A telling detail is that DoubleClick, along with almost all other ad networks, deposited its cookie whenever a user visited a webpage that contained an ad served by DoubleClick (unless, of course, the

request from the user's browser contained an existing DoubleClick cookie). In contrast, Google's ad network, AdSense, discussed in chapter 4, was much more sparing in its use of cookies, depositing a Google cookie only if the user clicked on an AdSense ad. When Google bought DoubleClick in 2008, it shifted to the latter's more expansive practices (Levy 2011: 334).

## Chapter 4 Hacking the System

1 As noted in chapter 1, there are most likely over two trillion ad auctions a day in total (see chapter 1, note 1, for the source and plausibility of that estimate). The number of in-app display auctions is now roughly equal to those of Web-display auctions (Paparo 2024a). We have no reliable estimate of, for example, the number of video/connected TV auctions, but it is most likely substantially lower. We are therefore estimating, probably conservatively, that a quarter of the two trillion are Web-display auctions.
2 Leonard (2024) reports that Google Search serves around 5.6 billion ads daily, which equates to one ad per day per internet user globally (see chapter 1, note 1). That seems likely to be an underestimate, even though, e.g., Google is not the leading search engine in Russia, and is partially blocked in China. Google Search, however, auctions multiple ad impressions in a single auction.
3 Two segments of Kawaja's talk are still available at https://www.youtube.com/watch?v=1oNBMCgxXf4, and they are what we are quoting in this and the next paragraph.
4 We owe this reference to Crain (2021: 141).
5 DART was the acronym of Dynamic Advertising Reporting and Targeting. Some publishers in 2007 were still using a version of DoubleClick's publisher's ad server called DART Enterprise, soon to be discontinued, which ran in their own computer rooms. DoubleClick also offered an advertiser's ad server, also re-engineered by Google, but for simplicity we do not discuss advertisers' ad servers.
6 DFP and AdX are now component parts of Google Ad Manager, but for simplicity we use those names throughout.

7 The reason why more than one bid is sometimes forwarded is that the highest bid might not always be successful, for example because the corresponding ad would violate "competitive separation": a publisher's undertaking, for example, not to show ads for Coca-Cola and Pepsi on the same webpage.
8 For clarity, we ignore complications such as whether more than one bid is forwarded at each stage.
9 A recording of the debate is available at https://www.youtube.com/watch?v=suszUQMJz3I
10 CMA (2020, appendix M: 109–10) describes why this is difficult.
11 Amazon's system, as far as we can tell, takes a hybrid form: the auction is triggered by the user's device but conducted by an Amazon server.
12 For an SSP to "de-duplicate" the flood of incoming ad requests is not straightforward, and would itself be a carbon-emitting computation. For the reason discussed below, it may not even be in the SSP's individual economic interest to do that.
13 See chapter 1, note 1, for why we think this is a plausible estimate.
14 The classic statement of the problem of collective action is Olson (1965). There is now an extensive literature on the topic, but for us to discuss it would divert us from the main themes of this book.
15 A small number of very large, elite publishers have been able stop selling their ad slots in the open marketplace, but withdrawing in this way from the megamachine is not an economically viable option for most publishers.
16 In Alphabet's financial reports, Google's display-ad revenue, such as from DFP and AdX, comes within a single aggregate heading, "Google Network." In 2023, Network advertising revenue was US$31 billion, a very large sum for most corporations, but only 13% of Alphabet's ad income, and slightly less than YouTube ad revenues. Search made up 74% of ad revenue (Alphabet Inc. 2024: 35).

## Chapter 5 Enfolding Your Phone

1. Sixty-one percent of smartphones in the United States are iPhones (Whitney 2024). For Apple's datacenters, see Apple Inc. (2024).
2. Ads are also often shown to people who have installed a game or other app but stopped playing/using it in the hope that they will return. The Apple privacy measures discussed below also disrupted this by making the targeting of ads to such people much harder.
3. For this basic constraint, see Nieborg (2017).
4. The course is "Modern Mobile Marketing at Scale": https://www.learn-mobile-marketing.com
5. On the heterogeneity of the data that platforms collect, and the way in which it goes beyond what Prey (2018: 1092) calls "fixed markers of identity," see, e.g., Cheney-Lippold (2017), Fisher and Mehozay (2019), and Prey (2018).
6. There is a useful discussion of the use in advertising of custom and look-alike audiences in Beauvisage et al. (2023).
7. A typical procedure was for the user's tap on an ad not to take them directly to the relevant app store, where they can install the app being advertised but via a mobile measurement platform. Such a platform is operated by a specialist firm that helps advertisers and ad networks measure the efficacy of their ads. That platform can then capture data about the ad and tap (including, at least prior to the Apple changes discussed later in this chapter, the IDFA or GAID of the phone in question). If the user shown the ad then installs the app, the latter reported the phone's IDFA or GAID and any subsequent app events to the measurement platform, so enabling it to connect up the ad, the install, and, e.g., subsequent in-app purchases.
8. The first mechanism is a "suppression list." An ad network will often offer a games studio or other app developer a fixed "cost per install," which simplifies their financial planning. There was and is, however, frequently a quid pro quo. In the words of interviewee DD, the ad network would say to the studio, "if you want me to ... sell you installs, you can't waste my money by [me] serving ads to people" who have already installed your game. So the ad

network would ask for a list of the IDFAs or GAIDs of all the game's existing users' phones (a "suppression list") on which ads would then not be shown. Such a list is a potentially very valuable addition to an ad network's data iceberg. The second mechanism is specific to what in chapter 6 we will call "walled gardens," such as the big social media platforms, and was described to us by interviewees DC and DR. Walled gardens' systems internally connect up ads and app installs, the latter via a "software development kit" that app developers add to their apps, which enables the gardens to produce their own measures of ads' efficacy (for this reason, participants often refer to walled gardens as "self-attributing networks"). If the advertiser is using a mobile measurement platform, as described in the previous note, that platform cannot itself directly measure the efficacy of walled-garden advertising. It has to send the walled garden's system the IDFA or GAID of each install that is reported to it, and ask that system whether it showed the relevant ad on the phone in question, so potentially increasing the system's accumulation of IDFA- and GAID-linked data.

9  In digital advertising, the term "deterministic" is often used to refer to high probability, not complete certainty. For example, one participant in a webinar we attended in January 2024 said, "we no longer expect deterministic attribution with 95% certainty."

10  Interviewee DD expressed this bid as a CPM (cost per mille) (per 1,000 ads), so the actual cost to the advertiser of showing the ad would be five cents, but that, as he says, is "very expensive in digital media considering the volumes [of ads]." A normal bid would be a small fraction of a cent.

11  Your tap assigns a value (*authorized* or *denied*) to the iOS/Swift variable *authorizationStatus*.

12  The history of the Facebook/Meta stock price can be found at: https://investor.fb.com/stock-info/

13  For details, see Friedman (2022).

14  SKAN is discussed in McGuigan, Sivan-Sevilla, Parham, and Shvartzshnaider (2023: 12–13).

15 Because cookies are a Web technology not available to mobile-phone apps, the "cookie phase-out" controversy did not involve the Android Privacy Sandbox, which did not become part of the CMA process.

## Chapter 6 Digital Advertising's Tensions

1 On matters of concern, see Latour (2004) and, for example, Geiger et al. (2014).
2 Two other market arrangements that we do not discuss to avoid making the book too complicated are direct deals between advertisers and publishers, and "private marketplaces," which employ open-marketplace mechanisms but allow only pre-selected participants to use them.
3 There is an English translation of this interview (Deleuze 1995).
4 Hennion and Méadel (1989) did not distinguish between mediators and intermediaries, but their notion of "mediation" – elaborated by Hennion in other contributions to the sociology of culture – may have influenced Latour's and Callon's.
5 On transparency, see Ananny and Crawford (2018).
6 In a footnote to his discussion of intermediaries and mediators, Latour (2005: 59) acknowledges the influence of his and others' earlier sociological/ethnographic studies of scientific laboratories and experiments in showing the mediated complexities of scientists' relations to "nature" in even "the most formatted settings of natural sciences." See, especially, Latour and Woolgar (1979).
7 For Callon, a "market encounter" is not always, and perhaps not usually, an interaction between human beings. For example, interactions of customers with supermarket shelves, their contents, and shopping carts are market encounters.
8 Caliskan and Callon (2010: 14) note that "organizing and framing [market encounters] is the product of the activity of mediators (we prefer this word to the less dynamic term 'intermediary,' since the idea of mediation stresses active participation in producing an outcome)." A recent use of the intermediary/mediator distinction

is by Goodchild and Ferrari (2024), who usefully apply it to property platforms such as Rightmove.

9   A similar study by the US Association of National Advertisers (ANA 2023) found that all costs could be traced in cases in which full log-level data on ad impressions was available. However, only 21 of the 67 corporations that wanted to take part in the study were able to do so; the remainder were not able to secure access to log-level data on the ad impressions they had bought.

10  The early Web portals, such as Yahoo and America Online, touched on in chapter 2, were also, at least to a degree, walled gardens. Today's big retailers (Amazon, and also, e.g., Tesco or Walmart) also operate walled gardens and directly sell advertising opportunities within them to advertisers, rather than sending ad requests out to the open marketplace. We will briefly discuss retail walled gardens in chapter 7.

11  As noted in chapter 2, these code snippets were originally implemented via tiny, transparent, single-pixel images on webpages. Although that would now be regarded as "old tech" (AC), the name has stuck.

12  Given the importance of Meta's auctions, it is remarkable how few sources there seem to be on them. Best is Sodomka (2015), a reference we owe to Viljoen, Goldenfein, and McGuigan (2021: 7), but see also Metz (2015) and Boyd and Sanchez (2018).

13  The one exception to this opacity in the academic literature of which we are aware is Vijoen et al. (2021: 3), who note that Facebook uses a Vickrey–Clarke–Groves auction, while Google Search employs "generalized second-price" auctions. The latter are simpler to understand but not theoretically optimal.

14  https://www.facebook.com/business/news/insights/boost-liquidity-and-work-smarter-with-machine-learning

15  In Ads Manager, the interface to Facebook's ads system that it makes available to advertising practitioners, an "ad set" is a subgroup of ads within a specific advertising campaign that share, e.g., a common budget allocation and intended audience.

16 https://en-gb.facebook.com/business/help/1153577308409919?id=1858550721111595 We owe the reference to Seufert (2024b).
17 https://adalytics.io/blog/search-partners-transparency

**Chapter 7 Conclusion**
1 See, for example, Callon (2021: 357–62).
2 See, for example, Meehan (1984), Ang (1991), and Napoli (2003, 2010). Smythe's (1977) article on the "audience commodity," with which we ended chapter 1 – along with the debate that article provoked (see, e.g., Murdock 1978, Jhally 1982, and Bermejo 2009) – was an important inspiration of work of this kind.
3 Nielsen, for example, is now combining its panel-based data with digital-advertising-style "big data" from streaming services.
4 In the United Kingdom, for example, there are sharp concerns over whether the traditional broadcast channels that are subject to the United Kingdom's legally enforceable "public service broadcasting obligations" are becoming difficult for viewers to find.
5 See, especially, O'Neil (2017). Other relevant work includes Seamster and Charron-Chénier (2017), who suggest that the rise of for-profit colleges, which have a much bigger share of the pool of Black undergraduates than of white, is a potential explanation for Black households' student debts having risen faster than white (on which see also Zaloom 2022: ch. 5). Such colleges, as O'Neil (2017) points out, often advertise extensively. A different example is Carter and Eger's finding that "tactics commonly thought to increase [social media] engagement metrics" are used by the convenors of "groups focused on prizes and giveaways" to increase the visibility of those groups and help drive traffic to external ad-supported websites, with the effect of increasing "the probability that users would reveal personal information, identities and experiences, including detailed descriptions of debt, unemployment and homelessness" (Carter and Eger 2021: 377, 383). Interviewee DH suggests that the social media ads that bring made-for-advertising sites their audience are cheap (which is necessary for those sites' "arbitrage" to be profitable) because they are shown to people who

are not in the market to buy anything, perhaps because they lack the money to do so and may be using social media simply because they are bored. So the platform's system is not targeting them on behalf of direct-response advertisers with products to sell.
6 On stickiness, see Hindman (2018).
7 Classic discussions of lock-in include Arthur (1989) and David (1992). Stickiness (see the previous note) can also be seen as a form of soft lock-in.
8 Power and money are often regarded as conceptually separate, for example, by Parsons (1967). His way of separating them, however, rests upon a definition of power too strongly inflected by his "functionalist" sociology: see below. Barnes, on whom we draw below, is right to point out that "[a]ccess to goods and services is access to power. . . . When we speak of 'purchasing-power' it is no metaphor" (1988: 82).
9 The classic sociological discussion of the importance of invisible forms of power is by Steven Lukes: see, e.g., Lukes (2021).
10 On the relationship between the literatures on infrastructures and platforms and the increasing real-world blurring of the two categories, see Plantin et al. (2018).
11 We owe the reference to Poell, Nieborg, and Duffy (2022: 1392).
12 Whether the agreement *actually* requires this is contested: see Stacey and Waters (2024).
13 The discussion of power in which discretion is most prominent is by Barnes (1988). Although his overall theoretical position is not at all Parsonian, he does define "the power of a society" as "its capacity for action." Power in that sense, however, is widely diffused: "capacity for action . . . is actually right down there amongst the supposedly powerless." Social power, however, "is *possessed* by those with discretion in the direction of social action," and "discretion in use . . . is strongly concentrated at the higher levels of society" (Barnes 1988: 58, 63; emphasis in original). Barnes's focus, however, is human actors (individual or collective), and the extension of the notion of "discretion" to the other-than-human

actors of actor-network theory introduces complexities that we cannot address here.

14 See van Dijck, Nieborg, and Poell (2019: 4) and also, for example, Chen (2021).
15 That court's Washington, DC location means that it is often the venue for cases involving the Federal government and its agencies.
16 Rockefeller persuaded the owners of companies operating competing oil refineries to transfer their shares to his Standard Oil Trust in exchange for part ownership of the latter (Orbach and Rebling 2012).

# References

Activision Blizzard. 2023. "Celebrating 20 Years of Gaming Excellence: King's Milestone Journey." Available at https://investor.activision.com/news-releases/news-release-details/celebrating-20-years-gaming-excellence-kings-milestone-journey

Adalytics. 2024. "'AI' Brand Safety Technology." Available at https://adalytics.io/blog/ai-brand-safety

Alaimo, Cristina and Kallinikos, Jannis. 2018. "Objects, Metrics and Practices: An Inquiry into the Programmatic Advertising Ecosystem," in Ulrike Schultze et al. (eds.), *Living with Monsters? Social Implications of Algorithmic Phenomena, Hybrid Agency, and the Performativity of Technology (IS&O 2018)*. Cham, Switzerland: Springer, pp. 110–23.

Alphabet Inc. 2024. "2023 Annual Report." Available at https://abc.xyz/investor/

ANA. 2023. "ANA Programmatic Media Supply Chain Transparency Study: First Look." Association of National Advertisers, June 19. Available at https://www.ana.net/miccontent/show/id/rr-2023-06-ana-programmatic-transparency-first-look

Ananny, Mike and Crawford, Kate. 2018. "Seeing without Knowing: Limitations of the Transparency Ideal and its Application to Algorithmic Accountability." *New Media & Society* 20(3): 973–89.

# References

Ananthanarayanan, Rajagopal, et al. 2013. "Photon: Fault-Tolerant and Scalable Joining of Continuous Data Streams." Available at https://dl-acm-org.eux.idm.oclc.org/doi/pdf/10.1145/2463676.2465272

Ang, Ien. 1991. *Desperately Seeking the Audience*. London: Routledge.

Angel, María P. and boyd, danah. 2024. "Techno-legal Solutionism: Regulating Children's Online Safety in the United States." Available at https://doi.org/10.1145/3614407.3643705

Anon. 2023. "Game Industry Layoffs." Available at https://publish.obsidian.md/vg-layoffs/Archive/2023

Apple Inc. n.d. "User Privacy and Data Use." Available at https://developer.apple.com/app-store/user-privacy-and-data-use/

Apple Inc.. 2023. "App Store Developers Generated $1.1 Trillion in Total Billings and Sales in the App Store Ecosystem in 2022." May 31. Available at https://www.apple.com/newsroom/2023/05/developers-generated-one-point-one-trillion-in-the-app-store-ecosystem-in-2022/

Apple Inc.. 2024. "Environmental Progress Report: Fiscal Year 2023." Available at https://www.apple.com/environment/pdf/Apple_Environmental_Progress_Report_2024.pdf

Arthur, Charles. 2010. "Apple Faces Suit over App Privacy Leaks." *The Guardian*, December 29. Available at https://www.theguardian.com/technology/2010/dec/29/apple-lawsuit-breach-of-privacy#:~:text=Apple's%20rules%20for%20applications%20says,the%20data%20will%20be%20used.%22

Arthur, W. Brian. 1989. "Competing Technologies, Increasing Returns, and Lock-In by Historical Events." *Economic Journal* 99(394): 116–31. Available at https://www.jstor.org/stable/2234208

Auletta, Ken. 2009. *Googled: The End of the World As We Know It*. London: Virgin.

Barnes, Barry. 1988. *The Nature of Power*. Cambridge: Polity.

Barroso, Luiz André, Dean, Jeffrey, and Hölzle, Urs. 2003. "Web Search for a Planet: The Google Cluster Architecture" *IEEE Micro* 23(2): 22–8.

Barroso, Luiz André and Hölzle, Urs. 2009. *The Datacenter as a Computer: An Introduction to the Design of Warehouse-Scale Machines.* Williston, VT: Morgan & Claypool.

Barry, Andrew. 2013. *Material Politics: Disputes Along the Pipeline.* Chichester, West Sussex: Wiley.

Battelle, John. 2005. *The Search: How Google and Its Rivals Rewrote the Rules of Business and Transformed Our Culture.* London: Brealey.

Bazeley, Michael. 2005. "Google Buying Web Analytics Company." *Mercury News*, March 28. Available at https://web.archive.org/web/20161109140133/http://www.siliconbeat.com/entries/2005/03/28/google_buying_web_analytics_company.html

Beauvisage, Thomas. 2023. "Sociologie du Cookie Publicitaire." Habilitation thesis: Université Paris Sciences et Lettres.

Beauvisage, Thomas, Beuscart, Jean-Samuel, Coavoux, Samuel, and Mellet, Kevin. 2023. "How Online Advertising Targets Consumers: The Uses of Categories and Algorithmic Tools by Audience Planners." *New Media & Society*. Early online.

Becker, Howard S. 1973. *Outsiders: Studies in the Sociology of Deviance.* New York: Free Press.

Bell, Emily. 2021."Do Technology Companies Care About Journalism?" in Anya Schiffrin (ed.), *Media Capture: How Money, Digital Platforms, and Governments Control the News.* New York: Columbia University Press, pp. 291–6.

Bender, Emily M., Gebru, Timnit, McMillan-Major, Angelina, and Shmitchell, Shmargaret. 2021. "On the Dangers of Stochastic Parrots: Can Language Models Be Too Big?" Available at https://dl.acm.org/doi/10.1145/3442188.3445922

Benes, Ross. 2017. "'I Just Wanted to Organize This Mess': An Oral History of the Lumascape." *Digiday*, September 12. Available at https://digiday.com/marketing/just-wanted-organize-mess-oral-history-lumascape/

Bensman, Joseph. 1967. *Dollars and Sense: Ideology, Ethics, and the Meaning of Work in Profit and Nonprofit Organizations.* New York: Macmillan.

Bermejo, Fernando. 2009. "Audience Manufacture in Historical Perspective: From Broadcasting to Google." *New Media & Society* 11(1 and 2): 133–54.

Berners-Lee, Tim. 1989–90. "Information Management: A Proposal." Available at https://cds.cern.ch/record/369245/files/dd-89-001.pdf

Berners-Lee, Tim. 2010. "Long Live the Web." *Scientific American* 303(6): 80–5. Available at https://www.jstor.org/stable/26002308

Beuscart, Jean-Samuel and Mellet, Kevin. 2008. "Business Models of the Web 2.0: Advertising or The Tale of Two Stories." *Communications & Strategies* (November): 165–81. Available at https://sciencespo.hal.science/hal-03459866/file/2008-beuscart-mellet-business-models-of-the-web-2-0.pdf

Beuscart, Jean-Samuel and Mellet, Kevin. 2013. "Competing Quality Conventions in the French Online Display Advertising Market." *Journal of Cultural Economy* 6(4): 402–18.

Birch, Kean. 2023. *Data Enclaves*. Cham, Switzerland: Palgrave Macmillan.

Boczkowski, Pablo. 2005. *Digitizing the News: Innovation in Online Newspapers*. Cambridge, MA: MIT Press.

Bogost, Ian and Madrigal, Alexis. 2020. "How Facebook Works for Trump." *The Atlantic*, April. Available at https://www.theatlantic.com/technology/archive/2020/04/how-facebooks-ad-technology-helps-trump-win/606403/

Boyd, Clark and Sanchez, Ximena. 2018. "Breaking Down the Facebook Auction." *Journal of Digital & Social Media Marketing* 6(2): 160–7. Available at https://www.ingentaconnect.com/contentone/hsp/jdsmm/2018/00000006/00000002/art00009

Braun, Benjamin. 2020. "Central Banking and the Infrastructural Power of Finance: The Case of ECB Support for Repo and Securitization Markets." *Socio-Economic Review* 18(2): 395–418.

Brin, Sergey and Page, Lawrence. 1998a. "The Anatomy of a Large-Scale Hypertextual Web Search Engine." Available at https://infolab.stanford.edu/pub/papers/google.pdf

Brin, Sergey and Page, Lawrence. 1998b. "The Anatomy of a Large-Scale Hypertextual Web Search Engine." *Computer Networks* 30: 107–17.

Brockhoff, Julia, Jéhanno, Bertrand, Pozzato, Vera, Buhr, Carl-Christian, Eberl, Peter, and Papandropoulos, Penelope. 2008. "Google/DoubleClick: The First Test for the Commission's Non-Horizontal Merger Guidelines." Available at https://web.archive.org/web/20220901040723/https://ec.europa.eu/competition/publications/cpn/2008_2_53.pdf

Bruns, Axel. 2019. "After the 'APIcalypse': Social Media Platforms and Their Fight Against Critical Scholarly Research." *Information, Communication & Society* 22(11): 1544–66.

Bryan, Kenza, Hodgson, Camilla, and Tauschinski, Jana. 2024. "The Battle Over Disclosing Pollution." *Financial Times*, August 14: 21. Available at https://ft.pressreader.com/v99f/20240814/281741274726840

Bucher, Taina. 2018. *If . . . Then: Algorithmic Power and Politics*. Oxford: Oxford University Press.

Burns, Tom. 1961. "Micropolitics: Mechanisms of Institutional Change." *Administrative Science Quarterly* 6(3): 257–81. Available at https://www.jstor.org/stable/2390703

Burrell, Jenna and Fourcade, Marion. 2021. "The Society of Algorithms." *Annual Review of Sociology* 47: 213–37. D

Caliskan, Koray. 2009. "The Meaning of Price in World Markets." *Journal of Cultural Economy* 2(3): 239–68.

Caliskan, Koray and Callon, Michel. 2009. "Economization, Part 1: Shifting Attention from the Economy towards Processes of Economization." *Economy and Society* 38(3): 369–98.

Caliskan, Koray and Callon, Michel. 2010. "Economization, Part 2: A Research Programme for the Study of Markets." *Economy and Society* 39(1): 1–32.

Caliskan, Koray, Callon, Michel, and MacKenzie, Donald. Forthcoming. *Economization: Markets, Platforms, and Ecologies*. New York: Columbia University Press.

Caliskan, Koray, MacKenzie, Donald, and Callon, Michel. 2024. "Stacked Economization: A Research Programme for the Study of Platforms." *Journal of Cultural Economy*. Early online. DOI: 10.1080/17530350.2024.2423687

Caliskan, Koray, MacKenzie, Donald, and Rommerskirchen, Charlotte. 2024. "Strange Bedfellows: Consumer Protection and Competition Policy in the Making of the EU Privacy Regime." *Journal of Common Market Studies* 62(5): 1296–313.

Callon, Michel (ed.). 1998. *The Laws of the Markets*. Oxford: Blackwell.

Callon, Michel. 2007. "What Does It Mean to Say that Economics is Performative?" in Donald MacKenzie, Fabian Muniesa, and Lucia Siu (eds.), *Do Economists Make Markets? On the Performativity of Economics*. Princeton, NJ: Princeton University Press, pp. 311–57.

Callon, Michel. 2021. *Markets in the Making: Rethinking Competition, Goods, and Innovation*. Brooklyn, NY: Zone.

Callon, Michel and Latour, Bruno. 1981. "Unscrewing the Big Leviathan: How Actors Macro-Structure Reality and How Sociologists Help Them to do So," in Karin Knorr Cetina and A. V. Cicourel (eds.), *Advances in Social Theory and Methodology: Toward an Integration of Micro- and Macro-Sociologies*. Boston: Routledge and Kegan Paul, pp. 277–303.

Caminade, Juliette and Borck, Jonathan. 2023. "The Continued Growth and Resilience of Apple's App Store Ecosystem." Analysis Group, May. Available at https://www.apple.com/newsroom/pdfs/the-continued-growth-and-resilience-of-apples-app-store-ecosystem.pdf

Canales, Jimena. 2009. *A Tenth of a Second: A History*. Chicago: University of Chicago Press.

Carter, Daniel and Eger, Elizabeth K. 2021. "Visibility and Vulnerability in Online Marketing Practices." *Journal of Cultural Economy* 14(4): 373–87.

Chafkin, Max. 2007. "How to Kill a Great Idea!" *Inc.*, June 1. Available at https://www.inc.com/magazine/20070601/features-how-to-kill-a-great-idea.html

Chavez, Anthony. 2024. "A New Path for Privacy Sandbox on the Web," July 22. Available at https://privacysandbox.com/news/privacy-sandbox-update/

Chen, Jiahong. 2021. *Regulating Online Behavioural Advertising through Data Protection Law*. Cheltenham, UK: Elgar.

Cheney-Lippold, John. 2017. *We Are Data: Algorithms and the Making of our Digital Selves*. New York: New York University Press.

Chowdhry, Amit. 2017. "How Jeff Green Took the Trade Desk from a Simple Idea to a Programmatic Ad Giant." *Forbes*, December 12. Available at https://www.forbes.com/sites/amitchowdhry/2017/12/12/how-jeff-green-took-the-trade-desk-from-a-simple-idea-to-a-programmatic-ad-giant

Cluley, Robert. 2018. "The Construction of Marketing Measures: The Case of Viewability." *Marketing Theory* 18(3): 287–305.

Cluley, Robert. 2020. "The Politics of Consumer Data." *Marketing Theory* 20(1): 45–63.

Cluley, Robert. 2025. *Marketing Science Fictions: An Ethnography of Marketing Analytics, Consumer Insight and Data Science*. Bristol: Bristol University Press.

Cluley, Robert and Brown, Stephen D. 2015. "The Dividualised Consumer: Sketching the New Mask of the Consumer." *Journal of Marketing Management* 31(1–2): 107–22.

CMA. 2020. "Online Platforms and Digital Advertising: Market Study Final Report." UK Competition and Markets Authority, July 1. Available at https://www.gov.uk/cma-cases/online-platforms-and-digital-advertising-market-study

CMA. 2021. "Notice of Intention to Accept Commitments Offered by Google in Relation to its Privacy Sandbox Proposals: Case Number 50972." UK Competition and Markets Authority, June 11. Available at https://assets.publishing.service.gov.uk/government/uploads/system/uploads/attachment_data/file/992975/Notice_of_intention_to_accept_binding_commitments_offered_by_Google_publication.pdf

Cochoy, Franck. 2002. *Une sociologie du packaging, ou l'âne de Buridan face au marché*. Paris: Presses Universitaires de France.

Cochoy, Franck. 2007. "A Sociology of Market-Things: On Tending the Garden of Choices in Mass Retailing," in Fabian Muniesa,

Yuval Millo, and Michel Callon (eds.), *Market Devices*. Oxford: Blackwell, pp. 109–29.

Cochoy, Franck, Trompette, Pascale, and Araujo, Luis. 2016. "From Market Agencements to Market Agencing: An Introduction." *Consumption Markets & Culture* 19(1): 3–16.

Crain, Matthew. 2021. *Profit Over Privacy: How Surveillance Advertising Conquered the Internet*. Minneapolis, MN: University of Minnesota Press.

Crain, Matthew and Nadler, Anthony. 2019. "Political Manipulation and Internet Advertising Infrastructure." *Journal of Information Policy* 9: 370–410.

Cronin, Anne M. 2004. "Regimes of Mediation: Advertising Practitioners as Cultural Intermediaries?" *Consumption Markets & Culture* 7(4): 349–69.

Crupi, Anthony. 2011. "How TV Got Sold: One Bourbon, One Scotch, and One Beer. The Art of Selling in the Upfront's Early Years." *AdWeek*, May 9. Available at https://www.adweek.com/brand-marketing/how-tv-got-sold-131385/

Curry, David. 2025. "Android Statistics (2025)," February 17. Available at https://www.businessofapps.com/data/android-statistics

data.ai. 2024. "State of Mobile 2024: The Industry's Leading Report." Available at https://sensortower.com/state-of-mobile-2024

David, Paul A. 1992. "Heroes, Herds and Hysteresis in Technological History: Thomas Edison and 'The Battle of the Systems' Reconsidered." *Industrial and Corporate Change* 1(1): 129–80.

Dean, Jeff. 2010. "Building Software Systems At Google and Lessons Learned." Talk at Stanford University, September 10. Available at https://www.youtube.com/watch?v=modXC5IWTJI

Dean, Jeffrey and Ghemawat, Sanjay. 2004. "MapReduce: Simplified Data Processing on Large Clusters." Available at https://research.google/pubs/mapreduce-simplified-data-processing-on-large-clusters/

Deleuze, Gilles. 1985. [Interview conducted by Antoine Dulaure and Claire Parnet]. *L'Autre Journal* 8 (October): 10–22.

Deleuze, Gilles. 1992. "Postscript on the Societies of Control." *October* 59 (Winter): 3–7. Available at https://www.jstor.org/stable/778828

Deleuze, Gilles. 1995. "Mediators." in Gilles Deleuze (ed.), *Negotiations: 1972–1990*. New York: Columbia University Press, pp. 121–34

Dourish, Paul. 2017. *The Stuff of Bits: An Essay on the Materialities of Information*. Cambridge, MA: MIT Press.

Duffy, Brooke Erin, Ononye, Anuli, and Sawey, Megan. 2024. "The Politics of Vulnerability in the Influencer Economy." *European Journal of Cultural Studies* 27(3): 352–70.

du Gay, Paul and Pryke, Michael (eds.). 2002. *Cultural Economy: Cultural Analysis and Commercial Life*. London: Sage.

Duhigg, Charles. 2024. "Silicon Valley, The New Lobbying Monster." *New Yorker*, October 7. Available at https://www.newyorker.com/magazine/2024/10/14/silicon-valley-the-new-lobbying-monster

Edelman, Benjamin, Ostrovsky, Michael, and Schwarz, Michael. 2007. "Internet Advertising and the Generalized Second-Price Auction: Selling Billions of Dollars Worth of Keywords." *American Economic Review* 97(1): 242–59.

Edwards, Douglas. 2011. *I'm Feeling Lucky: The Confessions of Google Employee Number 59*. New York: Houghton Mifflin Harcourt.

Elder-Vass, Dave. 2016. *Profit and Gift in the Digital Economy*. Cambridge: Cambridge University Press.

European Parliament and Council. 2022. "Regulation (EU) 2022/1925." *Official Journal of the European Union* 65 (October 12). Available at http://data.europa.eu/eli/reg/2022/1925/oj

Eyal, Gil. 2013. "For a Sociology of Expertise: The Social Origins of the Autism Epidemic." *American Journal of Sociology* 118(4): 863–907.

Facebook Inc. 2020. [Ad attacking Apple]. *Financial Times*, December 17: 7. Available at https://www.macrumors.com/2020/12/16/facebook-takes-out-full-page-ads-to-attack-apple/

Federal Trade Commission. 2023. "United States District Court, Western District of Washington, Case No. 2:23-cv-01495: Complaint," September 26. Available at https://www.ftc.gov/sys

tem/files/ftc_gov/pdf/1910129AmazoneCommerceComplaintPublic.pdf

Fiegerman, Seth. 2014. "Friendster Founder Tells His Side of the Story, 10 Years After Facebook." *Mashable*, February 3. Available at https://mashable.com/archive/jonathan-abrams-friendster-facebook

Fisher, Eran and Mehozay, Yoav. 2019. "How Algorithms See Their Audience: Media Epistemes and the Changing Conception of the Individual." *Media, Culture & Society* 41(8): 1176–91.

Flensburg, Sophie and Lai, Signe Sophus. 2023. "Follow the Data! A Strategy for Tracing Infrastructural Power." *Media and Communication* 11(2): 319–29.

Fourcade, Marion and Healy, Kieran. 2024. *The Ordinal Society*. Cambridge, MA: Harvard University Press.

Fourcade, Marion and Kluttz, Daniel N. 2020. "A Maussian Bargain: Accumulation by Gift in the Digital Economy." *Big Data & Society* 7(1): 1–16.

Friedman, Eran. 2022. "The Ultimate Guide to SKAdNetwork Privacy Thresholds," May 25. Available at https://www.singular.net/blog/skadnetwork-privacy-threshold/

Frier, Sarah. 2020. *No Filter: How Instagram Transformed Business, Celebrity and Culture*. London: Random House.

Fuentes, Christian and Sörum, Niklas. 2019. "Agencing Ethical Consumers: Smartphone Apps and the Socio-Material Reconfiguration of Everyday Life." *Consumption Markets & Culture* 22(2): 131–56.

García Martínez, Antonio. 2016. *Chaos Monkeys: Obscene Fortune and Random Failure in Silicon Valley*. New York: Harper.

Garfinkel, Simon. 1996. "Browser Cookies are Persistent, Not Necessarily Evil." *Wired*, December 11. Available at https://www.wired.com/1996/12/browser-cookies-are-persistent-not-necessarily-evil/

Geiger, Susi, Harrison, Debbie, Kjellberg, Hans, and Mallard, Alexandre (eds.). 2014. *Concerned Markets: Economic Ordering for Multiple Values*. Cheltenham, UK: Elgar.

Geiger, Susi, Mason, Katy, Pollock, Neil, et al. (eds.). 2024. *Market Studies: Mapping, Theorizing and Impacting Market Action*. Cambridge: Cambridge University Press.

Gillespie, Tarleton. 2018. *Custodians of the Internet: Platforms, Content Moderation, and the Hidden Decisions that Shape Social Media*. New Haven, CN: Yale University Press.

Goldman, David. 2012. "Microsoft's $6 billion Whoopsie." *CNN*, July 12. Available at https://money.cnn.com/2012/07/02/technology/microsoft-aquantive/index.html

Goodchild, Barry and Ferrari, Ed. 2024. "Intermediaries and Mediators: An Actor-Network Understanding of Online Property Platforms." *Housing Studies* 39(1): 102–23.

Google Inc. 2009. "The DoubleClick Ad Exchange: Growing the Display Advertising Pie for Everyone." September 17. Available at https://googleblog.blogspot.com/2009/09/doubleclick-ad-exchange-growing-display.html

Google LLC. n.d. "Search Quality Rater Guidelines: An Overview." Available at https://services.google.com/fh/files/misc/hsw-sqrg.pdf

Google LLC. 2020. "Online Platforms and Digital Advertising: Comments on the Market Study Interim Report." Available at https://assets.publishing.service.gov.uk/media/5e8c8290d3bf7f1fb7b91c2c/200212_Google_response_to_interim_report.pdf

Greenstein, Shane. 2015. *How the Internet Became Commercial: Innovation, Privatization, and the Birth of a New Network*. Princeton, NJ: Princeton University Press.

Hamburger, Tom and Gold, Matea. 2014. "Google, Once Disdainful of Lobbying, Now a Master of Washington Influence." *Washington Post*, April 12. Available at https://www.washingtonpost.com/politics/how-google-is-transforming-power-and-politicsgoogle-once-disdainful-of-lobbying-now-a-master-of-washington-influence/2014/04/12/51648b92-b4d3-11e3-8cb6-284052554d74_story.html

Heath, Teresa, Cluley, Robert, and O'Malley, Robert. 2017. "Beating, Ditching and Hiding: Consumers' Everyday Resistance to Marketing." *Journal of Marketing Management* 33(15–16): 1281–303.

Hennion, Antoine and Méadel, Cécile. 1989. "The Artisans of Desire: The Mediation of Advertising between Product and Consumer." *Sociological Theory* 7(2): 191–209.

Hercher, James. 2021. "How Facebook is Overhauling its Attribution Standards to Deal with Apple's ATT." Available at https://www.adexchanger.com/mobile/how-facebook-is-overhauling-its-attribution-standards-to-deal-with-apples-att/

Hercher, James. 2022. "Facebook Advertisers are Itching for Change as Bugs Infest its Attribution Tech." Available at https://www.adexchanger.com/platforms/facebook-advertisers-are-itching-for-change-as-bugs-infest-its-attribution-tech/

Hessler, Jennifer. 2021. "Peoplemeter Technologies and the Biometric Turn in Audience Measurement." *Television & New Media* 22(4): 400–19.

Hindman, Matthew. 2018. *The Internet Trap: How the Digital Economy Builds Monopolies and Undermines Democracy*. Princeton, NJ: Princeton University Press.

Humphrey, Caroline and Hugh-Jones, Stephen. 1992. "Introduction: Barter, Exchange and Value," in Caroline Humphrey and Stephen Hugh-Jones (eds.), *Barter, Exchange and Value: An Anthropological Approach*. Cambridge: Cambridge University Press, pp. 1–20.

Hwang, Tim. 2020. *Subprime Attention Crisis: Advertising and the Time Bomb at the Heart of the Internet*. New York: Farrar, Straus and Giroux.

IAB. 2014. "Viewability Has Arrived: What You Need To Know To See Through This Sea Change." Interactive Advertising Bureau, March 31. Available at https://www.iab.com/news/viewability-has-arrived-what-you-need-to-know-to-see-through-this-sea-change/

IAB. 2022. "Internet Advertising Revenue Report: Full-Year 2021 Results." Available at https://www.iab.com/wp-content/uploads/2022/04/IAB_Internet_Advertising_Revenue_Report_Full_Year_2021.pdf

Iliadis, Andrew and Russo, Federica. 2016. "Critical Data Studies: An Introduction." *Big Data & Society* 3(2): 1–7.

Indergaard, Michael. 2004. *Silicon Alley: The Rise and Fall of a New Media District*. New York: Routledge.

Isaacson, Walter. 2012. "The Real Leadership Lessons of Steve Jobs." *Harvard Business Review* 90(4): 93–102. Available at https://hbr.org/2012/04/the-real-leadership-lessons-of-steve-jobs

ISBA. 2020. "Programmatic Supply Chain Transparency Study." Incorporated Society of British Advertisers, May 6. Available at https://www.isba.org.uk/knowledge/executive-summary-programmatic-supply-chain-transparency-study

Jhally, Sut. 1982. "Probing the Blindspot. The Audience Commodity." *Canadian Journal of Political and Social Theory* 6(1–2): 204–10. Available at https://journals.uvic.ca/index.php/ctheory/article/view/13928/4701

Jobin, Anna and Ziewitz, Malte. 2018. "Organic Search: How Metaphors Help Cultivate the Web." Available at https://www.hiig.de/en/organic-search-metaphors-help-cultivate-web/

Johansson, Simon. 2024. "Minor Tweaks Can Produce Major Environmental Wins for the Advertising Industry." *AdExchanger*, July 8. Available at https://www.adexchanger.com/tag/simon-johansson/

Johnson, Lauren and Rittenhouse, Lindsey. 2022. "Amazon is Building an Advertising Behemoth – and It's Coming for Facebook." *Business Insider*, May 10. Available at https://redef.com/author/5c64a37eb5d039435ad4eb89

Jones, Meg Leta. 2016. *Ctrl+Z: The Right to be Forgotten*. New York: New York University Press.

Jones, Meg Leta. 2019. "The Development of Consent to Computing." *IEEE Annals of the History of Computing* 41(4): 34–47.

Jones, Meg Leta. 2020. "Cookies: A Legacy of Controversy." *Internet Histories* 4(1): 87–104.

Jones, Meg Leta. 2024. *The Character of Consent: The History of Cookies and the Future of Technology Policy*. Cambridge, MA: MIT Press.

Joseph, Daniel and Bishop, Sophie. 2024. "Advertising as Governance: The Digital Commodity Audience and Platform Advertising

Dependency." *Media, Culture & Society*. Early online. Available at https://doi-org.eux.idm.oclc.org/10.1177/01634437241237935

Joseph, Seb. 2024. "GARM and Ad Net Zero Launch New Standards to Transform Carbon Emission Measurement in Media." *Digiday*, June 17. Available at https://digiday.com/marketing/garm-and-ad-net-zero-launch-new-standards-to-transform-carbon-emission-measurement-in-media

Jounce Media. 2023. "The State of the Open Internet: A Data-Driven Perspective on the Forces that will Shape the Ad-Supported Open Internet in 2023." Available at https://static1.squarespace.com/static/553c03d0e4b08cd58585d2ec/t/661d12c197905f1c09f51d96/1713181382054/Jounce+Media+2023+State+Of+The+Open+Internet.pdf

Judiciary Committee, House of Representatives. 2024. "How the World's Biggest Brands Seek to Control Online Speech." Interim Staff Report, July 10. Available at https://judiciary.house.gov/media/press-releases/how-worlds-biggest-brands-seek-control-online-speech

K2 Intelligence. 2016. "An Independent Study of Media Transparency in the US Advertising Industry." Available at https://www.ana.net/content/show/id/industry-initiative-recommendations-report

Kirkpatrick, David. 2011. *The Facebook Effect: The Real Inside Story of Mark Zuckerberg and the World's Fastest Growing Company*. London: Virgin.

Knorr Cetina, Karin. 1999. *Epistemic Cultures: How the Sciences Make Knowledge*. Cambridge, MA: Harvard University Press.

Koetsier, John. 2021. "Apple Rejecting Apps with Fingerprinting Enabled as iOS 14 Privacy Enforcement Starts." *Forbes*, April 1. Available at https://www.forbes.com/sites/johnkoetsier/2021/04/01/apple-rejecting-apps-with-fingerprinting-enabled-as-ios-14-privacy-enforcement-starts/

Koetsier, John. 2024. "Singular's Quarterly Trends Report: Q2 2024," July 31. Available at https://www.singular.net/blog/quarterly-trends-report-q2-2024/

Kotila, Mikko. 2021. "How Much Does an Ad Impression Emit Carbon?" Available at https://medium.com/art-technology/how-much-does-an-ad-impression-emit-carbon-d31daea57184

Kristol, David M. 2001. "HTTP Cookies: Standards, Privacy, and Politics." *ACM Transactions on Internet Technology* 1(2): 151–98.

Lambrecht, Anja and Tucker, Catherine E. 2018. "Algorithmic Bias? An Empirical Study into Apparent Gender-Based Discrimination in the Display of STEM Career Ads." Available at https://ssrn.com/abstract=2852260

Latour, Bruno. 1991. "Technology is Society Made Durable," in John Law (ed.), *A Sociology of Monsters: Essays on Power, Technology and Domination*. London: Routledge, pp. 103–31.

Latour, Bruno. 2004. "Why Has Critique Run out of Steam? From Matters of Fact to Matters of Concern." *Critical Inquiry* 30(2): 225–48.

Latour, Bruno. 2005. *Reassembling the Social: An Introduction to Actor-Network-Theory*. Oxford: Oxford University Press.

Latour, Bruno and Woolgar, Steve. 1979. *Laboratory Life: The Social Construction of Scientific Facts*. Beverly Hill, CA: Sage.

Law, John and Mol, Annemarie. 2008. "Globalisation in Practice: On the Politics of Boiling Pigswill." *Geoforum* 39(1): 133–43.

Lawrence, Mathew and Laybourn-Langton, Laurie. 2018. "The Digital Commonwealth: From Private Enclosure to Collective Benefit." Institute for Public Policy Research. Available at https://ippr-org.files.svdcdn.com/production/Downloads/cej-platforms-sept18.pdf

Lebow, Sara. 2024. "5 Recent Charts Forecasting how Ad Spend is Changing, from Retail Media to Programmatic." Available at https://www.emarketer.com/content/5-recent-charts-on-forecasting-all-things-ad-spend

Lee, Denny. 2002. "Neighborhood Report: Silicon Alley; A Once-Evocative Name Falls Victim to the Bursting of the High-Tech Bubble." *New York Times*, March 24. Available at https://www.nytimes.com/2002/03/24/nyregion/neighborhood-report-silicon-alley-once-evocative-name-falls-victim-bursting-high.html

Leonard, Jay. 2024. "How Many Ads Does Google Serve in a Day?" May 16. Available at https://web.archive.org/web/20240916071035/https://www.business2community.com/online-marketing/how-many-ads-does-google-serve-in-a-day-0322253

Levy, Dan. 2020–21. "Speaking Up for Small Businesses." Available at https://www.facebook.com/business/news/ios-14-apple-privacy-update-impacts-small-business-ads

Levy, Steven. 2011. *In the Plex: How Google Thinks, Works, and Shapes Our Lives*. New York: Simon & Schuster.

Levy, Steven. 2020. *Facebook: The Inside Story*. London: Penguin.

Lewandowski, Dirk, Kerkmann, Friederike, Rümmele, Sandra, and Sünkler, Sebastian. 2018. "An Empirical Investigation on Search Engine Ad Disclosure." *Journal of the Association for Information Science and Technology* 69 (3): 420–37.

Lotz, Amanda D. 2007. "How to Spend $9.3 Billion in Three Days: Examining the Upfront Buying Process in the Production of US Television Culture." *Media, Culture & Society* 29(4): 549–67.

Lukes, Steven. 2021. *Power: A Radical View*. London: Bloomsbury.

MacKenzie, Donald. 1990. *Inventing Accuracy: A Historical Sociology of Nuclear Missile Guidance*. Cambridge, MA: MIT Press.

MacKenzie, Donald. 1996. *Knowing Machines: Essays on Technical Change*. Cambridge, MA: MIT Press.

MacKenzie, Donald. 2006. *An Engine, Not a Camera: How Financial Models Shape Markets*. Cambridge, MA: MIT Press.

MacKenzie, Donald. 2021. *Trading at the Speed of Light: How Ultrafast Algorithms Are Transforming Financial Markets*. Princeton, NJ: Princeton University Press.

MacKenzie, Donald. 2022. "Blink, Bid, Buy." *London Review of Books* 44(9): 21–3. Available at https://www.lrb.co.uk/the-paper/v44/n09/donald-mackenzie/blink-bid-buy

MacKenzie, Donald. 2023. "Short Cuts: A Puff of Carbon Dioxide." *London Review of Books* 45(2): 16. Available at https://www.lrb.co.uk/the-paper/v45/n02/donald-mackenzie/short-cuts

MacKenzie, Donald. 2024. "Hey Big Spender: What Your Smartphone Knows About You." *London Review of Books* 46(16): 25–7. Available at https://www.lrb.co.uk/the-paper/v46/n16/donald-mackenzie/hey-big-spender

MacKenzie, Donald, Caliskan, Koray, and Rommerskirchen, Charlotte. 2023. "The Longest Second: Header Bidding and the Material Politics of Online Advertising." *Economy and Society* 52(3): 554–78.

MacKenzie, Donald and Millo, Yuval. 2003. "Constructing a Market, Performing Theory: The Historical Sociology of a Financial Derivatives Exchange." *American Journal of Sociology* 109(1): 107–45.

MacKenzie, Donald and Wajcman, Judy (eds.). 1999. *The Social Shaping of Technology*. Buckingham, England: Open University Press.

Mann, Michael. 1984. "The Autonomous Power of the State: Its Origins, Mechanisms and Results." *Archives Européennes de Sociologie* 25(2): 185–213. Available at https://www.jstor.org/stable/23999270

Marchiori, Massimo. 1997. "The Quest for Correct Information on the Web: Hyper Search Engines." *Computer Networks and ISDN Systems* 29(8): 1225–35.

Markoff, John and Hansell, Saul. 2006. "Hiding in Plain Sight, Google Seeks More Power." *New York Times*, 14 June. Available at https://www.nytimes.com/2006/06/14/technology/hiding-in-plain-sight-google-seeks-more-power.html

McCambley, Joe. 2013. "Stop Selling Ads and Do Something Useful." *Harvard Business Review*, February. Available at https://hbr.org/2013/02/stop-selling-ads-and-do-someth

McCormick, Myles and Smyth, Jamie. 2024. "Microsoft in Three Mile Island Deal to Power AI." *Financial Times*, September 21–2: 15. Available at https://www.ft.com/content/ddcb5ab6-965f-4034-96e1-7f668bad1801

McCullough, Brian. 2018. *How the Internet Happened: From Netscape to the iPhone*. New York: W. W. Norton.

McDermott, John. 2014. "Google's Display Advertising Dominance Raises Concerns." *Digiday*, December 2. Available at https://digiday

.com/media/google-bundling-ad-tech-inventory-raising-anti-com petitive-concerns/

McFall, Liz. 2004. *Advertising: A Cultural Economy*. London: Sage.

McFall, Liz. 2014. "The Problem of Cultural Intermediaries in the Economy of Qualities," in Jennifer Smith Maguire and Julian Matthews (eds.), *The Cultural Intermediaries Reader*. Thousand Oaks, CA: Sage, pp. 42–51.

McGee, Patrick. 2021. "Snap, Facebook, Twitter and YouTube Lose Nearly $10bn after iPhone Privacy Changes." *Financial Times*, October 31. Available at https://www.ft.com/content/4c19e387-ee1a-41d8-8dd2-bc6c302ee58e

McGowan, Addie, MacKenzie, Donald, and Caliskan, Koray. 2024. "Intermediaries, Mediators and Digital Advertising's Tensions." *Journal of Cultural Economy* 17(5): 513–31.

McGuigan, Lee. 2023. *Selling the American People: Advertising, Optimization, and the Origins of Adtech*. Cambridge, MA: MIT Press.

McGuigan, Lee, Myers West, Sarah, Sivan-Sevilla, Ido, and Parham, Patrick. 2023. "The After Party: Cynical Resignation in Adtech's Pivot to Privacy." *Big Data & Society* 10(2): 1–14.

McGuigan, Lee, Sivan-Sevilla, Ido, Parham, Patrick, and Shvartzshnaider, Yan. 2023. "Private Attributes: The Meanings and Mechanisms of 'Privacy-Preserving' Adtech."*New Media & Society*. Early online. DOI: 10.1177/14614448231213267

McMahan, H. Brendan, et al. 2013. "Ad Click Prediction: A View from the Trenches." DOI: 10.1145/2487575.2488200

Meehan, Eileen R. 1984. "Ratings and the Institutional Approach: A Third Answer to the Commodity Question." *Critical Studies in Mass Communication* 1(2): 216–25.

Mehta, Amit P. 2024. "Memorandum Opinion: US District Court for the District of Columbia: Cases 20-cv-3010 and 2-cv-3715." Available at https://www.adexchanger.com/wp-content/uploads/2024/08/DOJ-Google-search-antitrust-Judge-Amit_Mehta-ruling.pdf

Meisner, Colten, Duffy, Brooke Erin, and Ziewitz, Malte. 2024. "The Labor of Search Engine Evaluation: Making Algorithms More Human or Humans More Algorithmic?" *New Media & Society* 26(2): 1018–33.

Mellet, Kevin. 2025. "Fragile Bridges: Identity Management and the Linked Ecologies of Marketing Technologies (MarTech)." *Journal of Marketing Management*. Early online. DOI: 10.1080/0267257X.2025.2459907

Mellet, Kevin and Beauvisage, Thomas. 2020. "Cookie Monsters: Anatomy of a Digital Market Infrastructure." *Consumption Markets & Culture* 23(2): 110–29.

Meta Platforms Inc. 2024. "Form 1-K (Annual Report)." Available at https://investor.fb.com/financials/default.aspx

Metz, Cade. 2015. "Facebook Doesn't Make as Much Money as It Could – On Purpose." *Wired*, September 21. Available at https://www.wired.com/2015/09/facebook-doesnt-make-much-money-couldon-purpose/

Milne, Richard. 2024. "Harness Data Centres to Heat Europe Cities, Says Danfoss." *Financial Times*, October 30: 9. Available at https://www.ft.com/content/a85a32a2-407a-42ec-930f-6809191236dd

Montulli, Lou. 2013. "The Irregular Musings of Lou Montulli: The Reasoning Behind Web Cookies." Available at http://montulli.blogspot.com/2013/05/the-reasoning-behind-web-cookies.html

Moore, Malcolm. 2024. "Google Orders Small Modular Nuclear Reactors for its Data Centres." *Financial Times*, October 14. Available at https://www.ft.com/content/29eaf03f-4970-40da-ae7c-c8b3283069da

Morris, Stephen. 2024. "Google Streamlines Structure to Speed up AI Efforts." *Financial Times*, April 18: 15. Available at https://www.ft.com/content/26d39c4a-a6c7-4703-8184-271fde7f717e

Mumford, Lewis. 1967. *The Myth of the Machine: Technics and Human Development*. London: Secker & Warburg.

Mumford, Lewis. 1971. *The Pentagon of Power*. London: Secker & Warburg.

Murdock, Graham. 1978. "Blindspots about Western Marxism: A Reply to Dallas Smythe." *Canadian Journal of Political and Social Theory* 2(2): 109–19. Available at https://journals.uvic.ca/index.php/ctheory/article/view/13744

Murgia, Madhumita and Waters, Richard. 2024. "How Google Lost Ground in the AI Race." *Financial Times* 6–7 (April): 9. Available at https://www.ft.com/content/4dfc113f-ccbe-4d11-82b5-761c77fbda24

Nakashima, Ellen. 2007. "Feeling Betrayed, Facebook Users Force Site to Honor Their Privacy." *Washington Post*, November 30. Available at https://www.washingtonpost.com/archive/national/2007/11/30/feeling-betrayed-facebook-users-force-site-to-honor-their-privacy/3854a177-7784-431e-93fb-7ee612539c38/

Napoli, Philip M. 2003. *Audience Economics: Media Institutions and the Audience Marketplace*. New York: Columbia University Press.

Napoli, Philip M.. 2010. *Audience Evolution: New Technologies and the Transformation of Media Audiences*. New York: Columbia University Press.

Nieborg, David B. 2015. "Crushing Candy: The Free-to-Play Game in Its Connective Commodity Form." *Social Media + Society* 1(2): 1–2.

Nieborg, David B. 2017. "Free-to-Play Games and App Advertising: The Rise of the Player Commodity," in James F. Hamilton, Robert Bodle, and Ezequiel Korin (eds.), *Explorations in Critical Studies of Advertising*. New York: Routledge, pp. 28–41.

Nieborg, David B. and Foxman, Maxwell. 2023. *Mainstreaming and Game Journalism*. Cambridge, MA: MIT Press.

Nielsen, Rasmus K. and Ganter, Sarah A. 2022. *The Power of Platforms*. Oxford: Oxford University Press.

Nishtala, Rajesh, et al. 2013. "Scaling Memcache at Facebook." Available at https://research.facebook.com/file/839620310074473/scaling-memcache-at-facebook.pdf

Nixon, Sean. 2003. *Advertising Cultures: Gender, Commerce, Creativity*. London: Sage.

Nolet, Mike. 2010. "The Challenge of Scaling an AdServer." Available at https://web.archive.org/web/20210427162314/http://www.mikeonads.com/2010/04/04/the-challenge-of-scaling-an-adserver/

NOYB. 2024. "Microsoft's Xandr Grants GDPR Rights at a Rate of 0%." Available at https://noyb.eu/en/microsofts-xandr-grants-gdpr-rights-rate-0

Nylen, Leah. 2023. "Apple Gets 36% of Google Revenue in Search Deal, Expert Says." *Bloomberg*, November 13. Available at https://www.bloomberg.com/news/articles/2023-11-13/apple-gets-36-of-google-revenue-from-search-deal-witness-says

Olson, Mancur. 1965. *The Logic of Collective Action: Public Goods and the Theory of Groups*. Cambridge, MA: Harvard University Press.

O'Neil, Cathy. 2017. *Weapons of Math Destruction: How Big Data Increases Inequality and Threatens Democracy*. London: Penguin.

Orbach, Barak and Rebling, Grace Campbell. 2012. "The Antitrust Curse of Bigness." *Southern California Law Review* 85(3): 605–56. Available at https://southerncalifornialawreview.com/wp-content/uploads/2018/01/85_605.pdf

Page, Larry and Brin, Sergey. 2006. "2006 Founders' Letter." Available at https://abc.xyz/investor/founders-letters/2006/

Paparo, Ari. 2024a. "Auction Trends from BidSwitch." Available at https://news.marketecture.tv/p/auction-trends-from-bidswitch

Paparo, Ari. 2024b. "How It All Started: The DoubleClick Acquisition." Available at https://monopoly.marketecture.tv/p/the-doubleclick-acquisition

Paparo, Ari. 2024c. "Scoop: We Found the Deck DoubleClick Used to Sell Itself to Google." Available at https://monopoly.marketecture.tv/p/the-deck-doubleclick-used-to-sell-to-google

Parsons, Talcott. 1967. *Sociological Theory and Modern Society*. New York: Free Press.

Pärssinen, Matti, Kotila, Mikko, Cuevas, Rubén, Phansalkar, Amit, and Manner, Jukka. 2018. "Environmental Impact Assessment of Online Advertising." *ScienceDirect* 73 (November): 177–200.

Philippon, Thomas. 2019. *The Great Reversal: How America Gave Up on Free Markets*. Cambridge, MA: Belknap.

Pink, Sarah, Ruckenstein, Minna, Willim, Robert, and Duque, Melisa. 2018. "Broken Data: Conceptualising Data in an Emerging World." *Big Data & Society* 5(1): 1–13.

Plantin, Jean-Christophe, Lagoze, Carl, Edwards, Paul N., and Sandvig, Christian. 2018. "Infrastructure Studies Meet Platform Studies in the Age of Google and Facebook." *New Media & Society* 20(1): 293–310.

Poell, Thomas, Nieborg, David B., and Duffy, Brooke E. 2023. "Spaces of Negotiation: Analyzing Platform Power in the News Industry." *Digital Journalism* 11(8): 1391–409.

Pragad, Dev. 2024. "Don't Cancel Brand Safety – Improve It." *AdExchanger*, August 19. Available at https://www.adexchanger.com/the-sell-sider/dont-cancel-brand-safety-improve-it/

Prey, Robert. 2018. "Nothing Personal: Algorithmic Individuation on Music Streaming Platforms." *Media, Culture & Society* 40(7): 1086–100.

Pritchard, Marc. 2017. "Better Advertising Enabled by Media Transparency." Talk at Interactive Advertising Bureau Annual Leadership Meeting, Hollywood, FL, January 29. Available at https://www.youtube.com/watch?v=NEUCOsphoI0

Pubmatic. 2023. "Pubmatic Announces Third Quarter 2023 Financial Results." Available at https://investors.pubmatic.com/news-releases/news-release-details/pubmatic-announces-third-quarter-2023-financial-results

PwC. 2023. "ISBA Programmatic Supply Chain Transparency Study II Summary: Test of the Taskforce Financial Audit Toolkit." Available at https://www.isba.org.uk/knowledge/second-programmatic-supply-chain-transparency-study

Ravel, Ann M., Woolley, Samuel C., and Sridharan, Hamsini. 2019. "Principles and Policies to Counter Deceptive Digital Politics." Available at https://legacy.iftf.org/fileadmin/user_upload/images/ourwork/digintel/IFTF_MapLight_Principles_and_Policies_to_Counter_Deceptive_Digital_Politics_02122019.pdf

Reese, Patricia. 2002. "DoubleClick, Inc.: A Strategic Transformation." Fontainebleau, France: INSEAD. Available at https://publishing.insead.edu/case/doubleclick-inc-a-strategic-transformation.

Reichert, Corinne. 2023. "iPhones Continue to Be a Bright Spot for Apple, Even in a Tough Economy." CNET, May 4. Available at https://www.cnet.com/tech/mobile/iphones-continue-to-be-a-bright-spot-for-apple-even-in-a-tough-economy/

Rieder, Bernhard. 2022. "Towards a Political Economy of Technical Systems: The Case of Google." *Big Data & Society* 9(2): 1–5.

Rogers, Richard. 2009. "Post-Demographic Machines." Available at http://www.govcom.org/publications/full_list/rogers_post-demographics_22Feb2009_withimages.pdf

Ruckenstein, Minna and Granroth, Julia. 2020. "Algorithms, Advertising and the Intimacy of Surveillance." *Journal of Cultural Economy* 13(1): 12–24.

Ruppert, Evelyn, Isin, Engin, and Bigo, Didier. 2017. "Data Politics." *Big Data & Society* 4(2): 1–7.

Ryan, Annmarie, Stigzelius, Ingrid, Mejri, Olfa, Hopkinson, Gill, and Hussien, Fairouz. 2023. "Agencing the Digitalised Marketer: Exploring the Boundary Workers at the Cross-road of (E)merging Markets." *Marketing Theory* 23(3): 463–87.

Schiff, Alison. 2020. "Apple WWDC 2020: A Version of Intelligent Tracking Prevention is Coming to the App World." *AdExchanger*, June 22. Available at https://www.adexchanger.com/privacy/apple-wwdc-2020-a-version-of-intelligent-tracking-prevention-is-coming-to-the-app-world/

Schiff, Alison. 2024. "The Bidstream is a Duplicative, Chaotic Mess – But It Doesn't Have to Be That Way." *AdExchanger*, September 30. Available at https://www.adexchanger.com/publishers/the-bidstream-is-a-duplicative-chaotic-mess-but-it-doesnt-have-to-be-that-way/

Schlissel, David and Wamsted, Dennis. 2024. "Small Modular Reactors: Still Too Expensive, Too Slow and Too Risky." Institute for Energy Economics and Financial Analysis, May. Available at https://ieefa.org/resources/small-modular-reactors-still-too-expensive-too-slow-and-too-risky

# References

Schwartz, John. 2001. "Giving Web a Memory Cost Its Users Privacy." *New York Times*, September 4. Available at https://www.nytimes.com/2001/09/04/business/giving-web-a-memory-cost-its-users-privacy.html

Scope3. 2023. "The State of Sustainable Advertising, Q2." Available at: https://scope3.com/news/the-state-of-sustainable-advertising-q2-2023

Seamster, Louise and Charron-Chénier, Raphaël. 2017. "Predatory Inclusion and Education Debt: Rethinking the Racial Wealth Gap." *Social Currents* 4(3): 199–207.

Seufert, Eric. 2017. "The Coming War between Apple and Facebook." *Mobile Dev Memo*, January 23. Available at https://mobiledevmemo.com/coming-war-apple-facebook/

Seufert, Eric. 2021. "Unpacking ATT's Impact on Facebook Revenue." *Mobile Dev Memo*, October 26. Available at https://mobiledevmemo.com/unpacking-atts-impact-on-facebook-revenue/

Seufert, Eric. 2022. "Twitter and the Quality of Brand Advertising Revenue." *Mobile Dev Memo*, November 9. Available at https://mobiledevmemo.com/unpacking-atts-impact-on-facebook-revenue/

Seufert, Eric. 2024a. "Meta's Turnaround, and the Opportunity and Risks Ahead." *Mobile Dev Memo*, February 7. Available at https://mobiledevmemo.com/metas-tailwinds/

Seufert, Eric. 2024b. "The Advertiser's Dilemma with PMax and Advantage+." *Mobile Dev Memo*, 31 January. Available at https://mobiledevmemo.com/the-faustian-bargain-of-pmax-and-advantage/

Seufert, Eric. 2024c. "The Big Economy of Small Advertisers." *Mobile Dev Memo*, April 3. Available at https://mobiledevmemo.com/the-big-economy-of-small-advertisers/

Silberling, Amanda. 2024. "Microsoft Lays Off 1,900 Employees in Activision Blizzard and Xbox Divisions." *TechCrunch*, January 25. Available at https://techcrunch.com/2024/01/25/microsoft-lays-off-1900-employees-in-activision-blizzard-and-xbox-divisions/

Slater, Don. 2011. "Marketing as a Monstrosity: The Impossible Place between Culture and Economy," in Detlev Zwick and Julien Cayla (eds.), *Inside Marketing: Practices, Ideologies, Devices*. Oxford: Oxford University Press.

Sluis, Sarah. 2022. "Google Ad Manager Builds a Bridge to Prebid – but Don't Call It a Two-Way Street." *Ad Exchanger*, April 27: 23–41. Available at https://www.adexchanger.com/platforms/google-ad-manager-builds-a-bridge-to-prebid-but-dont-call-it-a-two-way-street/

Smith, Mike. 2015. *Targeted: How Technology is Revolutionizing Advertising and the Way Companies Reach Consumers*. New York: American Management Association.

Smyth, Jamie. 2024. "Amazon Joins Nuclear Energy Rush." *Financial Times*, October 17: 10. https://www.ft.com/content/00776191-b010-4104-add4-8dc430386911

Smythe, Dallas W. 1977. "Communications: Blindspot of Western Marxism." *Canadian Journal of Political and Social Theory* 1(3): 1–27. Available at https://journals.uvic.ca/index.php/ctheory/issue/view/796

Sodomka, Eric. 2015. "How Machine Learning and Auction Theory Power Facebook Advertising." Talk at Simons Institute, University of California, Berkeley, November 17. Available at https://www.youtube.com/watch?v=94s0yYECeR8

Somers, James. 2018. "Binary Stars: The Friendship that Made Google Huge." *New Yorker*, 10 December: 28–35. Available at https://www.newyorker.com/magazine/2018/12/10/the-friendship-that-made-google-huge

Srinivasan, Dana. 2020. "Why Google Dominates Advertising Markets: Competition Policy Should Lean on the Principles of Financial Market Regulation." *Stanford Technology Law Review* 24: 55–175. Available at https://law.stanford.edu/publications/why-google-dominates-advertising-markets/

Stacey, Stephanie and Waters, Richard. 2024. "Microsoft to Revamp Windows after CrowdStrike IT Debacle." *Financial Times*, August 24–5: 12. Available at https://www.ft.com/content/71f6551a-90c5-4ba5-b314-7f3b0c000551

Stark, David. 2009. *The Sense of Dissonance: Accounts of Worth in Economic Life*. Princeton, NJ: Princeton University Press.

Stokel-Walker, Chris. 2013. "What is the Appeal of Candy Crush Saga?" BBC News, December 18. Available at https://www.bbc.co.uk/news/magazine-25334716

Story, Louise. 2007. "DoubleClick to Set Up an Exchange for Buying and Selling Digital Ads." *New York Times*, April 4. Available at https://www.nytimes.com/2007/04/04/business/media/04adco.html

Texas et al. 2022. "In re: Google Digital Advertising Antitrust Litigation. Third Amended Complaint." Available at https://texasattorneygeneral.gov/sites/default/files/images/child-support/20220114_195_0_States%20Third%20Amended%20Complaint.pdf

Thomas, David. 2023. "Yahoo's Chief Plots Revival with Return to Stock Market." *Financial Times*, July 5: 11. Available at https://www.ft.com/content/5c8c15ea-e495-4ab4-b535-e0ceef5030dd

Thurm, Scott and Kane, Yukari Iwatani. 2010. "Your Apps Are Watching You." *Wall Street Journal*, December 17. Available at https://www.wsj.com/articles/SB10001424052748704694004576020083703574602

Tunstall, Jeremy. 1964. *The Advertising Man in London Advertising Agencies*. London: Chapman & Hall.

Turow, Joseph. 1997. *Breaking Up America: Advertisers and the New Media World*. Chicago: University of Chicago Press.

Turow, Joseph. 2006. *Niche Envy: Marketing Discrimination in the Digital Age*. Cambridge, MA: MIT Press.

Turow, Joseph. 2011. *The Daily You: How the New Advertising Industry Is Defining Your Identity and Your Worth*. New Haven, CN: Yale University Press.

Unal, Sevde Nur, Koray Caliskan, Simone Polillo, and Donald MacKenzie. Forthcoming. "The Modes and Types of Performativity: A Meta-Theoretical Review." *Finance and Society*. Under review.

US Department of Justice, Virginia, California, Colorado, Connecticut, New Jersey, New York, Rhode Island, and Tennessee. 2023. "Case 1:23-cv-00108: Complaint." Available at

https://www.justice.gov/opa/pr/justice-department-sues-google-monopolizing-digital-advertising-technologies

van der Vlist, Fernando N., Helmond, Anne, Burkhardt, Marcus, and Seitz, Tatjana. 2022. "API Governance: The Case of Facebook's Evolution." *Social Media + Society* 8(2): 1–24.

van Dijck, José, Nieborg, David, and Poell, Thomas. 2019. "Reframing Platform Power." *Internet Policy Review* 8(2): 1–18.

Vargas, Anthony. 2024a. "Discover Wiped Out MFA Spend by Following these Four Basic Steps." *AdExchanger*, October 25. Available at https://www.adexchanger.com/programmatic/discover-wiped-out-mfa-spend-by-following-these-four-basic-steps

Vargas, Anthony. 2024b. "Readers are Flocking to Political News, Says WaPo – and Advertisers Are Missing Out." *AdExchanger*, September 27. Available at https://www.adexchanger.com/publishers/readers-are-flocking-to-political-news-says-wapo-and-advertisers-are-missing-out/

Verma, Abhishek, et al. 2015. "Large-Scale Cluster Management at Google with Borg." Available at https://dl.acm.org/doi/pdf/10.1145/2741948.2741964

Viljoen, Salomé, Goldenfein, Jake, and McGuigan, Lee. 2021. "Design Choices: Mechanism Design and Platform Capitalism." *Big Data & Society* 8(2): 1–13.

Vise, David A. and Malseed, Mark. 2005. *The Google Story*. London: Macmillan.

Vopson, Melvin M. 2021. "Estimation of the Information Contained in the Visible Matter of the Universe." *AIP Advances* 11(10): Article 105317.

Wakabayashi, Daisuke. 2019. "Google's Shadow Workforce: Temps Who Outnumber Full-Time Employees." *New York Times*, May 28. Available at https://www.nytimes.com/2019/05/28/technology/google-temp-workers.html

Webber, Jude and Moore, Malcolm. 2024. "Ireland Struggles to Consolidate Role as Data Centre Hub." *Financial Times*, October 10: 4. Available at https://www.ft.com/content/9ab958bf-41dc-4d38-81e1-b311c9e57332

Weber, Max. 1947. *The Theory of Social and Economic Organization.* Glencoe, IL: Free Press.

Whitney, Lance. 2024. "iOS vs Android Market Share: Do More People Have iPhones or Android Phones?" *Tech Republic*, July 25. Available at https://www.techrepublic.com/article/ios-vs-android-market-share/

Winner, Langdon. 1977. *Autonomous Technology: Technics-out-of-Control as a Theme in Political Thought.* Cambridge, MA: MIT Press.

World Federation of Advertisers. 2024. "WFA Discontinues GARM," August 9. Available at https://wfanet.org/knowledge/item/2024/08/09/wfa-discontinues-garm

Wolff, Josephine. 2024. "Software Crash Exposes Tensions between Security and Competition." *Financial Times*, July 29: 23. Available at https://www.ft.com/content/60dde560-194a-40d1-8c98-1d96d6d019a0

Wu, Tim. 2016. *The Attention Merchants: The Epic Struggle to Get Inside Our Heads.* New York: Knopf.

Zaloom, Caitlin. 2022. *Indebted: How Families Make College Work at Any Cost.* Princeton, NJ: Princeton University Press.

Zapolsky, David. 2023. "Read Amazon's Response to the FTC's Antitrust Complaint," September 26. Available at https://www.aboutamazon.com/news/company-news/amazon-response-to-ftc-antitrust-lawsuit

Ziewitz, Malte. 2019. "Rethinking Gaming: The Ethical Work of Optimization in Web Search Engines." *Social Studies of Science* 49(5): 707–31.

Zuboff, Shoshana. 2019. *The Age of Surveillance Capitalism: The Fight for a Human Future at the New Frontier of Power.* London: Profile.